# THEORY FROM THE SOUTH

# THEORY FROM THE SOUTH

or, How Euro-America Is Evolving Toward Africa

*Jean Comaroff and*
*John L. Comaroff*

*Paradigm Publishers*
Boulder • London

Copyright © 2012 by Paradigm Publishers

Published in the United States by Paradigm Publishers, 2845 Wilderness Place, Boulder, Colorado 80301 USA.
Paradigm Publishers is the trade name of Birkenkamp & Company, LLC, Dean Birkenkamp, President and Publisher.

Library of Congress Cataloging-in-Publication Data for this book is available from the Library of Congress.

ISBN: 978-1-59451-764-8 (hc. : alk. paper)
ISBN: 978-1-59451-765-5 (pbk. : alk. paper)

Printed and bound in the United States of America on acid-free paper that meets the standards of the American National Standard for Permanence of Paper for Printed Library Materials.

Designed and Typeset by Straight Creek Bookmakers.

16 15 14 13 12   5 4 3 2 1

The universe is no narrow thing and the order within it is not constrained by any latitude in its conception to repeat what exists in one part in any other part. Even in this world more things exist without our knowledge than with it and the order in creation which you see is that which you have put there, like a string in a maze, so that you shall not lose your way.

Cormac McCarthy,
*Blood Meridian, or the Evening Redness in the West,* p. 245

Social and political theory have been central to creating an understanding of how our society has functioned . . . [They must] take their place again at the leading edge of our struggle for transformation and development of South African society . . . At a deeper level, we also look to social scientists, philosophers, historians, artists and others to help us rebuild our sense of nationhood, our independence and our ability to take our place proudly in the community of nations. We should not only be consumers of theory from the developed world. We should become more active producers of social theory . . .

Ministry of Higher Education and Training, Republic of South Africa,
*Media Statement on the Development of a Humanities
and Social Sciences Charter, 10.vi.2010*

*for our son and daughter-in-law, Joshua*
*Adam Comaroff and Ong Ker-shing*
*and our daughter and son-in-law, Jane Anne*
*Gordon and Lewis Ricardo Gordon*

*who are cited in this book for their own scholarly work*
*who themselves embody theory from the south*
*and in whom the future of critical thought is safely vested*

*in appreciation for everything we have learned,*
*and continue to learn, from them*

# Contents

# Acknowledgments

We would like to thank our colleagues and graduate students at the University of Chicago, especially in the Department of Anthropology and the Chicago Center for Contemporary Theory, for the innumerable conversations that have shaped this volume of essays. Our scholarly work is nurtured in the extraordinary atmosphere and intellectual ferment for which Chicago is justly known. It has been both a pleasure and a privilege to count it as home for the past three decades. A major debt of gratitude is also owed the American Bar Foundation. Our colleagues there, too, have been a perennial source of critical insight and inspiration, and have given their enthusiastic support to our often unconventional interests over the past twenty or so years. In South Africa, our ongoing conversations with Achille Mbembe, Sarah Nuttall, Steven Robins, Jane Taylor, David Bunn, Dennis Davis, Hylton White, Kellie Gillespie, Bernard Dubbeld, and innumerable others have also had a major impact on our thinking and on the way we have come to see the world. Three individuals, in particular, have made signal contributions to the production of *Theory from the South.* Molly Cunningham, our research assistant, has tolerated our scholarly inquiries and requests, some of them not easy to deal with, with remarkable forbearance and insight. Lisa Simeone has played an important role as editorial assistant, especially in helping to ensure that the essays come together into a coherent collection. Finally, Dean Birkenkamp is responsible for the fact that the book exists at all. We have long had both deep affection for him as a person and enormous admiration for his contribution to academic publishing. Funding for the research on which the essays in this volume are based has been afforded, very generously, by the American Bar Foundation, by the Social Sciences Division and the Lichtstern Fund (Department of Anthropology) at the University of Chicago, and by the National Science Foundation under grants #0514207 (2004) and #SE S-0848647 (2009).

The introduction was written in the summer and fall of 2010 at STIAS, the Stellenbosch Institute for Advanced Study in South Africa, and the Internationales Forschungzentrum Kulturwissenschaften in Vienna. In both places we were warmly welcomed and supported as Visiting Fellows. We should like to express our wholehearted gratitude to all concerned—and to Lauren Coyle, who offered us an unusually insightful reading of the completed text.

CHAPTER 1

# Theory from the South

THE IDEA IS VERY SIMPLE REALLY, ALTHOUGH ITS IMPLICATIONS ARE quite radical. We have essayed it many times over the past two decades. So have many others.[1] Especially "other" others.

It is this. Western enlightenment thought has, from the first, posited itself as the wellspring of universal learning, of Science and Philosophy, uppercase; concomitantly, it has regarded the non-West—variously known as the ancient world, the orient, the primitive world, the third world, the underdeveloped world, the developing world, and now the global south—primarily as a place of parochial wisdom, of antiquarian traditions, of exotic ways and means. Above all, of unprocessed data. These other worlds, in short, are treated less as sources of refined knowledge than as reservoirs of raw fact: of the historical, natural, and ethnographic minutiae from which Euromodernity might fashion its testable theories and transcendent truths, its axioms and certitudes, its premises, postulates, and principles. Just as it has capitalized on non-Western "raw materials"—materials at once human and physical, moral and medical, mineral and man-made, cultural and agricultural—by ostensibly adding value and refinement to them. In some measure, this continues to be the case. But what if, and here is the idea in interrogative form, we invert that order of things? What if we subvert the epistemic scaffolding on which it is erected? What if we posit that, in the present moment, it is the global south that affords privileged insight into the workings of the world at large? That it is from here that our empirical grasp of its lineaments, and our theory-work in accounting for them, is and ought to be coming, at least in significant part? That, in probing what is at stake in it, we might move beyond the north-south

1

binary, to lay bare the larger dialectical processes that have produced and sustain it. Note the simultaneity of the descriptive and the prescriptive voice. It is critical to what follows in the following essays. Each is a reflection on the contemporary order of things approached from a primarily African vantage, one, as it turns out, that is full of surprises and counter-intuitives, one that invites us to see familiar things in different ways.

*   *   *

First, some background.

Euro-American social theory, as writers from the south have often observed (e.g., Chatterjee 1997; Chakrabarty 2000; Mbembe 2001), has tended to treat modernity as though it were inseparable from *Aufklarung,* the rise of Enlightenment reason. Not only is each taken to be a condition of the other's possibility, but together they are assumed to have animated a distinctively European mission to emancipate humankind from its uncivil prehistory, from a life driven by bare necessity, from the thrall of miracle and wonder, enchantment and entropy. Whether the Enlightenment is regarded as an epoch, as Susanne Langer (1942:12f) saw it, or, after Foucault (1997), as an "attitude," whether it be vested in Kantian philosophical critique or positivist science, in self-possessed subjectivity or civic democracy, in Arendt's (1958:4) "laboring society" or Marx's capitalist mode of production, in the free market, bioscience, or liberal humanism—or in various ensembles of these things—the modern has its *fons et origo* in the West; this notwithstanding the fact, as Scott Lash (1999:1; cf. Duara 2009) reminds us, that, in the West itself, the term has always been an object of deep contestation, polysemy, ambivalence. *Pace* Cheikh Anta Diop (1955), the Senegalese polymath for whom civilization arose in Egypt thence to make its way northward,[2] other "modernities" are, by implication, taken to be either transplants or simulacra, their very mention marked by ironic scare quotes. The accomplishment of anything like the real thing, the Euro-original, is presumed, at worst, to be flatly impossible, at best to be deferred into a dim, distant, almost unimaginable future—to which, as Fanon (1967:121) put it, if the colonized ever *do* arrive, it is "[t]oo late. Everything is [already] anticipated, thought out, demonstrated, made the most of." To the degree that, from a Western perspective, the global south is embraced by modernity at all, then, it is as an outside that requires translation, mutation, conversion, catch-up.

Take two diverse instances, both expressions of that exteriority, both involving economies of north-south representation. One is literary. It is J.M. Coetzee's (2003:51) story, "The Novel in Africa," set on a cruise ship called, tellingly, *Northern Lights*. The narrative hinges on a conversation between a Nigerian writer and Elizabeth Costello, the Australian novelist who, for all interpretive purposes, is Coetzee's alter ego. "[H]ow can you explore a world in all its depth," Costello asks the man, "if at the same time you are having to explain it to outsiders?" To Europeans, that is. From the standpoint of northerly enlightenment, African prose is taken, intrinsically, to be a performance of otherness; less an act of "self-writing" (Mbembe 2002) than an allegory of Africanity. As Žižek (n.d.) has observed, the universality presumed by Western liberalism "does not reside in the fact that its values (human rights, etc.) are [putatively] universal in the sense of holding for ALL cultures, but in a much more radical sense: in it, individuals relate to themselves as 'universal,' they participate in the universal dimension directly, by-passing their particular social position." The African author, by virtue of a genetic particularity, is foreclosed from writing in the cosmopolitan voice taken for granted by literati in Euro-America. If s/he speaks Out of Africa, it requires "explanation," a.k.a. conversion into the lexicon of liberal universalism and the humanist episteme on which it is based. The other instance is scholarly. It refers to the social sciences in the global south. For Dipesh Chakrabarty (2000:89), European historicism allows only one trajectory to non-Western societies if they are to be recognized as part of the grand human story: they must undergo a visible metamorphosis—fast or slow, effective or otherwise—to Western capitalist modernity. Their diverse, variously animated life-worlds have to be translated into the "universal and disenchanted language of sociology" whose telos decrees: "First in Europe, then elsewhere" (p.7). This, of course, alludes tacitly to the founding assumption of so-called modernization theory—the "social-science story of modernization as the theory of the true, the good, and the inevitable" (Appadurai 1996:11)—of which we shall have more to say later.

Coetzee and Chakrabarty, both of them from the antipodes, construe the exteriority of the non-West, its displacement from the Euromodern, in ways that echo a long, slowly rising tide of critique. To be sure, the object of much postcolonial theory, like other southern critical theory before it,[3] has been to disrupt the telos of modernity, to trouble the histories it presumes, to "provincialize Europe" (Chakrabarty 2000), to "renarrate" empire (Makdisi 1992)—all the better, Homi Bhabha (1994a:6) insists, to move the project of theory-making to an "ex-centric site," thus to capture the restless, re-visionary energy that comes from the vast reaches of the planetary population whose genealogies do not reach back directly into the European Enlightenment, whose lives-and-times either elude or exceed its verities, whose ways of apprehending the world make manifest their difference. Bhabha's call is echoed by those social scientists who argue for the distinctive forms of knowledge yielded by peripheral vision (Wedeen 2008; cf. Piot 2010). And by those who have pointed to the qualifications and question marks brought by non-Western experience to mainstream discourses about the nature of modernity itself (Ferguson 1999:17; Chalfin 2010). It is also echoed, as George Orwell (1933) and W.E.B. du Bois (1933) long ago reminded us so graphically, in

ex-centric site (?)

the life-stories of those *within* the metropole—southerners in the north, so to speak—who are largely excluded from its human fellowship (cf. Jones 1971). We shall return to the ex-centric as an angle of vision. It offers nuance to what we seek to do throughout much of this volume.

More immediately, though, despite decades of postcolonial critique, the modernist social sciences—not excluding those of more radical bent— tend still to "bypass ... the third world," its narratives of modernity and the work of its local intellectuals, in writing the planetary history of the present. Even critical theorists take the "driving engine" of late capitalism to lie wholly in Euro-America (Chakrabarty 2000:7), thus to "create fissures between worlds that [are] in fact intimately linked, that [are] part of precisely the same cultural and historical moments" (Gordon and Roberts 2009:4), the same intricately articulated political economy. In the upshot, the south continues to be the suppressed underside of the north. Which is why, in an important, early intervention on the topic, Gayatri Spivak (1988) censured post-structuralism for failing to give account of geopolitics in its analyses of "Power" and the "Sovereign Subject." By ignoring the impact of the international division of labor on discourse and consciousness everywhere, she argued, and by rendering ideology invisible, post-structuralist theory participated in an economy of representation that has kept the non-European other "in the Self's shadow" (p.280)—thereby allowing the Universal Subject to remain securely on Euro-American terrain, whether it be on the world map of 19th-century imperial rule or the global topography of "decolonized" capital.

Her point is well taken. However, when she goes on to dissect the technologies of Eurocentrism, Spivak (1988:281) seems to court the very psychic self-obsession that she takes to task in post-structuralism. By focusing on the colonial narcissism of Europe, a narcissism that obliterates "the trace of [the colonized] Other in its precarious Subjectivity," she herself puts social and material conditions more or less "under erasure." As a result, the subaltern is so fully eclipsed by an omnipotent Western selfhood as to be rendered inaudible, unspeaking and unspeakable. But *they*—the colonized were, and are, a *social* category, after all—are not quite that easily effaced, notwithstanding their multiple displacements. Why not? Because, being active, sentient human subjects, they were more than just a "necessary supplement" (Derrida 1974:146) or a "constitutive outside" (Butler 1993:39)[4] to the production of European consciousness, not to mention European material, moral, and political life. Even at their most inarticulate, the unsettling presence of those others has always agitated imperial aspirations, demanding constant oversight. Like Rochester's West Indian wife in the attic who, as Edward Said (1983:273) noted of Brontë's *Jane Eyre,* had to be exorcized from polite society at the metropole.

What is more, because colonial societies were complex socio-cultural and economic formations, they entered into complex, often unpredictable relations with Europe. Metropole and colony, after all, were co-constitutive elements in a rising world capitalist order—entailed, that is, in what Deleuze and Guattari call a double capture, "an encounter that transforms the disparate entities that enter into a joint becoming" (Toscana 2005:40). Hence the recognition on the part of Spivak (*ibid.*) and others that overseas "possessions" were critical sources of surplus value and cultural innovation for the modern nation-states of the north. At the same time, the colonized were excluded from full citizenship in those "imagined communities." Worse yet, colonial polities were sustained by acts of violence that flew in the face of the vaunted tenets of liberal European law and civility. This was owed to the fact that efforts to impose imperial sovereignty occurred in places of partial visibility, places where working misunderstandings bred reciprocal fetishisms, unwritten agreements, unruly populations, and protean social arrangements, many of which were taken to require unusual techniques of control (Pietz 1985–88; Stoler 2006:9).

Above all, these frontiers fostered conjunctures of Western and non-Western values, desires, conventions, and practices, fusions that fueled the destructive, innovative urges of Euromodernity, but with little of the ethical restraint that reined them in "back home." Sometimes, too, they were fertile staging grounds—even, as is often said nowadays, laboratories—for ways of doing things that were not possible elsewhere: experiments, for instance, in urban architecture and planning (Wright 1991), in brutally profitable methods of labor discipline (Worger 1987), in socially engineered public health regimes (Comaroff and Comaroff 1992:228ff), and in untried practices of governance and extraction, bureaucracy and warfare, property and pedagogy (cf. Mitchell 1988; Dirks 1992). Nor is this all in the distant past. In 2000, US Republican Senator and House Majority Whip Tom DeLay prevented legislation barring sweatshop conditions in the Northern Mariana Islands, an American territory in the Western Pacific; said DeLay to the *Washington Post,* "the low-wage, anti-union conditions of the Marianas constitute a 'perfect petri dish of capitalism' ...."[5] The edges of empire also allowed for bold forays across established lines of sexuality, sociality, race, and culture that opened up unfamiliar sorts of intimacy and modes of reproduction (Stoler 2002; Hoad 2007); sometimes, as for the 19th-century English literateur Charles Kingsley, the vigor and vitality of those frontiers threw light on the bloodless decadence of modernity on the home front (Wee 2003:37). Which, in turn, ensured that the traces of colonial others could never be fully removed or repressed. Just as Euromodernity sowed its seeds among those others, so the signs and spoils, the seductions and scandals, the indictments and injuries of the colony made themselves palpably present in the domestic politics and the moral imagination of the metropole, breaching its boundaries and inflecting its interiors (Bhabha, after Fanon, 1994b:116; Comaroff and Comaroff 1997).

As this underscores, modernity was, almost from the start, a north-south collaboration—indeed, a world-historical production—albeit a sharply asymmetrical one. Whatever its philosophical conceits, however hard it may seek to "purify" itself (Latour 1993), it has always been a composite of multiple significations, materializations, and temporalities, one that is perpetually contested, conceptually hard to pin down, historically labile. As an ideology, moreover, it has never been dissociable from capitalism, from its determinations and social logic (cf. Amin 1989); although, to be sure, fascism and socialism have sought to build their own versions. Hyphenated in many respects, capitalist-modernity has realized itself, if *very* unevenly, in the great aspirations of liberalism, among them the politico-jural edifice of democracy, the "free" market, civic rights and civil society, the rule of law, the separation of the public from the private, the secular from the sacred. But it has also *excluded* many populations from just these things, especially those in colonial theaters who have been subjugated to its modes of extraction—or have been rendered disposable by virtue of having no value to extract.

Precisely because it has plied its abrasive course in so many disparate contexts, at so many intersections of the capitalist imperium, in other words, modernity has always been both one thing and many, always both a universal project and a host of specific, parochial emplacements. This is self-evidently true in Europe, where national imaginings have never been all alike, neither within nation-states—a point made repeatedly by the "industrial novel" in British literature, from *North and South* (Gaskell 1855) to *Nice Work* (Lodge 1988)—nor between them (see, e.g., Therborn 1995, Eisenstadt 2002); hence the rise of a discursive domain dubbed, broadly, "comparative [a.k.a. 'multiple'] modernities."[6] But it has been even more so in Europe's distant "peripheries," where, in the shadow of various metropoles, modernity was made at a discount. Colonies were pale proxies, subsidiary holding companies as it were, for sovereign Western powers, at once dumping grounds for their superfluous people-and-products and sources of raw value, rare exotica, and racialized labor. Here the violence and the magic, the expropriation and alienation, the syncretism and archaism suppressed in Europe—hidden from view, like the woman in Rochester's attic—were often promiscuously visible. So, too, were the local inventions, accommodations, and hybrids produced in different colonial contexts: forms of domestic and urban life, of peasant-proletarianization, and of displaced cosmopolitanisms forged in the spaces between promise and privation, between inclusion and erasure, there to assert their own contemporaneity, their own ... modernity.

Here, then, is the point. To the degree that the making of modernity has been a world-historical process, it can as well be narrated from its undersides as it can from its self-proclaimed centers—like those maps that, as a cosmic joke, invert planet Earth to place the south on top, the north below. But we seek to do more than just turn the story upside down, thus to leave intact the Manichean dualism that holds Euro-America and its others in the same, fixed embrace. Or to displace an established telos with its opposite, leaving teleology itself intact. We also seek to do more than note that many of the emergent features, the sublimated structures, and the concealed contradictions of capitalist modernity were as readily perceptible in the colony as in the metropole. Or that the former was often a site of production for the ways-and-means of the latter. What we suggest, in addition, is that contemporary world-historical processes are disrupting received geographies of core and periphery, relocating southward—and, of course, eastward as well—some of the most innovative and energetic modes of producing value. And, as importantly, part or whole ownership of them. Which is one of the things that makes contemporary capitalism distinctive, thus to alter the lineaments of global modernity *tout court.*

Arg

It is in this light that we offer a prolegomenon to the essays to follow, to their central claim: that, because the history of the present reveals itself more starkly in the antipodes, it challenges us to make sense of it, empirically and theoretically, from that distinctive vantage. This, of course, is merely to put into the indicative voice the interrogative posed at the outset. In making this claim, *Theory from the South* is built on two closely interwoven arguments. We develop them, as we intimated earlier, by taking Africa as our point of departure. In the final analysis, however, our horizons extend to the global order at large.

## Mise en Scène, in Two Parts

### *Afromodernity, In Practice and Theory*

The first argument is that modernity in the south is not adequately understood as a derivative or a *doppelganger,* a callow copy or a counterfeit, of the Euro-American "original." To the contrary: it demands to be apprehended and addressed in its own right. Modernity in Africa—which, as Masilela (n.d., 2003) shows, has a deep history—is a hydra-headed, polymorphous, mutating ensemble of signs and practices in terms of which people across the continent have long made their lives; this partly in dialectical relationship with the global north and its expansive capitalist imperium, partly with others of the same hemisphere, partly intra-continentally, partly in localized enclaves. As in the north, it has manifest itself in a number of registers at once, from the literary to the lay, the philosophical to the pragmatic. And, as in the north, it has been mired in ambivalence, contestation, and "entangled meanings" (Deutsch, Probst, and Schmidt 2002; Nuttall 2009; Táíwò 2010:13). Should Afromodernity be part of a universal enlightenment, of Christianity and civilization, of Shakespearean English and scientific reason—the very things long presented to Africa as the epitome of Western culture—as some black South African intellectuals argued in the early 20th century (Masilela n.d.:6)? Should it choose only "the good things" of that civilization and discard the rest, as R.V. Selope Thema once put it?[7] Or should it "combine the native and the alien, the traditional and the foreign, into something new and beautiful," as H.I.E. Dlhomo (1977) wrote in 1939? In point of fact, there has been a steady move from the first to the third; a move, that is, toward the mimetic, understood here as a process that "establish[es] similarities with something else while at the same time inventing something original" (Mbembe 2008:38f, after Halliwell 2002). Like its European counterpart, modernity in Africa entailed a re-genesis, a consciousness of new possibilities, and a rupture with the past—a past that, in the upshot, was flattened out, detemporalized, and congealed into "tradition," itself a thoroughly modern construct.

[rupture w/ the past (margin note)]

African modernity, in sum, has always had its own trajectories, giving moral and material shape to everyday life. It has yielded diverse yet distinctive means with which to make sense of the world and to act upon it, to fashion social relations, commodities, and forms of value appropriate to contemporary circumstances—not least those sown by the uneven impact of capitalism, first colonial, then international, then global. In so doing, it has been at once productive and destructive in flouting, reconstructing, repudiating, remaking European life-ways; Thema's prescription turns out to have been more or less descriptive. Sometimes the process has been strikingly self-conscious, as among Xhosa intellectuals of the 1880s (Masilela 2003:506f) and, later, black South Africans of the New Africa Movement, not least Pixley ka Isaka Seme (1905–06), who famously insisted, in "The Regeneration of Africa," that the continent not be compared with Europe since it had its own genius; that it was a "giant ... awakening," about to "march to the future's golden door"; that, being "part of the new order of things," it was entering "a higher complex existence, ... a unique civilization" founded on "precious creations of its own," creations alike "spiritual and humanistic, moral and eternal"— creations, we might add, that were to be inseminated by other influences from the south, from the likes of Mohandas Gandhi and the African diaspora in the New World.

Much the same rhetoric was to suffuse anticolonial movements and post-independence nationalisms. Kwame Nkrumah, for example, quoted Seme at length in opening the First International Congress of Africanists in 1964. That rhetoric is also audible in the assertive alterities of Pan-Africanism, Ethiopianism, Negritude, and Afrocentrism; in musical genres, Nollywood movies, and surrealist art that spell out profoundly local aspirations; in experiments with communitarianism, democracy, born-again belief, and Pentecostal prosperity cults; in high-minded visions, like *Ubuntu,* the call for a generically "African humanity" and, even more ambitiously, the "African Renaissance." At other times, Afromodernity has lain implicit in signs and practices, dispositions and discourses, aesthetic values and indigenous ways of knowing. Nor is it best labeled an "alternative modernity."[8] It is a *vernacular*—just as Euromodernity is a vernacular—wrought in an ongoing, geopolitically situated engagement with the unfolding history of the present. And, like Euromodernity, it takes many forms.

It is important, in this respect, to distinguish modernity from modernization (cf. Appadurai 1996), a point that takes us away from Africa and onto more general terrain for a moment. Allow us a digression, therefore, before we go on to the second of our arguments. It will return us squarely to the central thesis of *Theory from the South*.

Modernity refers to an orientation to being-in-the-world, to a variably construed and variably inhabited *Weltanschauung,* to a concept of the person as self-actualizing subject, to an ideal of humanity as species-being, to a vision of history as a progressive, man-made construction, to an ideology of improvement through the accumulation of knowledge and technical skill, to the pursuit of justice by means of rational governance, to a restless impulse toward innovation whose very iconoclasm brings a hunger for things eternal (cf. Harvey 1989:10). Modernization, by contrast, posits a strong normative teleology, a unilinear trajectory toward a future—capitalist, socialist, fascist, African, whatever—to which all humanity ought to aspire, to which all history ought to lead, toward which all the peoples ought to evolve. This telos has expressed itself in self-styled progressive movements, both secular and religious, in expansive models of improvement, and in "objective" scientific paradigms, among them "modernization theory" in sociology. It has also been censured for the contradictions between its promises and the effects of practices pursued in its name: between, for example, the promise of a more equal humanity and the burgeoning biopolitics of difference across the world; between the promise of global economic development and the reality of spiraling underdevelopment for the populations of the south, of rising Gini coefficients, and of increasingly violent modes of extraction everywhere. We are less concerned here with these contradictions—they are the subject of a large literature—than with the confusion itself between modernization and modernity. It underpins a recent debate about the latter, about modernity as category of critical analysis, and raises a clutch of theoretical issues salient to this volume.

Frederick Cooper (2005:113), whose own scholarly *oeuvre* is also deeply rooted in Africa, has recently complained that modernity is ever more imprecisely used as a technical term in the academy. We agree, having remarked ourselves on its vagueness, its tendency to melt into air under scrutiny (1993:xii). We concur, too, with his observation that its analytic and everyday connotations are often confused and conflated (*ibid.*:xiif); although this is as true of other constructs in the vocabulary of the human sciences, like colonialism, identity, politics, liberalism (cf. Duara 2007:295). Even theory. In point of fact, it is precisely the protean quality of modernity that has made it so productive as a trope of worldly claim-making, as a political assertion, and as an *object* of analysis. "Modernity," plainly, is a shifter (Silverstein 1976), whose meaning derives from the context of its use. It serves to situate people— recursively, in mutually reinforcing oppositions (Irvine and Gall 2000)—on the near or the far side of the great divide between self and other, the present and prehistory, here and there, the general and particular; oppositions that are mobilized in a range of registers from theological treatises to party platforms, from policy documents to black letter law, from cartographies of social space to the bureaucratic management of populations.

The positivist social sciences have also deployed this grammar of oppositions, of course; hence their embrace of such foundational antinomies as mechanical:organic solidarity, ascription:achievement, status:contract, *gemeinschaft:gesellschaft,* savage:civilized, precapitalist:capitalist, and so on and on. Modernization theory, ascendant in sociology from the 1950s, was no exception; it set out to isolate, define, and measure the variables according to which human populations might be placed along an imagined continuum from the pre- to the modern, the past to the present. Despite having been subjected to repeated critique, Cooper (2005:9ff) argues—and this takes us to the nub of the debate—both the conceptual foundations and the Eurocentric telos of that paradigm linger on in colonial and postcolonial scholarship. As a result, he says, the latter "reinforce[s] the metanarratives [it] pretend[s] to take apart" (p.9), thereby muddying rather than illuminating the question of African modernity, of what it actually is and how we might typify it. For him, the problem is to be solved by a strong dose of "rigorous historical practice" (p.13), as though a protean, contested phenomenon of this sort might finally be laid bare by recourse to frank empiricism,[9] as though the empirical itself can be read without a theoretical frame to focus it.

Ironically, by the canons of rigorous historical practice, colonial and postcolonial studies are not so easily dismissed. Some work in that tradition *has* taken pains to transcend the assumptions and methods of modernization theory. And to do so with reference to carefully grounded histories and ethnographies that do not confuse the empirical with brute empiricism. Constructs like "alternative modernities" have their limitations, as we have intimated. But they were developed precisely to move *beyond* the binary opposition between the premodern and the modern,[10] to capture complex facts on the ground, to repudiate the telos that was held to chart the course from one to the other, and to avoid conflating modernization with Westernization—although there have been historical movements outside Europe, like the 19th-century Arab modernism of Jamāl-al-din al-Afghāni (Hourani 1983), that *have* taken the European version as their model.

But there is something else here, something more general. Cooper's effort to counter indiscriminate uses of the term underscores why it is so important not to mistake modernity for modernization. Or to treat modernity as an analytical construct without also considering the conditions of its material existence. Cooper laments that, with the repudiation of modernization theory and its telos, "everything" tends to be treated as "simultaneously modern" (p.132). But that, in part, was the very object of the critique: to show that, while modernization as Western ideology might have represented non-Western worlds as just so many not-yet-modern outsides, the capitalist imperium *has* no exteriors, although it has many peripheries. Its exclusions and its margins, as critical theorists of various stripes have stressed, are a requisite condition for the growth of its centers.

In that light, it is necessary to take seriously the reality that many disadvantaged people across the world desire much of what *they* understand by the modern. And, to the degree that they can, to fashion their own versions of it, even as they live with its constraints and contradictions, absences and aporias. Which is where the *empirical* fact of "multiple modernities"—a fact that Cooper himself recognizes in another work (Stoler and Cooper 1997:32)[11]—came from to begin with. Acknowledging the widespread yearning for the elusive promise of "progress," patently, does not preclude recognizing its destructive effects or challenging the Eurocentric myth that there is only one authentic instance of it. Nor is the demand for its fruits among those deprived of them negated by accepting that there may be more than one modernity, a fear expressed by James Ferguson (2006:33, 176f), who cautions that, in celebrating "alternative modernities," we may all too easily scant the very real inequalities that exist in the world; inequalities, one might add, to be found as much in the *lumpen* heart of global metropoles as in some of Africa's most remote regions. It is not that people in the global south "lack modernity." It is that many of them are deprived of the bounty of modernization by the inherent propensity of capital to create edges and undersides in order to feed off them.

Modernity, as we said earlier, is a concrete abstraction. It has realized, marked forms in the world, being a product of human activity, but also exists as a reified order of imagined, transactable value. It is a Big Idea: the term refers *both* to something general and to things particular, *both* to the singular and to the plural. And to the relations between them. It embraces the social, economic, cultural, and moral dimensions of life in specific times and places— and, simultaneously, is invoked to describe the epochal and the universal. Popular constructs of this kind are as integral to theory-work in the social sciences, history among them, as they are to the everyday discourses of mass culture; the need to make sense of their practical semiosis would appear self-evident. Can one really argue, as Cooper (2005:116) does, that to use "modernity" in the plural rather than the singular, to treat it as more than a vernacular category and/or a strategy of claim-making, or to elevate it to an abstraction at all, is to give it "artificial coherence"? What exactly is artificial about it, beyond the fact that *every* concept interrogated by the human sciences is, ultimately, an artifice? Why should it be that to recognize modernity to be one thing and many is to fall into "confusion" (*ibid.*)?[12] To bring this back to present concerns and to our own argument, it follows from what we have been saying that African modernity is *both* a discursive construct and an empirical fact, both a singularity and a plurality, both a distinctive aspiration and a complicated set of realities, ones—as the likes of Pixley ka Isaka Seme said long ago—that speak to a tortuous endogenous history, one still actively being made. A history, as it turns out, not running behind Euro-America, but ahead of it.

## The Global South: Hyper-Extensions of the Present, Harbingers of Future-History

This brings us to the second argument of the volume. Contrary to the received Euromodernist narrative of the past two centuries—which has the global south tracking behind the curve of Universal History, always in deficit, always playing catch-up—there is good reason to think the opposite: that, given the unpredictable, under-determined dialectic of capitalism-and-modernity in the here and now, it is the south that often is the first to feel the effects of world-historical forces, the south in which radically new assemblages of capital and labor are taking shape, thus to prefigure the future of the global north. It is this that we seek to capture in our pointedly provocative, partially parodic, counter-evolutionary subtitle, *How Euro-America Is Evolving Toward Africa*. In using the trope of the "counter-evolutionary," we repeat, we do not intend simply to reverse the telos at the heart of modernist reason. We mean, instead, to call into question the epistemic reflex on which that reason is founded.

It scarcely needs to be said that the received narrative itself has always been flawed. The north has long adopted techniques, knowledges, and practices that have prior histories in Africa and elsewhere. British industrialization, for example, as Jack Goody (2006:210) shows, drew on means of mechanization and mass production developed earlier in China and India. Subsequently, many northern innovations emerged directly out of the colonial encounter, the impact of which on the metropoles of Europe has been expansively documented. Not only did this include the repatriation, appropriation, and mimicry of vernacular "talents," like cuisines, couture, and creative arts. It also ran to more weighty things, from medical expertise and technologies of the body to spiritual beliefs and modes of managing publics. Even more, the in-migration of formerly colonized populations has brought with it species of difference that have transformed Euromodern nation-states, testing the limits of their liberal foundations. But there are also other ways in which the global north is becoming more like the south. These owe less to north-south encounters than to historical exigencies of different kinds. We shall give any number of examples in the chapters to follow. They stretch from the nature of personhood and participatory democracy through the politics of identity and occult economies to sovereignty over life and death.

✳ The point—that the place of Africa in the received narrative of Universal History is fundamentally flawed—need not be labored further. Here, as we said a moment ago, we seek to stress something else: that, while Euro- [Arg] America and the south are currently caught up in the *same* all-embracing world-historical processes, it is in the latter that the effects of those processes tend most graphically to manifest themselves. Old margins are becoming new frontiers, places where mobile, globally competitive capital—much of it, these days, southern and eastern—finds minimally regulated zones in which to vest its operations; where industrial manufacture opens up ever more cost-efficient sites for itself; where highly flexible, informal economies have long thrived; where those performing outsourced services have gone on to develop cutting-edge info-tech empires of their own, both legitimate and illicit; where new, late-modern idioms of work, time, and value take root, thus to alter planetary practices. Which is why, in the dialectics of contemporary world history, the north appears to be "evolving" southward. Put another way, as we do in Chapter 3, Africa, South Asia, and Latin America seem, in many respects, to be running slightly ahead of the Euromodern world, harbingers of its history-in-the-making.

This cuts to the very heart of contemporary capitalism: to the means of primary production associated with it, to its preferred forms of labor extraction, to its modes of accumulating and circulating wealth, to its political and legal geographies, to its interpolation in the institutions of governance. In recent decades, capital, with its stress on flexibility, liquidity, and deregulation, has yet again found untapped bounty in former colonies, where postcolonial states, anxious to garner disposable income and often in desperate need of "hard" foreign currency, have opened themselves up to business; specifically, to corporations that have little compunction in pressuring ruling regimes to offer them tax incentives, to relax environmental controls, to remove wage restrictions and worker protections, to limit liability and discourage union activities, even to allow them to enclave themselves—in short, to bow to the tenets of *laissez-faire* at their most extreme, their most sovereign. As a result, it is increasingly in the south, Tom DeLay's preferred "petri dish," that the practical workings of neoliberalism have been tried and tested, in them that the outer bounds of its financial operations have been explored—thence to be exported to Euro-America.

The north, of course, is now experiencing those practical workings ever more palpably as labor markets contract and employment is casualized, as manufacture moves away without warning, as big business seeks to coerce states to unmake ecolaws, to drop minimum wages, to subsidize its infrastructure from public funds, and to protect it from loss, liability, and taxation;[13] this, often, over the unavailing protests of various sectors of civil society. Which is why so many citizens of the West—of both laboring and middle classes—are having to face the insecurities and instabilities, even the forced mobility and disposability, characteristic of life in much of the non-West; also its massively widening wealth gap, which, by some accounts (e.g., Wilkinson and Pickett 2010; Jackson 2009),[14] is seriously destabilizing economies and societies across the globe under the alibi of unimpeded growth. Which is why, too, we are beginning to see public intellectuals in the USA publish books with titles like *Third World America* (Huffington 2010).

At the same time, some nation-states in the south, by virtue of having become economic powerhouses—India, Brazil, South Africa—evince features of the future of Euro-America in other ways, having opened up frontiers of their own and having begun to colonize the metropole: *vide* the seizure of global initiative in the biofuel economy by Brazil, or the reach of the Indian auto industry into Britain, or the impact of the Hong Kong banking sector on the development of new species of financial market. Or, in another register, the emergence of South Africa, a major force in the international mineral economy, as the America of Africa, an African-America eager to experiment with constitutional law, populist politics, and, if hesitatingly, post-neoliberal forms of redistribution. Or, in yet another, the rise of new forms of urbanism, as in Nigeria, where, observe Joshua Comaroff and Gulliver Shepard (1999), "many of the trends of canonical, modern, *Western cities can be seen in hyperbolic guise* ... Lagos is not catching up with us. Rather, we may be catching up with Lagos." That city, adds Rem Koolhaas, is "a paradigm for [the] future" of *all* cities. A "megalopolis of 18 million" whose prime real estate is as expensive as comparable property in Manhattan (Guo 2010:44), it is, he says, at "the forefront of globalizing modernity" (Koolhaas and Cleijne 2001:652–53). Not of an alternative modernity. Of modernity *sui generis*. The irony of this will be obvious to those familiar with Johannes Fabian's *Time and the Other* (1983). The question now is not whether the West eschews, ignores, or misrecognizes the "coevalness"—i.e., the contemporaneity—of the non-West with the West, which is what Fabian accused anthropology of doing. It is whether the West recognizes that *it* is playing catch-up in many respects with the temporality of its others.

But this is a different aspect of the story. In large part, it is its undersides, its *lumpen* ends, that are worked out first in the south, where much of the working class of the world is dispersed. This, perhaps, accounts for the fact that some of the earliest, most trenchant populist critiques of the neoliberal turn—and the most skeptical responses to free-market triumphalism—have come from those very undersides (see, e.g., Lomnitz 2006; Desai 2002; Amin 2010), this being yet another respect in which the global north has tracked behind its antipodean counterparts.[15]

But why? Why has Africa in particular, and the south in general, come, in significant respects, to anticipate the unfolding history of the global north? Why, for good or ill, are the material, political, social, and moral effects of the rise of neoliberalism most graphically evident there? We have already begun to address the question, and will return to it below. Suffice it to say here that the answer begins with the past, with the fact that most colonies were zones of occupation geared toward imperial extraction (see above). To the degree that neocolonial politics and economics have conspired, more or less coercively, to keep them that way, postcolonies have remained dependent and debt-strapped, tending still to export their resources as raw materials and unskilled labor rather than as value-added commodities or competencies; this even as some of them—like Nigeria, Morocco, Egypt, Tunisia, and, again, South Africa—have experienced real growth in their manufacturing industries, in their service sectors, in home-grown finance capital, and in urban consumer spending.[16] Furthermore, (i) because large sectors of their populations have long worked under conditions designed to depress wages and disempower potentially dangerous classes, (ii) because market forces in Africa have never been fully cushioned by the existence of a liberal democratic state and its forms of regulation, and (iii) because governance here has frequently been based on kleptocratic patronage—all of these things also being in part legacies of colonialism and its aftermath—African polities have been especially hospitable to rapacious enterprise: to asset stripping, to the alienation of the commons to privateers, to the plunder of personal property, to foreign bribe-giving. In sum, to optimal profit at minimal cost, with little infrastructural investment.

The rapid increase of foreign direct investment (FDI) south of the Sahara over the past decade[17]—capital inflows to Africa rose by 16 percent to $61.9b in 2008, while falling 20 percent worldwide (Guo 2010:44)—has led Ferguson (2006:41), among others, to speculate that African countries might be less sites of "immature forms of globalization" than "quite 'advanced' and sophisticated mutations of it." A recent technical report on African economies by the McKinsey Global Institute (Roxburgh *et al.* 2010; see n.16) supports this view. So, too, does Brenda Chalfin's (2010) case study of Ghana, which, she shows, has become a "neoliberal pacesetter" (p.29), putting into play new regulatory techniques at a time when customs mandates are expanding everywhere in response to burgeoning transnational trade. With the involvement of multilateral agencies, "Ghana Customs ... functions in many respects as a laboratory for the testing out and ... shaping of global modalities of governance" (p.29–30). Again, for better or for worse, Africa is ahead of the curve. It is precisely the mélange of its inherited colonial institutions and its postcolonial availability to neoliberal development that make Ghana, and other nations of the south, a vanguard in the epoch of the market. As *Newsweek* put it in early 2010, Africa is "at the very forefront of emerging markets ... Like China and India, [it is] perhaps more than any other region, ... illustrative of a new world order" (Guo 2010:44), a multi-focal order whose *axis mundi* is no longer self-evidently in the north.

The US and Europe have colluded in this by seeking to impose their future-vision—infamously, under the sign of structural adjustment—on Africa, Asia, and Latin America, inadvertently giving early warning of what would lie in store for themselves. George Stiglitz (2002) has argued that the doctrinaire insistence on the liberalization of trade and capital markets, on high returns to financial investment, and on the privatization of public assets is especially unsuited to developing economies. In his view, this precipitated the Asian crisis of 1997, a history of failed development in sub-Saharan Africa, and the meltdown in Argentina. The fallout—epidemic bankruptcies, massive unemployment *sans* a social safety net, downwardly mobile middle classes, and so on—provides a chilling preview of the effects of the global economic implosion of 2008. In terms that now sound prophetic, Stiglitz described how the nations of the East were thrown into material and social chaos; how, in order to protect international markets, the International Monetary Fund (IMF) rushed in with massive bailouts directed mainly at foreign creditors, leaving ordinary citizens to carry the costs; how financial stabilization rather than job creation became the prime objective; how money was available to save banks but not to compensate unemployed workers or pay for essentials like education and health care. In its staunch ideological advocacy of *laissez-faire,* the IMF ignored critical knowledge in economics about the conditions under which self-regulating markets actually operate (Stiglitz 2002:73):

> ... these conditions are highly restrictive. Indeed, more recent advances in economic theory—ironically occurring precisely during the period of the most relentless pursuit of the Washington Consensus policies—have shown that whenever information is imperfect and markets incomplete, which is to say always, and especially in developing countries, then the invisible hand works most imperfectly. Significantly, there are desirable government interventions which, in principle, can improve upon the efficiency of the market.

What Stiglitz was pointing to, patently, are fundamental flaws in the precepts and practices of neoliberalism (see also Chang 2008, 2011); also to the fact that our incapacity—or faith-based refusal—to understand those flaws, not least when they manifest themselves in the "petri dish" of developing countries, blinds us to the economic history of our own present. Small wonder, then, that he should express similar sentiments (Stiglitz 2008) in a mass-mediated symposium, prompted by the events of 2008, on *How to Save Capitalism: Fundamental Fixes for a Collapsing System,* itself the sort of topic more usually associated with the third world than the first. How was it that the over-analyzed Asian and Latin American financial crises, or the ill effects of structural adjustment in Africa, sounded no warning bells for the future of the global north? Could it be because these things occurred in the antipodes? Or because, blinkered by our own narratives of Universal History, we have simply been unable to see the coming counter-evolution, the fact, so to speak, that the north is going south? Is there any other explanation for our failure to recognize in Africa, Asia, and Latin America the traces of things about to happen, things sometimes destructive, sometimes productive, sometimes a mixture of both?

To be sure, the north had foretaste of the downsides of market fundamentalism, and of the forms of neoliberal governance that orchestrate it, well before the crisis of 2008; according to Immanuel Wallerstein (2009), in fact, the USA has been in decline since the 1970s. The contradictions that brought this to a head, after all, were long in the making: the relentless reduction of manufacturing heartlands into rust-belt wastelands has traced the steady de-industrialization of Euro-America—and have recently given rise to calls for re-industrialization, ironically, by emulating Fordist manufacture exported to, and significantly re-engineered in, the south and east; in Britain, it is referred to as "re-balancing" the economy (Seabrook 2010:68),[18] probably a vain hope under northern conditions in which competitive production seems no longer possible. Those contradictions also flash into the public eye more dramatically from time to time, sparked by ruptures in the flow of everyday life. In the US, the implosion of Enron in 2004 is a notable instance, one that made plain the fragility of an economy built on unregulated corporate greed and voodoo accounting. A year later, Hurricane Katrina revealed to middle Americans the extreme poverty, abjection, and inequality in their midst, the hidden effects on national infrastructure of the retraction of the resources of state, the absence of a commonweal, the deep fissures of race and class among them, the ruthlessness of police in dealing with the indigent, the callousness of power in the face of human catastrophe. Brutal conflict in the *banlieues* of Paris, attacks on immigrants in the United Kingdom, and the repression of Muslims in the Netherlands have played out similar themes, making clear how, despite the triumphal fetishism of democracy and human rights, of neoliberal deregulation and the freedom to be, the nations of the north are witnessing rising tides of ethnic conflict, racism, and xenophobia, of violent criminality, social exclusion, and alienation, of rampant corruption in government and business, of shrinking, insecure labor markets, afflicted middle classes, and *lumpen* youth, of executive authoritarianism, popular punitiveness, and much more besides (Comaroff and Comaroff 2006a, 2006b). Talk, even moral panic, about the imminent breakdown of order is to be heard in places as pacific as Sweden and Scotland—and read, tellingly, in their socially conscious, creatively diagnostic crime fiction.[19] Africa, it seems, is becoming a global condition.[20] Or, at least, Africa as imagined in Euro-America. Its reality is rather more complex. And not all darkness.

Just as it has been in the past, the continent is also a source of inventive responses to the contingencies of our times, responses driven by a volatile mix of necessity, possibility, deregulation, and space-time compression. Hence, among other things—and in addition to the vibrant, if uneven, growth of its formal sectors and its endogenous capital—the extraordinary expansion here of "informal" commerce, the growth of economies built on more or less licit practices of counterfeit, and the emergence of new modes of service provision; Hardt and Negri (2000:292) dub this last, misleadingly perhaps, "immaterial production," the traffic in care, security, intimacy, affect.[21] The south has also led the way in the efflorescence of "ethnoprise," what elsewhere we term *Ethnicity, Inc.* (Comaroff and Comaroff 2009): the incorporation of identity and the commodification of culture–as–intellectual property, this by appeal to the natural copyright of indigenous knowledge, by deploying sovereign exclusion, and by exploiting markets in difference, not least via the tourist industry, the media, and the Internet. The boom in the identity economy is having thoroughgoing implications for the ways in which ordinary people experience collective being, social capital, and political attachment. And it is steadily diffusing northward, toward those metropoles that once saw themselves as beyond ethnic parochialism or "tradition." In the face of the structural violence perpetrated in the name of neoliberalism, as this suggests, the global south is producing and exporting some ingenious, highly imaginative modes of survival—and more.

Not that the fruits of this ingenuity have reversed the radical privation from which it springs. As Zygmunt Bauman (2005:88f) reminds us, the creative destruction endemic to modernity has always produced poverty in its wake (see above). All the more so in neoliberal times. Hence the emergence in the south of new forms of human immiseration, new forms of alienation, new means through which human life and work are devalued or rendered redundant (cf. Mbembe 2006); hence, concomitantly, the rise of an assertive politics of "the poors" (Desai 2002) and of new social movements of various sorts across the planetary south (see below).[22] At the same time, those most adversely affected are taking modernity to places it has never been before, thus also to bring to light elements of its intrinsic nature long suppressed. Indeed, it is precisely this dialectic that has pushed Africa, Asia, and Latin America to the vanguard of the epoch, making them at once contemporary frontiers and new centers of capitalism—which, to reiterate, in its latest, most energetically voracious phase, thrives in environments in which the protections of liberal democracy, of the rule of law, of the labor contract, and of the ethics of civil society are, at best, uneven.

It is here that our two theses converge: here where the first, the ontological claim that Afromodernity exists *sui generis,* not as a derivative of the Euro-original, meets the second assertion that, in the history of the present, the global south is running ahead of the global north, a hyperbolic prefiguration of its future-in-the-making.

Let us move on, then, to specifics: to introduce the various domains into which we take our two lines of argument—and the ways in which those lines of argument are further developed—in the following chapters. This will lead, in turn, back to the larger question at the core of this volume: how might *Theory from the South* inform the ways in which we are to interrogate the present and future of global capitalism and its many mediations?

## INTO AFRICA, AGAIN: MAPPING THE V-EFFECT

G.K. Chesterton, one of the great aphorists of English letters, once remarked that "the function of the imagination is not to make strange things settled, so much as to make settled things strange."[23] In taking up some of the critical concerns of the present age—concerns about personhood, identity, difference, and belonging, about the state, sovereignty, governmentality, citizenship, and borders, about law, liberalism, and democracy, about labor and the politics of life, about history and memory—we seek to do just that: to make settled things strange.

Critical estrangement, of course, has long been an autonomic reflex of anthropology, the discipline that, at its best, seeks what Bertolt Brecht famously spoke of as *Verfremdung,* or the V-effect: the effort to defamiliarize, distance, astonish, thus to strip the ordinary of its self-evident ordinariness (see, e.g., Mumford 2009:60–62). Our effort to make other—largely African—facts undermine established verities about the nature of the contemporary order of things is an enterprise that, perforce, juxtaposes social processes of different kinds, different temporalities, different geographies, different dimensions, riding the gaps between them (cf. Tsing 1993:207). This, as we shall see, relies on an ethnographic praxis of various scales, to which we return, either explicitly or implicitly, in several of the following chapters. But let us begin at the beginning.

## On Personhood, Difference, and ID-ology

The beginning, at least for liberal constructions of modernity, lies with personhood, the elemental "atom" of social being. Chapter 2 reflects on this foundational Western precept from a contemporary African vantage. It was written in response to a provocation on the part of a circle of philosophers and anthropologists at the University of Heidelberg: "Is the idea of the autonomous person a European invention?" they asked. On the face of it, the question appeared, beguilingly, to voice late-modern doubts about the universality of the individual postulated in liberal political philosophy: the individual, that is, as an essentially Hegelian being, potentially capable everywhere of recognizing, claiming, and affirming an unencumbered right to liberty on his or her own account, a being at once self-reflective, self-possessed, rationally self-motivated. But the provocation carried within it another, less charitable possibility. If the "autonomous person" was indeed a European invention, were the non-European antipodes yet again to be defined by its absence, by an innate antipathy to liberalism, to its foundational principles of free will and democracy, of enlightened self-interest, unfettered markets, and value-neutral knowledge? Are these principles nurtured only by a relatively small, fragile fraternity of freedom-loving societies, societies locked in global combat with "civilizations"—ironic scare quotes, again—driven by fundamentalist faiths, primordial passions, authoritarian constraints, communitarian impulses? Or, worse yet, is the non-West populated by others who may aspire to better things, but are congenitally incapable of the enlightenment required to accomplish truly "autonomous personhood"?

In taking on the question—well, *is* the "autonomous person" a European invention?—we resist a time-worn anthropological move: the repudiation of Eurocentricism by recourse to cross-cultural comparison. There is, after all, little polemical power left in the insistence that people "are the same the whole world over, except when they are different," as the incorrigible British critic Nancy Banks-Smith once put it.[24] That personhood takes many manifest forms is indisputable; so is the fact that it evinces similarities, parallels, resemblances, and affinities across time and place. But this does not answer the question one way or the other. Nor does it tell us anything much about the theoretical status of the concept itself, which, in Western social thought, refers at once to a philosophical postulate, a normative ideal, and a regime of bourgeois values.

But is it a "European *invention*"? The very idea implies two things. One is that the "autonomous person" arose, anew and unabetted, from within the genius of Euromodern thought. The other is that it actually exists as a lived form in the West and not—at least not indigenously, nor until imported— elsewhere. Both claims are dubious.

The historical anthropology of colonialism has shown repeatedly that modernist ideas of personhood were not simply an endogenous Western creation. *Per contra,* they were the product of a dialectic of the long-run between a European self very much under construction from the late 18th century onward and divers others. Nor were those others merely a necessary supplement to the process, a *tabula obscura* onto which assertive Euro-agency inscribed the person it found when it looked into the colonial mirror. To be sure, humans everywhere take on their subjectivity within more or less structured webs of relations. As Durkheim observed in *The Elementary Forms of Religious Life* ([1912]2001:200f), in a note on Kant and Leibniz, "what makes man a person is what he shares with other men ... Individuation is not the fundamental character of the person. A person is ... a being to [whom] relative autonomy is attributed in relation to [a] setting." As Durkheim and many others have said, personhood may be *attributed* autonomy, but it can never be *ontologically* autonomous (cf. Mauss 1990; Butler 2004). Here the Hegel of free will is to be placed alongside the Hegel who understood well that lordship is indissoluble from bondage, that a master and his slave are conditions of each other's possibility.

Intrinsic to the positive dialectic that yielded the "autonomous person" of Euromodernity was the negation of anything that might be taken as resembling it elsewhere. The putative invention of that self for Europe meant inventing an Africa that lacked it (cf. Mudimbe 1988). The stakes in so doing were not trivial. The enlightened individual, as both archetype and ideal-type, has served as the grounding of liberal society *ab initio,* notwithstanding the fact that, sociologically speaking, personhood within the north has varied widely, and certainly has not always conformed to this ideal-type. The latter, however, has remained enshrined in a range of discursive constructs and civic institutions—from the idea of free labor to the Lockean social contract, from rights-bearing citizenship to the rule of law—that underpin the very meaning of liberty. But what of the claim that Africa, and other European elsewheres, lacked a concept of autonomous personhood? And what might it have to do with theory from the south, or the counter-evolution of Europe toward Africa?

A great deal on both counts, as it turns out.

Take the Southern Tswana peoples of South Africa. These peoples, as we shall see in Chapter 2, have long had an elaborate theory about the nature of the self. They also sustain a qualified idea of "autonomous personhood"; qualified, that is, by the notion, quite close to Durkheim's, that "what makes man a person is what he shares with other men." *Motho ke motho ka batho,* a person is a person (by virtue of other) people, is the indigenous translation of the same point. Most Tswana would probably agree, too, that "individuation ... is not the fundamental character of the person." At the same time, they are wont to say that people make themselves and their social identities through various, linguistically marked forms of labor (*tiro*); performance theory, reminiscent of Judith Butler (1990), has vernacular echoes here. For as long as there is historical record, the Tswana world appears to have been highly individualistic in many respects—and palpably competitive. The trope of the self-possessed subject was captured in the concept of *itirela,* or self-construction, the accumulation of personal "name" (*leina*) or "fame" (*tumo;* also "noise") by dint of political acumen, economic patronage, social management, oratorical skill. But the manner of that self-construction was, and is, subject to a fan of ethical possibilities, stretching from work that is purely self-interested to that which enriches not only the self but socially significant others as well.

This performative conception of personhood, by extension, has it that human beings live in a constant state of becoming, a process that ends only at death. It is also predicated on a highly partible notion of selfhood: people retain their autonomy, and protect themselves from being "eaten" by rivals, by taking pains not to open up their bodies, their enterprises, their dependents, or their possessions to undue scrutiny. Or to any intrusion whatsoever. In a manner oddly resonant with Erving Goffman's *Presentation of Self in Everyday Life* (1959), they show to others only those aspects of themselves they deem relevant, as Durkheim (*ibid.*) put it, "to the setting with which [they are] most immediately in contact," secreting other facets of their being. In other words, they perform themselves as fractal subjects, as persons whose very partibility is part of the social fabrication of their selfhood.

Protestant missions in the 19th century sought to replace this species of personhood—which was taken to be a by-product of primitive kinship arrangements—with an inward-turning *in*dividualism, one that sought salvation and worldly success strictly as a private pursuit. For their part, Southern Tswana were quick to draw a sharp contrast between the latter, glossed as *sekgoa,* European ways, and *setswana,* their own cultural practices. *Setswana* was to be transformed by the colonial encounter, by its contradictions and exclusions, by a brutal system of labor migration that ruptured families and domestic lives, by the kinds of double consciousness bred in a world in which Europeans lived with Africans in intimate interdependence while denying them a common humanity. Over the long 20th century, too, the line between *setswana* and *sekgoa* was endlessly redrawn. In the upshot, the content of Tswana personhood altered. But, if anything—as everyday life was rendered ever more insecure under a regime of racial capitalism—the sense that selfhood is always under construction, always fragile, always socially embedded, became, if anything, *more* compelling. So did the notion that humans could only protect themselves from forces that would undo them by carefully managing those parts of their partible selves that they opened up to others.

The point? It scarcely bears repeating that the liberal modernist conception of autonomous personhood, a philosophical postulate that sought to factualize a bourgeois fiction, was the historical artifact of a particular epoch in the Euro-American past. Far from being the sole species of selfhood that lies at the End of History, it describes a parochial cultural form, one that had quite elaborate parallels and alternatives elsewhere. It also describes an artifact that seems, once again, to be undergoing at least partial reconstruction. Which is where the thrust of this theoretical incursion from the south lies. Our objective is not just to historicize or to relativize a Western concept, important though that remains in a world that continues to universalize and proselytize northern parochialisms. It is also to return to the counter-evolutionary argument of the book.

Baldly stated, the Southern Tswana conception of the self that has survived into the postcolonial era seems to have foreshadowed recent shifts in Euro-American ideas of personhood. Not only does their sense of the individual as a constant labor of becoming, of ethical self-construction, call to mind the obsession with "personal growth" in various new wave movements across the north. More seriously, it conjures up the figure of the "entrepreneurial self" that Foucault (2008) associates with the rise of neoliberalism; the self who is her or his own capital *an und für sich*. Similarly, the Tswana notion of partible personhood, honed under colonialism, appears to have anticipated the fractal human subject with which late-modern Lacanian theory was to be so concerned. Indeed, it presaged the fixation of much post-structuralist writing, and postmodern cultural production, on the contingent, fragmentary, polymorphous, ungrounded nature of contemporary being-in-the-world—with its concomitant stress on identity as the accomplishment of a performing, performative individual.

The stress on the human subject as an entrepreneur of the self, as author of his or her own being-in-the-world, has itself to be contextualized. That subject, in its *collective* aspect, takes on its sociality, at least in its own psycho-cognized experience, by virtue of identification with others connected through putative biogenetic substance, choice, contract, and/or other forms of shared affect, predicament, interest. In Euromodernist states, however, the primary, most pervasive form of identification, normatively speaking, has long lain in secular, universal citizenship. Hence Benedict Anderson's (1991) depiction of the nation as an "imagined community" founded on cultural homogeneity and horizontal fraternity—within which "personal" differences, a.k.a. identities, were subsumed, if never fully dissolved. However, as we show in Chapter 3, precisely *because* human subjects construct and perform themselves ever more explicitly in terms of those differences, nation-states are having to deal increasingly with the hard facts of heterogeneity. This—in tandem with other historical processes of the medium term—is, we submit, changing the nature of the modernist polity. And changing it in ways, again, in which the global south is running palpably ahead of Euro-America. In ways, too, that raise fundamental questions about the limits of liberalism.

The encounter of nation-states with ever more strident claims of difference is manifesting itself in the rise of what we term, in Chapter 3, *policultural- ism*. This refers to a politicization of diversity that expresses itself in demands not merely for recognition, but also for a measure of sovereignty against the state and against the idea of the universal citizen, now less a citizen *of* the polity than a citizen *in* it—and likely to be possessed of multiple identities. Multiculturalism might have been declared dead in many European contexts, especially those plagued by xenophobia. Policulturalism, however, is making itself felt with mounting vigor, be it in African countries where chiefs seek unencumbered autonomy to rule their realms, or in places where communities of faith seek to enclave themselves and live by their own law—as in the United Kingdom, where the Archbishop of Canterbury recently suggested that Sharia be officially recognized because it already *is* the basis for the governance of everyday life among many Muslim groupings.

The rise of policulturalism has been part of a more embracing transformation of the nation-state *form,* the critical symptoms of of which—discussed in this chapter and again, in a different key, in Chapters 4 and 6—run to the very heart of the workings of governance, politics, economics, the law, and citizenship. If we may be excused a rather stark inventory for summary purposes here, those symptoms include, though are not exhausted by, (i) the displacement from public life of ideology, the -ology of the Idea, by ID-ology, the -ology of Identity, itself part of an escalating assertiveness, and will to sovereignty, of communities of faith and culture; (ii) a tendency for partisan national politics to hinge less on differences of belief or conscience than on the pursuit, on one hand, of the material interests of party elites and, on the other, on populist mobilization founded on the promissory rhetoric of a better life for all, of less intrusive government, of greater technical efficiency and service delivery, of tighter control of borders and closer protection of the commonweal through the mechanisms of the market; (iii) the fetishism of the law and the judicialization of politics, in which class actions become a common species of collective deployment and in which the constitutionally rooted language of rights provides the universal argot of social and economic life; (iv) the metamorphosis of the state into a mega-corporation—part franchising authority, part holding company, part venture capitalist business—accompanied by the outsourcing of many of its operations, like the regulation of violence, the conduct of warfare, the exploitation of natural resources, and the management of the fiscus; and, consequently, (v) the fracture and parsing of its sovereignty through a series of displacements of its authority. Taken together, these features of the nation-state form—plainly visible in the postcolonies of the south but becoming more so in the global north—suggest that we have entered a post-Weberian moment in the *longue durée* of modernity, one in which the "imagined community" of the 19th and 20th centuries demands re-imagination. Following the history of the present in the antipodean world, it would seem, is an appropriate place to begin the theory-work that this entails.

Chapter 3 was originally written in 2003. Since then, little has given us cause to rethink its argument. But one thing *does* stand out: the economic "meltdown" of 2008–09, which, although global in its ramifications, was felt less in those parts of the south that had already been through their own crises and, hence, were familiar with the downsides of deregulation, of the reliance on wealth *sans* work, of shrinking job markets, of credit without collateral; which is why, concomitantly, one of its effects was to curtail growth more severely in the "developed" economies of the north than in Africa, Asia, and Latin America (see above). In its immediate wake, as we have noted, government in the US, then in Europe and beyond, fell over itself to rescue large finance houses; politicians endorsed massive stimulus packages and called for oversight of the so-called shadow banking system—even as they tended to ignore the plight of ordinary citizens, who, as "entrepreneurs of themselves," were left to make do. Coming on the heels of three decades of rising market fundamentalism, these moves posed questions about the role of the state in contemporary capitalism. Were we, in Euro-America, in the midst of a return to the Keynesian past? The transfusion of tax revenues to banks and corporations deemed "too big to fail" prompted talk of a return of interventionism.[25] In the US, it reignited populist fears of creeping "socialism," a sentiment that grew more agitated—*vide* the rise of the Tea Party movement—as the Obama administration steered its national health care legislation through Congress. Less often noted was that this is a curious kind of Keynesianism, since it did not restore even the hint of a welfare state for citizens, preferring rather to redistribute public funds into private hands. What is more, government went into business on its own account as a major holding company, a move referred to by the *Economist* as "Leviathan Inc." and dismissed, derisively, as "déjà voodoo."[26] Which simply underscores our point, above, about the collapse of the lines of separation between the state and the market. And, ultimately, as Ralph Miliband noted some years ago, the inability of the state to tame capitalism any longer.[27]

Time will tell whether we are actually seeing the dawn of a new epoch in the history of capital and, in particular, the role in it of the nation-state. For now, however, there is little reason to expect a retreat of the precepts and practices of neoliberalism, even though its triumphal assertion as ideological paradigm may be more muted at the moment. Governments continue to secure the field of play for corporate commerce and venture capital much as before.

For all their promises to curb excesses, they have not yet circumscribed the risk-laden, inscrutable, and ultimately unaccountable operations of the finance "industry." Nor are they likely to,[28] even as commodity speculation conduces, among other things, to a growing global food crisis, exacerbated by the strident, well-funded efforts of agribusiness to block any legislative reform that might ease it.[29] What is more, states almost everywhere continue to endorse the market as the ultimate mechanism both for solving social problems and for creating value. In the USA, the Supreme Court has removed all limits on the capacity of corporations to determine the "democratic" political process by means of campaign contributions, ironically on the ground of protecting their right to free speech—as though an abstract legal fiction were a sentient political subject. The growing autonomy of the corporate sector in Euro-America and the capillary effects of the privatization of the media, of scientific research, and of bureaucratic state services, among many other things, have rendered the neoliberal habitus—its cultural fabric, its ethical argot, its moral economy—endemic to much of the late modern world.[30] As Susan Watkins (2010:14) has put it, "The widely proclaimed end of neoliberalism looks more and more like the continuation of its agenda by other means." We return to some of these issues later in the volume. Most immediately, in Chapters 4 and 5, we explore three other aspects of the changing character of the nation-state in the history of the present.

### The Demos and Its Demons: Borders, Belonging, and Bodies Politic

The first, addressed in Chapter 4, has to do with the relationship between its interiors and its exteriors, with borders and belonging. Published in an earlier, very different version a decade ago (Comaroff and Comaroff 2000b), it was framed by concerns, at the time, with the integrity of the modernist polity under the impact of globalization; globalization, that is, not as a loose metaphor of planetary articulation, but as a topologically complex overlay of supranational economic, administrative, legal, cultural, and techno-electronic flows, networks, domains, commons. What, in the circumstances, was happening to sovereign boundaries? Were they dissolving? Hardening? And what of citizenship within them? Was it becoming more fluid, especially with the heightened mobility of populations in pursuit of work, enterprise, expatriate property? Or the opposite?

We came to these broad issues somewhat circuitously, as anthropologists are often wont to do. It began with a fire in South Africa, a catastrophe that gave voice to popular, if partly submerged, anxieties about the amorphous threat of "the alien"; this in what represented itself as a rainbow nation, one founded on its tolerance of difference and, especially, on "non-racialism." The postcolonial preoccupation with things foreign first expressed itself, at least openly, in an antipathy to so-called invasive flora, which were said to imperil the indigenous plant kingdom and its life-giving bounty. Spirited efforts to rout out non–South African species soon followed. We suggested then that the rising ambivalence of autochthons toward outsiders of all sorts—floral, animal, and human—spoke with new intensity to deep questions about national belonging and the status of borders under conditions in which culture and identity were coming to be jealously regarded as collective heritage, even branded property. In the circumstances, we argued, the alien embodied the inchoate forces that threatened national patrimony, identity, commonality, sovereign integrity.

As it turned out, this horticultural patriotism was highly effective as an allegory of nation-building in a land afflicted with barely suppressed racial animosity, epidemic unemployment, widening economic disparities, rampant fears of crime, and porous international frontiers. Political and scientific commentators collaborated, if unwittingly, in calling forth a chauvinism, clothed in the language of autochthonous nature, that resonated uncomfortably with rising resentment toward refugees and migrants from elsewhere in Africa. How long, we wondered, before righteous indignation against "alien species," fanned as well by belligerent government rhetoric, would leap the species barrier and become an inferno of human hatred and extirpation? Not long, sadly. Our worst fears were confirmed as deadly attacks on foreigners gathered momentum, culminating in May 2008 when, in a frenzy of violence, scores of people lost their lives as the world watched on its TV screens. These attacks—ascribed popularly, if too simplistically, to xenophobia—arose out of material and political conditions that, among other things, produced the paradox of national borders simultaneously open *and* closed. In the cause of deregulation, itself essayed strongly by the Washington Consensus, frontiers had to be permeable to business from outside, thus ostensibly to reap the benefits of the new global economy, *and* sealed to secure zones of domestic advantage; open, more or less licitly, to expatriates whose labor undercuts that of enfranchised citizens, profiting local producers and feeding the public demand for cheaper goods, yet closed to "aliens" who, in the eyes of many South Africans, are stealing their jobs. In sum, the border had become the living sign, and the material objectification, of the contradiction between globalized *laissez-faire* and national priorities, protections, and proprieties. It is hardly happenstance, then, that, in a straitened economy, the border-crosser—again, human, animal, or anything else—would become a standardized nightmare, a living expression of that very contradiction and the deep ambivalences induced by it.

In revisiting the original essay some years later, we were struck by the degree to which our African story anticipated things to come in the north, where antagonism toward outsiders was to rise dramatically after the millennium;

intensified there, often to violent effect, by the "War on Terror," with its in-built Islamophobia and deep distrust of all difference. The implications of economic liberalization—among them, again, the escalating mobility of people in search of incomes, the evolution of free-trade agreements, the growth of the global electronic commons, and the workings of supranational institutions—are everywhere altering the way in which Euromodernist polities manage their sovereign integrity. Like southern postcolonies, whose frontiers were breached and buttressed under the imperatives of structural adjustment, they too are now faced with the paradox of frontiers at once open and closed; all the more when they rely on foreigners to address labor needs by serving as an internal colonial workforce. In the upshot, the lines that count nowadays seem less and less coterminous with geopolitical boundaries. On one hand, nation-states extend *beyond* their physical limits it for a variety of purposes: some of the powerful, for example, do so in the name of preemptive security, interpolating themselves onto the terrain of others in order to conduct both overt and covert warfare; others do so via their corporate enterprises. Legal jurisdictions, too, often exceed those of the political community, prime instances being the International Criminal Court, the European Courts of Justice and Human Rights, the Inter-American Court, and, in the USA, those courts to which recourse is sought under the Alien Tort Claims Act, which allows judicial processes that transect, transcend, and sometimes offend national sovereignties.[31] On the other hand, internal frontiers *within* countries tend increasingly to reinforce racial and ethnic cleavages, seeking to secure the "homeland" by dividing citizens from outsiders wherever they might be. Hence the highly controversial, contested law passed by the state of Arizona in the US, in April 2010, designed to make it easier, in the depths of the American heartland, to identify, criminalize, and deport unwelcome foreigners.

In the north, in short, just as in South Africa, antipathy toward foreigners tends to flare into full-blooded xenophobia—and into the exorcism of aliens whose bodies become a means of distinguishing inside from out—when adverse economic conditions, especially rising unemployment, mock the promises of citizenship. All too often that antipathy is interpolated into "narratives of national decline," prompting public figures to join "the nativist bandwagon … against the immigrant enemy" (Finnegan 2010:20). This is likely to accelerate yet further in a mobile, multicentric global ecumene, one whose populations and migrant hubs follow the magnetic pathways of capital, one whose space-time dynamics outrun the mechanics of modernist government. As Western states struggle with the conundrum of borders and belonging, as legal jurisdictions map ever less easily onto sovereign national space, as political rhetoric resorts audibly to the language of birthright and exclusion, as terms like "apartheid planet" circulate freely in the media, we may be forgiven for thinking that the colonial and postcolonial societies of the south were not so much historical inversions of the metropole as templates of what, in a postmodern world, the north would become.

But what of the political *interiors* of the Euromodernist nation-state, the public sphere so jealously protected as their own by its citizens? Democracy, participatory politics, and representative government, broadly conceived, are the topic of Chapter 5, originally written in 1996. The 1990s, recall, were the Decade of Democratization, especially in postcolonial and post-Soviet societies, a decade in which it was commonplace to bespeak the global triumph of liberalism. But it was also a time when a rising swell of social commentary had it that the world was witnessing the end of politics. Albeit counter-intuitively, it seemed to us that the two things were related: that democracy was asserting itself precisely to the extent that politics and power were migrating away from the state and its institutions. Which raised an obvious question: under such conditions, in what did it actually consist? In point of fact, a very thin idea of "government by the people," one largely measured by the presence or absence of national elections, was being exported to the non-Western world, often coercively, by the USA and its allies; freedom, went the mantra, inheres above all in the right to choose. This species of minimalist democracy was also being advocated by some political scientists—whose philosophical orientation, not coincidentally, derived from rational choice theory (e.g., Przeworski 1991, 1999).[32] It was accompanied by the equally insistent imposition of free market capitalism, although capital has often flourished sans democratic governance. It still does. Increasingly.

The chapter begins with an antipodean critique of the minimalist version of participatory government sold to the south by the north. It cites, as its prologue, a literary confection in which it is argued—by a fictional female character from Latin America—that democracy is a small idea, one that promises the world and delivers cheap consumer goods. But what kind of idea is it? What might it *mean* in cultural contexts, like those in Africa, in which freedom is *not* reducible to the exercise of choice, the equivalent to *homo politicus* of shopping to *homo economicus?* In which the political subject, as we will see in Chapter 2, is not an "autonomous" individual but a social being? In which, also, the rights of citizens—among them the right not just to speak but also to be heard, the right to the basic necessities of life, the right to protection *from* the state—are taken to be more important than, well, political shopping? In which, in other words, democracy is presumed to be more than a procedure, more a matter of substance?

Our first encounter with these questions was in Botswana in the 1970s, where, in observing two national elections from close up, we were struck by a paradox. On one hand, this country was taken at the time to be the *ur*-model of a popular African democracy. And yet, in the run-up to the ballot, we heard and read—in the media, on the streets of the capital, in rural villages—challenges posed to the prevailing order of things. They called for the replacement of the multiparty system with a single-party government; this on the ground, contrary to everything assumed in the West, that the latter is *more* democratic, the former more prone to authoritarianism. In the vibrant political culture of the indigenous communities of this nation, democracy depends not on *who* rules, nor on their ideological dispositions, but on *how* they rule. Good government, *bogosi yo bontle* in the Setswana vernacular, is measured in the performance of regimes in power: in their capacity to abide by *vox populi;* in their commitment to promoting an active public sphere and participatory politics according to established administrative and parliamentary means; in the pursuit of a better life for their citizens as indexed in the effort to bring "development"; in the existence of a just and fair system of courts; and, most of all, in the ongoing accountability of the sovereign to the demos. The habitual abrogation of these imperatives could, often did, lead to the removal of a ruler. As this implies, there existed elaborate modes of evaluation and sanction, and a public court, the *kgotla,* in which such things played themselves out.

It all sounds like democracy as idyll. But there were no elections. Chiefs, after all, were not chosen by universal franchise. This was a culture of participation without parties, of government, *bogosi,* without ballots. During the 1970s and 1980s, we could not help but observe how national political processes, formally an extension of the British Westminster model, were actually mimicking that vernacular culture; the then president, Sir Seretse Khama, was known as *Tautona,* "Great Lion," and commonly likened to a paramount. While popular debate about the quality of his regime was very active, and often quite critical, the vote was much less salient to most people. For them, it only had a point if there was need to remove a sovereign who failed consistently to meet the standards of good government; publically attested performance, not the polling booth, was the ultimate source of legitimacy. Largely in response to demands for open civic discourse, and for perennial accountability, so-called freedom squares—postcolonial versions of the *kgotla*—were created all over the country. Botswana as imagined community, in other words, became a projection, at least in part, of a political order founded on a highly substantive conception of democracy. Against this, the thin, procedural version proffered by Euro-America seemed an alienated, alienating alternative, a point made to us repeatedly by citizens of the country back in those days.

Beyond a critique of some of the basic tenets of liberal political theory, and of its export to Africa, what does our Botswana story add to *Theory from the South?*

A parenthetical comment here. The global south in general, Africa in particular, is often said to be intrinsically (culturally? genetically?) averse to democracy; Botswana tends to be cited as an outlier in this respect. The sheer number of African dictatorships, kleptocracies, and "failed states" is often given as evidence of the fact. This is in spite of the democratization wave of the 1990s and after; in spite of recent research, reported in *Afrobarometer,* which shows that "many more" Africans want and are "getting" democracy than did before; in spite also of the enactment of almost forty constitutions, since 1989, founded on liberal principles and the rule of law;[33] in spite of the reality that several nascent democracies on the continent have been destroyed at the behest of Euro-America foreign policy, especially during the Cold War, and/or by the rapacious incursions of mega-corporations, typically leaving behind them recurring cycles of violence and illicit collusions between states and organized crime; in spite of the risks to life and limb taken by many Africans in the cause of freedom, be it in South Africa, Namibia, Nigeria, Kenya, Zimbabwe, or elsewhere.

No wonder, in these circumstances, that there would be frank disillusion in many quarters—contempt, even—for market-friendly democracies that obsess over elections, but pay less attention to good government, accountability, or the rights and protections of their subjects. And that, as a result, appear remote, uncaring. Or that, in opinion surveys conducted by political scientists, respondents across the continent would have placed highest priority on the performance of their leaders, economic delivery, education, and the like—and much lower stress on the vote (Shechtel 2010:54–56),[34] all of which makes our Botswana case less singular than it might have seemed. Elsewhere in the south, for example, Indians dream of a nation with immediate, unmediated e-access to governmental processes (Mazzarella 2006). Back in Africa, South Africans spend inordinate amounts of time in a national conversation on FM radio, a conversation in which they demand answers from the ruling African National Congress (ANC). And often receive them. Significantly, when they meet denials of responsibility, not least for administrative functions that have been outsourced, they lament the seepage of authority away from the state, its institutions, and "the people"—and speak of it as a violation, a democratic deficit. Democracy, patently, *has* become a kind of fetish in much of the south. It is widely regarded as an enchanted force, one that, if only it could be fully domesticated, not hijacked by those who seek to empower and enrich themselves, might solve real problems in the world. But its true substance remains just out of reach, an elusive desire, a promise that fades into abstraction before it can actually be grasped, leaving behind it a thin procedural residue. No wonder, finally, that, throughout much of the south, one hears talk to the effect that the time has come for civil society to demand more of the state, not less.

End of parentheses. Back to the question we raised a moment ago about the relevance of our Botswana story for *Theory from the South.*

What has happened in Africa, epitomized by the Botswana case, appears to have anticipated a gathering sense of discontent throughout Europe and America with its own democracies. Hartmut Wasser (2001), surveying the findings of political science in this respect over the last years of the 20th century—there is a large literature on the topic—offers a terse synopsis of its most prevalent symptoms: a withdrawal, save in exceptional circumstances, from the electoral process; a "collapse of ... engagement with political parties" and, with it, a steady "de-alignment" from them; a dramatic drop of confidence in the executive branch everywhere; the almost universal view that government is run by "big interests" with no concern for the common good or for the well-being of citizens; the growing perception of an uncaring state, expressed in a broad "loss of faith in its institutions and the entire political class"; and so on and on. He might have added other sources of disaffection. One is that, with the spread of neoliberalism deep into the capillaries of public life, political parties have converged ideologically, congealing into competing coalitions of economic interest with little of real principle to separate them (see Chapter 3). Which might account for some of the de-alignment from them. So might the frequency with which they have been caught up in scandals arising from corruption, impropriety, and malfeasance in recent years; in this respect, at least, the north is no longer tracking behind Africa (Comaroff and Comaroff 2006b). But disenchantment with democracy, arguably, is also owed to the unassailability asserted by ruling regimes, even when they willfully mislead or defraud their populations; also by their flight away from transparency into regimes of secrecy, usually under the murky sign of security or the national interest. In addition, as we mentioned earlier, with rising unemployment and social alienation, growing numbers of the poor, *lumpen* youth, and racially marked populations feel themselves more excluded than ever before from public life—and often are by virtue of their relatively high rates of incarceration.

There is a counterpoint to this political narrative, a point that has also been made before but is worth reiterating. It lies in the relationship between capital and government. The more assertive corporations become, in particular global corporations, the more they find substantive democracy an impediment to their operations, preferring, and often colluding with, more authoritarian, wealth-conscious regimes—regimes willing to license and protect business without the encumbrance of parliaments or publics. Where such regimes are not available to them, it goes without saying, they are perfectly happy to bend those in place as far as they can to serve their interests, typically rationalized as a proxy for the national good. In sum, driven *both* by politics and economics, Euro-America's move toward a thinned-out version of participatory government seems, ironically, to be mimicking the very minimalist version exported to Africa some three or more decades ago. And, as in the south, that move appears to be evoking similar longings for a "thicker," less abstracted, more immediate version. After all, it is not democracy-as-ideal that has suffered a loss of faith. That, by all reliable accounts, remains firm in the north. It is the manner of its common practice. Hence the simultaneity of desire for and disaffection with it: like any fetish, its sustained enchantment lies in the fact that it remains a panacea whose promise is yet to be fulfilled. Hence, too, Wasser (*ibid.*) notes in conclusion, the call in some circles for "strong democracy"—following Benjamin Barber (1984)—embodied in robust "participatory institutions" rather than in "mere representation." For substance, that is, rather than for the proceduralism of the polling booth. Echoes, again, of Botswana.

In the meantime, everyday politics has migrated elsewhere. As in Botswana, with its *kgotla*s and freedom squares—African versions, these, of the Habermasian public sphere—it finds its voice in civil society, there to take up the space left by the democratic deficit (cf., on Yemen, Wedeen 2008). Thus the assertive rise and/or return of the town hall meeting, of talk radio, faith-based associations, and professional guilds, of grassroots organizations, anti-privatization coalitions, and eco-networks, even stand-up comedy and the likes of Tea Party rallies in the USA; these things sometimes fade into each other and are not mutually exclusive. And sometimes they grow into mass mobilizations, as did the one that overthrew the Mubarak regime in Egypt in early 2011. These movements constantly seek out new modes of recruitment, engagement, and deployment. Alongside and behind them has lain the liberalization of the means of communication, a virtual explosion that has spawned highly decentralized, highly accessible "social" media that facilitate instant interaction across time and space by way of Web-based and mobile technologies. These technologies create their own kinds of commons, their own communities of consciousness. Some of them, as in the Egyptian instance, have global reverberations. Others are more modest, yet also noteworthy for both their intent and their content. In September 2010, for example, a virtual collective of poets, protesting the deep cuts in public spending set in motion by the new Conservative-led coalition government in Britain, collaborated in the production of an online protest anthology, *Emergency Verse*. It mounted a "defence of the welfare state" at once lyrical and urgent. Within a few days of posting, according to press reports, the site had 300,000 visitors and submissions from across the planet.[35] Initiatives of these kinds all share the same impulse: a desire to engage in a participatory politics that might bring democracy to ground by finding a register in which the demos can argue and speak out. And might have a real impact on an otherwise unresponsive state. Perhaps their affective power stems from the heady sensation, the effervescence even, of creating a public with practical purpose, something that replaces the alienating abstraction of contemporary political life with the "close distance" (Benjamin 1968; Mazzarella 2003:256–57), the communitas, that inheres in mass-mediated public intimacy (J. Comaroff n.d.). That said, of course, their capacity to work transformation in and of themselves remains distinctly uneven; they cannot be understood apart from the particular historical circumstances that shape their mobilization and condition their effects.

But there are also other places to which politics takes flight. One of them, increasingly, is the law. Which takes us on to our next chapter.

*On Law, History, Memory, and Fetishes, of Various Sorts*

The judicialization of politics—and its concomitant, lawfare—has drawn a great deal of scholarly attention in recent times. Our own *Law and Disorder in the Postcolony* (2006b) takes it up directly, exploring how and why it is that litigation has become an autonomous reflex of political life in recent times. Government agencies and functionaries, social movements and NGOs, businesses, churches, political parties, ethnic corporations, charities, and ordinary citizens take to the courts with rising frequency. So do classes defined by interest, identity, injury, immiseration, lifestyle, desire, or predicament, seeking either authorization or restitution for an ever wider spectrum of claims, from the violation of bodies, psyches, memories, and intimacies, through the disposition of commodities, properties, propensities, and public policy to the determination of citizenship and civil rights, life and death. The spectacle of a suit between the president of the USA and one of its states over the right to regulate immigration is just one striking instance of the judicialization of politics in ways hitherto unknown or very rare (*The United States of America v State of Arizona and Janice K. Brewer*, #2:2010cv01413). Patently, resort to the law as political instrument is not unprecedented. What is, however, is its frequency and the range of differences that are being brought within its purview.

The turn to the law as a site of political contestation accords closely with the neoliberal propensity to re-situate most domains of life in the market and, thus, in the realm of contract, right, interest, entitlement—which, when violated, may be redressed through the courts. At least in principle. It is perhaps for this reason, too, that the world is seeing a realignment in the relationship between criminal and civil law. In Euro-America, the latter is encroaching upon the former, to the extent that it is no longer unusual to see felony proceedings followed by, or taking on elements of, personal injury actions.[36] The line between them, always porous, is rapidly collapsing, says John Coffee (1992:1875); to wit, the shrinkage of the criminal law in favor of the civil is being avidly advocated by some legal theorists (see Mann 1992). This fits well with the reduction of sociality to a commerce of rights and assets. And it makes sense of the growing support for the idea that victims should be given some say in determining the severity of sentences and settlements. Significantly also, for our purposes, it is foreshadowed in African vernacular jurisprudence, which is wont to treat most breaches, even homicides, as torts, not as offences against the state. And to put primary stress on negotiating ruptured relationships by ordering that restitution be made to wronged parties. The first resort to civil law to deal with social, material, and political conflict, in sum, is yet another axis along which Euro-America is evolving toward Africa.

It is to the judicialization of politics, civil law, and identity-as-injury that we turn in Chapter 6. It explores political subjectivity in the postcolony—in particular, its interpellation in the past. In South Africa, claims to the rights of citizenship, and especially to the reversal of old inequities, are overwhelmingly made with reference to damages inflicted by apartheid and the struggle to end it. Which raises a critical question: what role is to be accorded to memory—as inviolable possession, as a property of the human, as a vehicle of truth and redemption—in compensating for the costs inflicted by the *ancien régime;* this at a juncture, some would say, when History, in the upper case, has reached its end. And what difference does it make that the act of recall, in hopes of redress, is subjected ever more to the scrutiny of the courts, there to be assessed in the idiom of the evidentiary?

These questions must be parsed in light of a shift, most evident in the south, in the ways that nationhood lives with the past. Time was when Renan's (1882) foundational insight reigned supreme. It was necessary for modern nation-states to forget: to supplant "memory," a particular experience of place and pastness, with "history," whose communal, open-ended horizons gesture toward things to come (Koselleck 2002). Strategic forgetting, said Nietzsche (1957:6f), is a requisite condition for all action. Yet the late modern world, having lost confidence in collective possibilities ahead, seems preoccupied with the obligation to remember. In more and more places, the recovery of community, justice, and humanity is vested in public recall of old injuries. Not to lay them to rest, but to sustain them as means of *producing* a viable future. Iconic of the process is the vocal recognition accorded to the trauma of citizen-victims, a feature of restorative justice in periods of political transition; witness the over thirty truth commissions of the last three decades—and the move to insurgent class actions where they fail to heal festering wounds. In part, this reflects the cumulative impact of "global civil society," now armed with human rights jurisprudence, in pressing would-be democracies to deal with past crimes in the "court of public assessment."[37] It also accounts for the appeal of mechanisms like the US Alien Tort Claims Act, under which plaintiffs from across the world make hard-nosed demands on those held culpable for their pain. Again, personal recollection is the signal vehicle of these suits, memory its unalienated currency. While widely regarded as raw renderings of suffering, the narratives to which they give voice are shaped by unstated conventions of "truthfulness" and by the norms of legal testimony and claim-making.

The cogency of the forensic as a cultural idiom is evident in the fact that all those truth commissions, though technically extra-judicial, have relied heavily on the aura of legal procedure for their authorization. But there is more to this than merely authority. The judicialization of the past, and of its contemporary politics, is part of its transformation into established truths. And into property at once privatized and partisan. History, through the fetish of memory, has become, above all, a possession; the commodified substrate of subjectivity, as it were. Perhaps its putative demise, in the modernist form we have long known it, is due less to its irrelevance than to the alluring utility of the archive—living and literary, popular and professional—as heritage, as marketable legacy, and as the basis of lawful claims on the long-suffering present.

Which takes us back to truth commissions. While not new, they have taken on fresh salience in late modern times, where they aim to make peace with violence past and usher in a liberal, constitutional order that is generative of social solidarity, consensus, tolerance, and forgiveness. Theirs is the lexicon of civil law, of individual guilt and innocence—although, as restorative processes, couched in ethico-religious talk, their object is less to secure prosecutions or material damages than to broker amnesty in exchange for confession and apology. Nor do they investigate the structural conditions of past oppression, let alone traffic in redistribution. It is these limitations that have provoked class actions by victims who feel unrequited; like the South Africans, discussed in Chapter 6, whose case against corporations that colluded in apartheid is being pursued in a US district court. This kind of lawfare, notwithstanding the popular faith in it as a means of getting justice, is no more capable than are truth commissions of redressing legacies of structural inequity. But it does hold out the hope of restitution for a history of violation and trauma, a history that courts have the authority to recognize as the rightful possession of its claimants.

Truth commissions and insurgent lawfare may draw on jurisprudence and jurisdictions developed in Euro-America. But they have taken their late modern shape in antipodean sites, first in Latin America and later, charismatically enriched, in South Africa—thence to return to the north. The former Yugoslavia held one in 2002, for instance. So did Germany, a decade earlier, in respect of the former East. The latest is in Canada, where one was convened to address the grievances of First Peoples abused as children in Reservation Schools (Weiss n.d.). Many of the features of this extra-judicial form of restorative justice—identity-as-injury, the acknowledgment of culpability, and the plea for forgiveness—resonate culturally in a world in which declarations of sincerity and respect for dignity, couched in psychological terms, stand in for concrete social, political, and material action. Note, in this respect, the rash of public apologies of late (Trouillot 2000). They cover everything from the crusades to slavery. In 1997 Bill Clinton apologized to the survivors of the notorious Tuskegee Syphilis Study (1932–72) that left 399 African Americans untreated after a cure for the disease became available. In 1992 Pope John Paul II even apologized to Galileo for the churlish reaction of the Church to his insistence that the earth was not at the center of the universe.[38] It is hard not to conclude that the sheer frequency of these ritual performances, these confessions *sans* consequences, are displacements that sustain inequalities by hiding them in plain sight, where they are left unredressed, unrepaired, and unrequited.

Recourse to the law in repossessing the past—and in authorizing memory—is not unique to the south either. It has also migrated northward. As nationhood becomes more heterodox in Euro-America, as the politics of identity gather momentum, claims against the commonweal in recognition of historic rights denied or violations suffered challenge sovereign narratives there, too. Such claims brook no ambiguity. They prefer the language of legal certainty to that of social history, with its inherent indeterminacy, its subversive potential, its "attachment to the bud of awkward alternative outcomes," as Simon Schama puts it.[39] And because they rely on partisan experience as their alibi for authenticity, they resist incorporation in the belly of the Leviathan. "History is everywhere," says Yasmin Alibhai-Brown of Britain, "but whose history is it?"[40] Others in the UK note that teachers in "particular settings . . . are unwilling to challenge highly contentious or charged versions . . . in which pupils are steeped at home, in their community or in a place of worship."[41] Similar observations have been made in the US and Canada,[42] where debate has flared over the place of history in teaching about "citizenship and patriotism," in the rise of "multiculturalism" and "critical separatism," and in the struggle over creationism. Under these conditions, in which history is endangered less by authoritarian reductionism than by its unrestrained diffusion, the reliance on the law, the one national language of commensuration in which difference can be negotiated and claims made in its name, appears over-determined.

This is not, we stress, a lament for the end of national historiography. Quite the opposite. It is an observation that, as history becomes cacophony, as it is "experienced in fragments" (Schama, after Benjamin, see n.39), as it gives voice to political subjectivities under reconstruction, it shifts its epistemic ground. It becomes a celebration of identity *sui generis* rather than a critical instrument with which to give account of the conditions under which specific identities, as concrete abstractions, emerge, prosper, empower, discriminate, exclude. After all, history-as-learned grew up as part of a modernist regime of knowledge whose point was to interrogate the changing lineaments of the world, not merely to echo history-as-lived, whose narrative impulse is to make claims in that world. Now the received order of things is reversed. It is the latter, history-as-experienced, that speaks truth to history-as-learned, rendering its habitations unhomely, its northern orthodoxies heterodox, its universalities parochial, and its authority eroded—leaving politics an impassioned clamor for position, possession, right, and recognition.

## Political Economies of Exclusion: Zombies, Bare Death, and the Politics of Life

Let us turn from those who lay claim to the present by conjuring with the past to those for whom the present is already rife with conjurers of a very tangible sort, conjurers with unexpected northern counterparts. Chapter 7, first drafted in the late 1990s, bore the title "Alien-nation." The word, which had not yet coursed through global pop culture, continues to capture the existential undersides of the present age of capital, the age in which finance takes precedence over the productive economy. So, too, does its subtitle, "Zombies, Immigrants, and Millennial Capitalism," with its hint of nightmares and necropolitics (Mbembe 2003). In retrospect, the essay seems to have been haunted by the future, by events then still in gestation. Shot through with forebodings of economic crisis, it anticipated the backlash that was to follow against rampant deregulation and wealth accumulated by "instruments ... so opaque [that] nobody understands them."[43] This takes us back to the second argument of the volume: the south as frontier in the unfolding history of neoliberalism.

Our original essay described the *angst* of many South Africans in the wake of the economic liberalization of the 1990s, a process whose origins lay in global transformations that preceded the end of apartheid and were implicated in its demise. The avid espousal of free markets and private enterprise by those charged with bringing the postcolony into step with the world may not have been inevitable. But few were able then to imagine a national economy that did not accommodate itself to the neoliberal turn. As a result, the transition to democracy was accompanied by intensive downsizing, deregulation, the casualization of labor, and, with it, the steady disappearance of wage employment in its older forms—creating a void into which entered a rush of migrants from across the continent, many of them ready to toil at a deep discount. In this environment, augmented by positive efforts to transfer at least some of the reins of capital into black hands, a great deal of cash was made from immaterial property and new kinds of rentier rights; a significant proportion of it derived from privatized public assets. At the same time, millions of citizens, most of them poor people of color, lost their previous means of livelihood. Speculation of all kinds was rife. So, too, was a swelling sense that the country had been opened up as never before to occult forces, forces that yielded money without material effort, whether it was the inscrutable sorcery of finance, the magic of pyramid schemes and prosperity gospels, or the capricious capacity of the economy itself to deliver abundance in some places and to impoverish others. All of which was exacerbated by a rash of fraudulent get-rich schemes aimed alike at the affluent and the abject. South Africa had its own prefigurations of American con-artist *extraordinaire* Bernie Madoff—like Sibusiso Radebe and his Miracle 2000 Fund[44]—whose promises to earn vast profits for credulous investors were made plausible by the fact that, in the Brave Neo World, productive work and the production of wealth looked to be inversely related.

We have plumbed the lineaments of millennial capitalism in another context (2000a). Here it is sufficient to note that, in Africa, the new age of entrepreneurialism has proven exhilarating to many, especially those recently liberated from totalitarian austerity. But others, schooled in the belief that durable value comes of self-possessed effort (see Chapter 2), have been suspicious from the first of the sudden appearance of riches by largely inscrutable means. It smacked of ill-gotten gains, of witchcraft and sleight-of-hand, of toxic wealth gained by draining the lifeblood of the vulnerable and gullible. These conditions nurtured the figure of the zombie in South Africa during the late 1990s, lending credence to the idea that all this mysterious wealth was being reaped for the new rich, spectrally and invisibly, by eviscerated phantoms. The living dead, after all, toil ceaselessly without pay. They are truly cost-free labor, pure profit. Here was Marx's dread image of the ultimate achievement of capitalism: production without human workers, the final alienation, as it were, of their species being. The zombie gave ghostly meaning to an oxymoron favored by neoconservative apologists for South Africa's postcolonial road to development: jobless growth.

The apprehensions made manifest in this phantasmic figure ran parallel to fears in the north of the growing gap between the dazzling feats of finance capital and the "real" economy; of unrestrained speculation in domains formally associated with sober investment (banks, mutual funds, pension schemes) that had made people into unwitting gamblers on their own futures; of the delirious faith that fast, vast fortunes can be accumulated by creating mechanisms that abstract money from its more tangible forms, "rebundle" it, and pass it on at accelerating speeds. Even professional observers were moved to speak of the technicians of this phantasmic global economy as "financial alchemists" (Stiglitz 2008:37; Packer 2009:80); alchemy, after all, refers to the antique art that sought to change base metals into gold. And to discover the secret of life eternal, of which the zombie is a misbegotten freak. Speaking of the African context, we had referred to this broad species of alchemy, and the practices to which it gives rise, as an "occult economy" (1999a).

It is no coincidence, then, that talk of zombies should be heard amidst the frantic efforts of the governments of advanced capitalist nations to tether money to more substantial forms of wealth, exorcising "toxic" assets and bailing out banks. The trope of the living dead seemed splendidly appropriate to those struggling to grasp opaque means-ends relations as vast riches were conjured up—only to melt into air as solid "property" (savings, houses, companies) became tokens in a shell game that eliminated assets in ways that mock regular business. Hence the image of "zombie banks"[45] that feed fraudulently off bailout money; of "zombie debt" that is repeatedly resold, such that a settled account may come back to life and haunt people again; of "zombie funds" that promise risk-free returns but "plod along like the walking dead";[46] and, in Ireland, of "zombie hotels" built with insecure finance, run by lenders at no profit, and described as a "potent symbol of the profligacy ... that has plunged the Irish economy deep into crisis."[47]

We are in the realm, here, of critical poetics, of a reality made strange by *unheimlichkeit,* the denaturing of once dependable, solidly bourgeois institutions: banks, hotels, personal savings. At issue is the credibility of a credo that seduced people across the planet into believing that they had entered an era in which fortunes, fame, and virtue might be made by gaming with the equity of everyday life, with dwellings, bodies, identities, commodities. All of these things came to be treated as assets, equipping even the most humble to think of themselves as entrepreneurs; indeed, entrepreneurs, once more, of the self. In the last decades of the 20th century, what was once pariah profiteering—unfettered speculation, gambling, retailing contagious assets—was deemed legitimate, even esteemed enterprise. To the skeptical, it all seemed too good to be true. It was, of course. When the implosion eventually hit, it let loose a flood of dialectical images, zombification among them, which played on the primitive magic that has always haunted frontiers, including the frontiers of capital; all the more so as efforts to plumb its latest crisis have taken on divinatory, even theological, proportions. Many of those images draw heavily on the African occult. Not for the first time, either. After all, its lively history—in which different regimes of wealth production have long intersected, often disjunctively (Guyer 2004)—yielded the concept of fetishism, one that served critical thinkers well in earlier quests to probe the unfolding mysteries of the market (Pietz 1985–88).

The figure of the zombie—whose existence has always evoked ambivalence, uncertainty, agnosticism—resonates with a loss of confidence in the signal manifestations of what passes for the real: in the genuine value of specie, in the true meaning of signs, in the legibility of relations among humans, in the facticity of non-fiction, in the credibility of ethical commitments, and, especially, in the authenticity of capital itself as it comes to appear increasingly phantasmic, alchemic, abstract, capricious. In places like South Africa, moreover, the living dead serve as mute witnesses to—indeed, as iconic of—the deployment of ever more brute technologies in the extraction and accumulation of that capital. Also, to the power of the new masters of the universe to take charge of most forms of wealth in the world, to hollow out bodies, property, and institutions, and to leave behind only their facades. In short, zombies seem to stand in for what is left behind by the fitful, perverse, accelerated movement of money, jobs, and commodities, a process that subverts the received certainties of everyday experience—and, *in extremis,* pushes many to the limits of bare life, not to mention bare death.

But the limits of bare life breed their own positive possibilities. And their own species of political action that congeal in the space between a poetics of estrangement and politics in a more conventional sense of the term. That species of action, which tends to be more visible in the south than in the north, takes on many guises: mobilizations against the privatization of the means of subsistence; against rising homelessness and, in particular, against mass evictions from either commons rendered into real estate or zones of abandonment gentrified; against deepening poverty, unemployment, and the absence or withdrawal of government services; and so on. They often transcend old lines of class, race, and cultural difference, often produce new social categories (like "the poors" in South Africa; see above), citizens' movements (like *La Coordinadora* in Bolivia and the Landless Workers' Movement in Brazil), coalitions (like the Urban Poor Consortium in Indonesia), even political parties (like Evo Morales's *Movimiento al Socialismo*) and official identities (like *Beghar,* or homeless, in India). And they often conjure with new modes of collective action, new notions of political subjectivity and community, new sorts of sociality and citizenship. Of these mobilizations, among the most striking—because it deals most comprehensively in the calculus of life and death—has been the response to the global AIDS pandemic. Which takes us to Chapter 8.

Some years back, the South African activist Adam Levin (2005:226) declared that "the world has AIDS." To be sure, whatever its epidemiology, the entire planet is implicated in its spread and caught up in its effects—more or less directly. HIV *is,* in many ways, a quintessentially late modern, global phenomenon, the yield of accelerated circulation, communication, commensuration, and commerce of various kinds—local and translocal, licit and illicit, productive and destructive, contained and contagious. As the signal pandemic of the age, it is an unwelcome by-product of some of the major forces that have converged to make the 21st-century world: the advent of a vision of economies *sans* frontiers, of fluidity, flexibility, and the free flow of labor and capital; the unprecedented crossing of geopolitical, racial, social, sexual, and viral boundaries; the rise of a culture of commodified desire and liberal experimentation; the coexistence, in this world, of almost infinite human opportunity with ever-intensifying forces, indeed fortresses, of exclusion; the counterpoint between a spirited sense of deregulation and a politico-moral conservatism that resists challenges to established modes of social reproduction.

Like little before it, AIDS has made visible the stark distinctions of privilege and vulnerability that divide and unite the contemporary global order; distinctions, some would say, on which that order rests. Patently, the implications of the disease in the south are very different from those in the north—although there are atypical populations in each—which, in turn, have conduced to differences of political consciousness. And aspiration. In Euro-America, the appearance of a medieval-like scourge in an antiseptic universe coincided with the unraveling of the Cold War world order and, with it, the dawn of an age of creeping anxiety, then terror. Here AIDS served as an allegory for new fears and uncertainties, spawning a defensive politics of "intense moral purity" (Watney 1990:100). Fixated on family values as the means of communal regeneration, this moral impulse made "responsible" sexuality a prime index of virtue—and AIDS its obverse, the poisonous fruit of wanton depravity and amoral desire. As in the case of epidemics before and since, this one was deflected, in Euro-America, onto its primal others: "perverts" at home and Africans abroad. Energetic initiatives were mounted by sufferers and their supporters in the north to counter stigmatization, to fight for civil rights, and to push the quest for a cure. But, for the most part, AIDS remained a special-interest struggle, even more so as medical advances transformed it from a death sentence into a chronic condition. At least, for those who could afford the drugs.

Meanwhile, the disease went south. Mounting awareness of soaring infection rates in Africa, Asia, and Latin America made it synonymous with third-world abjection. There it remained a death sentence for the millions excluded from pharmaceutical salvation. Notwithstanding some successful south-north collaboration in opening up access to treatment, humanitarian empathy continues to run head-on into the realities of reproductive politics and corporate protectionism. For some, the southern AIDS sufferer has come to epitomize Giorgio Agamben's (1998) figure of *homo sacer,* a disposable being who, stripped to "bare life," might readily be killed without being granted sacrificial value. Suggestive as it is in metaphysical terms, however, the trope of bare life fails to capture the irreducible sociality of human existence, for good and ill, or the inexorable will to life-in-the-world of even the most destitute, deprived, disempowered.

In fact, AIDS has been singularly successful in giving rise to a self-conscious, critical biopolitics, not least among those very people who most often go unrecognized—and tend to be treated as disposable—by sovereign authority. Educated by the stark realities of the disease itself, southern sufferers have come to realize that healing requires that they lay bare the social etiology of the pandemic, exposing its vectors of causality; the structural conditions, that is, that render bodies vulnerable and stand between the ill and life-prolonging drugs. Their organic, practical sociology also charts a ground plan for action. AIDS politics, in the likes of South Africa and Brazil, has been driven by a passionate inventiveness, sharp in its analytical grasp and creative in its ways and means. Here, activists have found strategies to tap into the capillaries of neoliberal governance, like the private-public, multinational collaborations that control resources crucial to their survival and the legal means that undergird them. Working with a range of allies and tactics—mass mobilization, insurgent lawfare, the media, the politics of spectacle—AIDS activism has been notably effective, as Biehl (2004:111) attests for Brazil, at both coopting and challenging the state.

In South Africa, AIDS politics, famously typified by the Treatment Action Campaign, has also made common cause with grassroots movements fighting for basic services, education, and social equality. Here collective action centers on what Arendt (1958:100), after Locke, termed "the condition of human life itself." Not bare life, nor even "health citizenship" (Petryna 2002), but life vested in rights to full membership in the polis, something not entirely grasped by the notion of biopolitics, especially not biopolitics reduced to the logic of governmentality. Like similarly assertive movements elsewhere, from Cochabamba to Mumbai, Chiapas to Cairo, the South African ones seek to secure the minima of a dignified existence: clean water, housing, electricity, medical care, sanitation (Olivera 2004; Appadurai 2004). This species of "living politics" (Chance n.d.) has become a force to be reckoned with as unemployment and homelessness burgeon, as the indigent find themselves displaced and unheeded, as the discarded struggle, in the words of a South Durban tenement dweller (Chari n.d.), to find "a piece of oxygen" in the ruins of an age of industrialization and development past.

The popular politics of life draws on a diverse global archive, from Marx, Gandhi, and Fanon, through the Book of Revelations, Black Consciousness, Act Up, and the Zapatistas, to born-again faiths and human rights crusades. Movements given to this sort of social action often set out explicitly to develop a critical (self-)consciousness, to foster debate about the nature of theory, and to take up the question of who rightly ought to be producing it (Desai 2002); they also decry the limited horizons of procedural democracy and politics-as-usual (Chapter 5). In large part, theirs is a postcolonial, post-totalitarian enterprise, informed by a legacy of struggle that tends to instill both a deep historical sensibility and a commitment to the quest for collective emancipation. This is in sharp contrast to the north, where critics nowadays frequently bemoan the loss of the political (see above)—"politics without politics," Žižek calls it[48]—or rue the brute cynicism that surrounds the very idea of a public good. AIDS campaigners in Euro-America, who have sought to broaden their fight for the rights of the unprotected, have long implored their supporters to learn from the south (Watney 1990). So have champions of other progressive projects; among them, the push for society-wide basic income grants, which, according to the Carnegie Council, has been gaining momentum alike in "developed" as in "developing" countries.[49] Or, if not basic income grants, something akin to them. Again, the south provides a paradigmatic model: Brazil's *Bolsa Família,* a massive cash transfer program initiated in 2003 that uses debit cards to make small monthly payments to poor families, usually to women, which are then augmented if they invest in such things as educational and health services for their children (Morton n.d.). This scheme, incidentally, underscores our point about the extent to which the neoliberal habitus, its cultural practices and forms of political subjectivity, have come to pervade the global ecumene. Even under Brazil's Worker's Party regime, the payments are described as "investments" rather than wages for the unemployed, thus making the latter, like everyone else, into entrepreneurs of themselves.

In sum, just as neoliberalization, deindustrialization, and eco-degradation are crystallizing new forms of culture and sociality, new economies of exchange, and new survival strategies in the nether reaches of the north, so they are producing new modes of mobilization, species of ethical action that often elude the conventional bounds of politics. Like in the south, these address a wide spectrum of things, from healthcare, education, and basic income, through the recommissioning of urban space, the exploitation of nature, and the absence of police protection, to the predicament of the jobless and the homeless. As beggars, vagrants, migrants, and alumni of asylums and other institutions become more visible on the streets of Euro-America, as churches and shelters can no longer cater to the sheer numbers of hungry, unwaged, and unhoused people, as the capillaries of organized crime extend further and further, as relict populations expand in the derelict zones of the US and the idle shipyards of the UK, in the mining towns of South Wales and the scrap cities of eastern Germany, so we see the accelerated growth of precisely the same kinds of coalitions, campaigns, and citizens' movements, the same politics of life, that we have been seeing across the south for some time now; thus, for example, the sweep of anti-austerity actions across Europe in the fall of 2010. And so the cycle comes full circle. As the contemporary capitalist world order—at once global and local and everything in between—catches all and sundry in its web, as its peripheries become its vanguard and its centers mimic its peripheries, so the world *is* turned upside down. Modernity may be at once creative and destructive. But it is often both in quite perverse, counter-intuitive, counter-evolutionary ways. For better *and* worse, the south does seem to be tracking at the front end of history, there to challenge us to understand the world from *its* vantage: to make it, as the South African Ministry of Higher Education and Training put it—*vide* the epigraph at the beginning of the volume—an "active producer of social theory."[50]

This raises two final, fundamental, formidable questions: What, where, exactly *is* "the south"? And what, precisely do we mean by "theory"?

## ENDPOINTS: ON THE SOUTH, AND THEORY

For all the fact that "the global south" has replaced "the third world" as a more or less popular term of use, the label itself is inherently slippery, inchoate, unfixed. At its simplest, the shift is an effect of the end of the Cold War, during which the global map was clearly triangulated. The "first" and "second" worlds were blocs[51] sedimented around the USA and USSR, respectively, each founded on an ideological paradigm for configuring the political economy of modernity; each had its third term, its "less developed" others—and a telos for their futures, which, in turn, shaped their national aspirations, their *realpolitik,* and their economic objectives. So-called non-aligned countries faced massive pressures to fall into line, to look to left or right, and to situate themselves along one or another axis of the macro-geometry of the period.

That was then. In the age of neoliberal capitalism, of the "end of ideology,"[52] those aspirations and objectives are more crass: they lie everywhere in success or failure in the global marketplace and its sacred indicators. In the upshot, "the south," technically speaking, has more complex connotations than did the World formerly Known as Third. It describes a polythetic category, its members sharing one or more—but not all, nor even most—of a diverse set of features. The closest thing to a common denominator among them is that many were once colonies, protectorates, or overseas "possessions," albeit not necessarily during the same epochs (cf. Coronil 2004). "Postcolonial," therefore, is something of a synonym, but only an inexact one. What is more, like all indexical signs, "*the* global south" assumes meaning by virtue not of its content but of its context, the way in which it points to other things. Of these, the most significant, obviously, is its antinomy with "*the* global north," an opposition that carries a great deal of imaginative baggage congealed around the contrast between centrality and marginality, capitalist modernity and its absence. Patently, this opposition takes on a hard-edged political and economic reality in some contexts, among them, the politics of aid (and, yes, AIDS), the distribution of influence in the likes of the United Nations, the World Bank, and the IMF, G-8 deliberations and decisions, international courts of various jurisdictions, and perhaps most importantly, the fiscal arithmetic of influential credit rating institutions. But it obscures as much as it describes.

Two things in particular.

We have already alluded to both. The first is that a number of nation-states of the south, far from being marginal to global capitalism, are central to it. Recall that, in speaking of the many mushrooming economies of Africa, Guo (2010:44) observed that foreign multinationals report some of their most impressive returns there—which is likely to continue because those economies are expected to continue their growth at rates exceeded only by

Asia. And perhaps Brazil. Although this is not reducing mass immiseration or lowering Gini coefficients, it *does*—along with rapidly expanding endogenous production and consumption—ensure that the continent will become ever more integral to the operations of Euro-American commerce and the cultural life of neoliberalism. However it may be imagined, as Balibar (2004:14; cf. Krotz 2005:149) puts it, "the line of demarcation between 'North' and 'South,' between zones of prosperity and power and zones of 'development of underdevelopment,' is not actually drawn in a stable way." *Per contra,* that line is at best porous, broken, often illegible. Even if it could be definitively drawn, moreover, many nation-states defy easy categorization: On which side, for example, do the smaller countries of the former USSR fall? Or, if brute economic development is the primary criterion, where are we to place those powerhouses to which we keep returning, the likes of India, Brazil, South Africa, and Nigeria, which seem to cross the cleavage between hemispheres? This is not even to mention Japan or the most portentous player of them all, China, which greatly profits from playing in the interstices between worlds. And has interpolated itself into *both* north and south without being truly either, all the while promising, some time off into the future, to alter the political economy, and the geo-sociology, of the entire planet. On one hand, these are among the more dynamic economies and cultural worlds of our times. Yet, on the other, still being highly polarized within, they are geo-scapes in which enclaves of wealth and order feed off, and sustain, large stretches of scarcity, violence, and exclusion. This is also true, increasingly, of Euro-America. In short, there is much south in the north, much north in the south, and, as we argue throughout the volume, more of both to come.

The second thing, which follows as both cause and effect of the fuzziness of the line between the hemispheres, is the structural articulation—indeed, the mutual entailment—of their economies; which, we stress, subsumes their political economies, their cultural economies, their techno-economies, their moral economies. It is this, after all, that makes our counter-evolutionary story really a dialectical one; this, too, that makes global capitalism global, not merely international. It also reiterates our point, at the outset, that, in its aspiration and its reach, capitalist modernity has few, if any, exteriors, that its exclusions and its outsides are integral to its inner workings. Not only are the laboring classes of Euro-America, those who produce its means of consumption, situated ever more at southern margins, but, and this is critical, southern capital buttresses, even owns, many signature Euro-American firms (see above); all of which is further complicated by the world of finance and the ramifying electronic commons, whose labyrinthine capillaries defy any attempt to unravel them along neat geopolitical coordinates. This is true, as well, of the underside of the global economy, the spectacular expansion of transnational organized crime in its deregulated interstices, sometimes in collusion with legitimate business, whose own practices often tack along the outer limits of the law. Thus, for example, a good deal of the kleptocracy associated with government in the south involves bribe-givers from the north, among them large, respectable multinational companies (Comaroff and Comaroff 2006b:18); so much so that some African regimes have come to root their sovereignty on the management of external cash flows, often from corporations with an interest in keeping them in power, thus to sustain their right to disburse the very licenses and contracts that those corporations seek to acquire from them—including licenses and contracts to perform outsourced functions of government. In both its licit and its illicit dimensions, then, in the complex hyphenation that links economy to governance and both to the enterprises of everyday life, the contemporary world order rests on a highly flexible, inordinately intricate web of north-south synapses, a web that both reinforces and eradicates, both sharpens and ambiguates, the lines between hemispheres. As a result, again, what precisely is north and what is south becomes harder to pin down. All the more so, again, as the counter-evolution of Euro-America gains pace.

This is why "the south" cannot be defined, *a priori,* in substantive terms. The label bespeaks a *relation,* not a thing in or for itself. It is a historical artifact, a labile signifier in a grammar of signs whose semiotic content is determined, over time, by everyday material, political, and cultural processes, the dialectical products of a global world in motion. This, incidentally, is why, for certain purposes but not for others, some or all of the "the east" may be taken to be part of it. Analytically, though, to return to the point made by Homi Bhabha (1994b:6), whatever it may connote at any given moment, it always points to an "ex-centric" location, an outside to Euro-America. For our purposes here, its importance lies in that ex-centricity, in all senses of the term: in the angle of vision it provides us from which to estrange the history of the present in order better to understand it. As such, whatever else it may be presumed to be, whatever political or economic ends its invocation may serve, "the south" is a window on the world at large, a world whose geography, *pace* Kant and von Humboldt, is being recast as a spatio-temporal order made of a multitude of variously articulated flows and dimensions, at once political, juridical, cultural, material, virtual—a world that, ultimately, transcends the very dualism of north and south. *Theory from the South,* then, is about that world. And the effort to make sense of it.

Which, patently, is where the question of theory poses itself.

It is a matter of observation that, throughout much of the global north, there has been something of a flight from theory, a re-embrace both of methodological empiricism and born-again realism; also a return to the ethical and theological. At its simplest, this is a corollary of the postmodern, post-structuralist, post-Marxist disillusion with grand narratives and with systemic abstraction of all sorts. And of the tendency to see them—from the vantage of a neoliberal, anti-systemic, deregulatory present—as authoritarian, functionalist, over-determined, whatever; dismissive adjectives abound. For the global south, the refusal of theory has long been an unaffordable luxury. The need to interrogate the workings of the contemporary world order—to lay bare its certainties and uncertainties, its continuities and contingencies, its possibilities and impossibilities, its inclusions and exclusions—has become increasingly urgent. For, while it holds out the promise of new ways of knowing, new means of control, new techniques of accumulating wealth, that order has also yielded rising inequality and inequity, joblessness and homelessness, poverty and disempowerment, corruption, criminality, and xenophobia. Hence the call of the Ministry of Higher Education and Training in South Africa for "social theory" and "critical skills" (see above). This comes at a time when political classes across the north are evincing disturbingly anti-intellectual, anti-critical tendencies, seeking to shut down public discourse about the undersides of life in the here and now. And when many, unionists and scholars and journalists and ordinary people alike, are cowed into silence for fear of losing jobs, and worse. What the South Africans, and southerners elsewhere, seem to have grasped is that this is not an option: that the courage to criticize, the courage to theorize, is indispensable to any effort at making the history of the future different from the history of the present. If, indeed, rather south-like conditions have become the "grim New Normal" in Euro-America,[53] there is clearly a need there too for a return to Theory. Perhaps this is a respect in which Euro-America *ought* to evolve more rapidly toward Africa.

By theory, we stress, we do not intend grand theory in the high modernist tradition. Ours is not a flight into pure abstraction or into philosophical anthropology. We mean *grounded* theory: the historically contextualized, problem-driven effort to account for the production of social and cultural "facts" in the world by recourse to an imaginative methodological counterpoint between the inductive and the deductive, the concrete and the concept;[54] also, in a different register, between the epic and the everyday, the meaningful and the material—and, here in particular, between capitalism and modernity, the fitful dialectic at the core of our present concerns. In short, our predilection is for theory that neither is an all-embracing meta-narrative nor is microcosmically, myopically local, but tacks on the awkward scale between the two, seeking to explain phenomena with reference *both* to their larger determinations and their contingent, proximate conditions—by plumbing the complex, often counter-intuitive points of articulation among them. This, as we go on to say in our final chapter, implies a respect for the real that does not conflate the empirical with empiricism. And a respect for the abstract that does not mistake theory-work for theoreticism; a praxis, that is, whose object is to arrive at a principled sense of the connection between what it is that constitutes the lived world and how that world is affectively and cognitively experienced, acted upon, inhabited by sentient human subjects. *Theory from the South,* in sum, is an argument for just this kind of grounded theory.

A final thought. A reprise, really. We began by reflecting critically on the genealogy of enlightenment liberalism, on its presumption that universal truths and philosophical wisdom derive from Euro-America—whose others, by extension, are objects to be theorized. All of this goes back at least to Plato, to *The Philosopher and His Poor* (Rancière 2003), to the conceit that there is one class that reflects while others should do only their work, not think analytically about the world. Ours is a different genealogy. For us, theory, particularly critical theory, is immanent in life itself. Which to a greater or lesser extent *always* implies a degree of reflection, abstraction, generalization. Theory-work, with apologies to Veblen (1899), is not the sole prerogative of a leisured class. It need not be an elite or an elitist practice, even though it is often dismissed as such. To the contrary, it often derives, as much, from a lived praxis, one that may occur anywhere and everywhere. And does, not least at the frontiers of the contemporary world order—and, yes, in its petri dishes. These, again for better and worse, are rich sites of new knowledges and ways of knowing-and-being, ways of knowing-and-being that have the capacity to inform and transform theory in the north, to subvert its universalisms in order to rewrite them in a different, less provincial register. All the more so as Euro-America evolves southward, toward Africa. And Asia, and Latin America.

# CHAPTER 2

# On Personhood

*A Perspective from Africa*

Is the idea of "the autonomous person" a European invention? This conundrum, posed to us by colleagues in philosophy and anthropology at the University of Heidelberg in June 1997, seems straightforward enough. Even ingenuous. But hiding beneath its surface is another, altogether less innocent question, one that carries within it a silent claim: to the extent that "'the autonomous person" *is* a European invention, does its absence elsewhere imply a deficit, a failure, a measure of incivility on the part of non-Europeans? And what of the corollary: is this figure, this "person," the end point in a world-historical telos, something to which non-occidentals are inexorably drawn as they cast off their primordial differences? Is it, in other words, a universal feature of modernity-in-the-making, a Construct in the upper case? Or is it merely a lowercase, local euro-construct?[1]

We begin our excursion into African conceptions of personhood in a decentering, relativizing voice: the voice often assumed by anthropologists to discomfort cross-disciplinary, transcultural, suprahistorical Western categories, their provenance and putative universality. From our disciplinary perspective, "the *autonomous* person," that familiar trope of European bourgeois modernity (Taylor 1989), *is* a Eurocentric idea. And a profoundly parochial, particularistic one at that.[2] To be sure, the very notion that this generic person might constitute a universal is itself integral to its Eurocultural construction, a part of its ideological apparatus. What is more, "*the* autonomous person"—the

51

definite, singular article—describes an *imaginaire,* an ensemble of signs and values, a hegemonic formation: neither in Europe, nor in any place else to which it has been exported, does it exist as an unmediated sociological reality (Comaroff and Comaroff 1991:60f). Neither, of course, does the classical contrast between (i) the self-made, self-conscious, rights-bearing individual of "modern Western society," that hyphenated Cartesian figure epitomized in the Promethean hero of Universal History (Carlyle 1842:1), and (ii) the relational, ascriptive, communalistic, inert self attributed to premodern others. As we shall see, African notions of personhood are infinitely more compli-cated than this tired theoretical antinomy allows (Fortes 1973; La Fontaine 1985; Lienhardt 1985).[3] So, too, is the telos of Afromodernity, which, as we stressed in Chapter 1, is not moving, in a fixed evolutionary orbit, toward Euromodernity. To the degree that the continent, as diverse as it is large, has spawned its own modernit*ies,* often explicitly named as such, very different notions of selfhood, civility, and publicity have taken root within it. In this respect, too, there is a strong counter-teleological case to be made: a case for the radically revisionist thesis that, in some critical respects, Euro-American personhood is evolving toward Africa, not the other way around. Which, of course, echoes the central narrative of the present volume.

As this suggests, we shall call into doubt the universality of "the autono-mous person" by recourse to an anthropological insistence on cultural and historical specificity. But this does not exhaust either our objectives here or the interrogative that frames them: ... *A European Invention?* Phrased thus, the question mark points toward two further problems: Is the idea of "the autonomous person" properly regarded as an invention at all? If so, is it to be attributed to Europe? The first, patently, depends on the manner in which we understand processes of cultural production; the second, on the extent to which we allow that anything in European modernity was ever fabricated endogenously—rather than in hybridizing encounters with significant, usually colonized, others. We shall return, in due course, to the historical dialectics underlying the rise of post-enlightenment Western constructions of selfhood and, with them, to the answers to these questions.

First, however, let us turn to Africa. Note that we do not seek to arrive at a generic account of "*the* African conception of personhood." There is no such thing. Our purpose is to take one good, historically situated case: that of the Southern Tswana peoples of South Africa during the late colonial period. As it happens, much of what we shall have to say about Tswana imaginings of being-in-the-world, and about their historical anthropology, has broad resonances elsewhere across the continent. But, more to the present point, by illuminating the contrasts and consonances between African and European discourses of personhood, this case casts a sharp, prismatic light on received Western notions of the modernist self and its antinomies.

## Personhood and Society
## in the Interiors of South Africa

Among those peoples who, during the colonial encounter came to be known as "*the* Tswana,"[4] personhood was everywhere an intrinsically social construction. This in two senses. First, nobody existed or could be known except in relation and with reference to, even as part of, a wide array of significant others.[5] And, second, the identity of each and every one was forged, cumulatively, by an infinite, ongoing series of practical activities. *Pace* Tonnies, selfhood was not ascribed: status and role were determined by factors other than birth or genealogy, although social standing was typically represented in genealogical terms (Comaroff and Roberts 1981:37–46).[6] For reasons having to do with its internal workings—anthropologists have long noted that the coexistence of an ideology of patrilineal descent with endogamous marriage yields social orders of this sort[7]—the Tswana world of the time was at once highly communal and highly individuated. From within, it was perceived as a rule-governed, hierarchical, and ordered universe, and yet as an enigmatical, shifting, contentious one: a universe in which people, especially men, had to "build themselves up"—to constitute their person, position, and rank—by acquiring "wealth in people," orchestrating ties of alliance and opposition, and "eating" their rivals. Potentially at least, selfhood and social status, which were reckoned in terms of agnatic seniority, were always negotiable, an observation that Gluckman (1963) once claimed to be true of all African "tribal" societies. For Tswana of the colonial era, in sum, "the person" was a constant work in progress; indeed, a highly complex fabrication, whose complexity was further shaded by gender, generation, class, race, ethnicity, and religious ideology. Among other things.

But we are running ahead of ourselves. A bit more background first.

The Tswana peoples today compose one of the largest ethnic groupings in South Africa.[8] At least from the late 18th century onward, and probably for a good time before (Legassick 1969:98), the majority of them lived in expansive chiefdoms in the central, semi-arid interior of the country; although, for more than 130 years, many have either migrated to cities and towns across the subcontinent or have lived in small decentralized rural communities (Schapera 1953). Until the colonial state went about subverting their autonomy, the chiefdoms were a substantial political presence on the landscape, their economies founded on cultivation, cattle, hunting, and trade (Shillington 1985). Each was centered on a densely populated capital, with thousands of residents ordered into family groups and wards, surrounded by fields and cattle-posts; polities (*merafe*) stretched as far as chiefs and their subjects could pasture and protect their animals (Comaroff and Comaroff 1990). In the spaces between were tracts of "bush" (*naga*), cross-cut by pathways that linked the capitals.

These trails served as vectors of trade and alliance, of warfare and raiding, and of the exchange of cultural knowledge over long distances.

With the arrival of Protestant evangelists and European settlers from the 1820s onward, the region became increasingly populated. And contested. White farms, trading posts, and villages began to dot the countryside. Along with the missions—themselves augmented by schools, shops, and other signs of "civilization"—they soon asserted a visible presence on the "bushveld." Inexorably, roads and transport routes followed. Inexorably, autochthonous populations found more and more of their land expropriated. With the mineral revolution, Southern Tswana, already schooled by the civilizing mission in bourgeois ideas of property and progress, would learn the lessons of colonial capitalism first hand. Many migrated as neophyte proletarians to the burgeoning mining settlements just beyond the edges of their territory; some benefitted greatly from the opening up of markets for their produce and their services; all became embroiled in a rapid process of class formation, in which new patterns of social distinction and ideological difference, partly phrased in the polite language of the Protestant ethic, came to divide old communities. Finally, in the 1880s, overrule inserted the British state onto this terrain. Its functionaries located themselves either in the white towns at the hub of farming districts or in newly erected administrative centers, from which nearby "natives" could be governed. Often these centers were sited close to Tswana capitals and brought in yet more Europeans, generally in pursuit of trade and business; the building of a railway line across the territory in the 1890s made it accessible to people and goods otherwise unlikely ever to have entered it. This, in turn, exacerbated the ingress of Southern Tswana into the racialized, class-fragmented world of colonial economy and society—with all that it entailed (see, e.g., Shillington 1985; Molema 1966).

The most obvious thing that it entailed was a complicated, contradictory sociology. On one hand, colonialism spawned relations that transected the lines of race, class, and culture, creating hybrid identities and unexpected patterns of consociation (Comaroff and Comaroff 1997:24–25).[9] On the other, it came to be represented as a sharply sundered, Manichean world, in which the cleavage between black and white, ruler and ruled, African and European was cast in st    Elsewhere (*ibid.*:24–29), we have argued that this schismatic imagin      as endemic to the construction of colonial societies. We have also sho    at, in its representation here—wrought largely as a result of the encou    between Southern Tswana and colonial evangelists—this irredeemable opposition came to be phrased as a contrast between *sekgoa*, European ways and means, and *setswana*, their Tswana counterpart; each being reduced from a dynamic, evanescent, open-ended, historically expansive order of signs and practices to an ahistorical essence, a fetishized object, a tradition. A culture.

In point of historical fact, the content subsumed by these two constructs, by *setswana* and *sekgoa,* changed a great deal over time. That much is clear from the documentary record. However, they continued to stand in stark epistemic antinomy throughout the colonial epoch. To be sure, their residues persist today—even as they are encompassed within an increasingly heterotopic postcolonial cultural politics. It is out of this contrast that we may begin to draw our description of what personhood, as framed in *setswana,* may be taken to have meant during the late colonial period; to have meant, that is, both as a stereotypic representation and as a set of intersubjective practices.

## Of Being and Becoming

As we said a moment ago, the Southern Tswana world was a socially fluid, evanescent field of social relations: one in which, despite the stress on genealogical placement, the onus was on citizens, especially adult males, to "build themselves up," to protect themselves from their enemies and rivals, to negotiate their rank and status,[10] and to extend themselves across social space by accumulating wealth in people. Of course, not everybody was equal in this respect. For one thing, there were, until well into the colonial period, various forms of servitude to be found in most chiefdoms (Schapera 1938; cf. Tagart 1933). Slaves and servants, who were regarded as semi-social beings (Moffat 1842:383), lacked the right to own property or possessions—indeed, to be self-possessed. For another thing, women were jural minors, subject to the representation of their senior male kin. In the context of everyday social life, as well as in political processes that played themselves out away from the public eye, females were anything but inert or impotent. Quite the opposite. But, legally speaking, they lived in the passive voice. For example, where a man might marry (*go nyala*), a woman *was* married (*go nyalwa*). For a third thing, status made a difference. Kings and commoners, the rich and the poor, ritual experts and supplicants enjoyed varying capacities to act upon the world; not least, as we shall see, because the empowering activities of some people had the effect of reducing the potency and potentiality of others.

This qualification aside, however, most Southern Tswana adults found themselves engaged constantly in a praxis of self-construction. Given the scaffolding of their universe, it could not be otherwise. Either people acted upon the world or the world acted upon them. Or both, in some proportion. Every now and again this involved dramatic confrontations over property, possessions, or position. For the most part, however, it entailed the unceasing, quotidian business of cultivating relations and fields, of husbanding animals and allies, of raising offspring and avoiding the malign intentions of others, of gradually accumulating cultural capital and cash to invest in the future. Here, then, is the first principle of contemporary Tswana personhood: it referred not to a state of being but to a state of becoming. No living self could be static. Stasis meant social death.

The principle of personhood as a mode of becoming expressed itself in every aspect of social existence. Take, for instance, marriage, an ensemble of practices often treated as the site, *par excellence,* of social formation and reproduction.[11] Earlier generations of anthropologists were wont to say that, in Africa, wedlock was a process rather than "an event or condition" (Radcliffe-Brown 1951:49); that, as Murray (1976) has observed of Lesotho, the salient question was not whether two people were married, but how much. Among Southern Tswana, the creation of a conjugal bond, and of the parties to it as fully social adults, took the form of a protracted, cumulative succession of exchanges, sometimes ending only after the death of the spouses. What is more, the status of that bond was always open to (re)interpretation—as casual sex, concubinage (*bonyatsi*), living together (*ba dula mmogo*), marriage (*nyalo*)—this being facilitated by the fact that the terms used between partners (*monna* [m], *mosadi* [f]) were unmarked; they might as well have referred to someone with whom an individual cohabited the night before as to a mate of long standing. Nor, in the flow of everyday life, was any effort made to clarify such things. Relations might go undefined because, in the normal course of events, they were growing, developing, becoming. As were the human beings involved in them. It was only at moments of rupture, when the continuing present came to an abrupt end, that there was any necessity to decide what they *had been.* Or, rather, had become. And this only because different kinds of partnership involved a different disposition of assets on dissolution (Comaroff and Roberts 1981:151–53).

Much the same stress on becoming rather than being, on persons and relations as the unfolding product of quotidian social construction, was evident in patterns of inheritance as well. By contrast to European convention, the devolution of estates across the generations was not tied to death. It began, rather, as soon as an individual reached adulthood, set about establishing a conjugal union, and had children. And it continued, as an ongoing process, throughout the life cycle. Indeed, its success was measured not by how much of a residue of property one had at death, but by how much had been distributed before—and how little had been kept back to become the object of argument among heirs (Comaroff and Roberts 1981:175–215). Through the cumulative, gradual disposal of property, men and (to a lesser extent) women realized themselves as parents, spouses, citizens of substance, ancestors in the making. By these means they insinuated, objectified, and embodied themselves in their offspring. And ensured their perpetuity as persons.

As this suggests, the foundational notion of being-as-becoming, of the sentient self as active agent in the world, was so taken for granted that it went largely unsaid. Throughout life (in embodied form) and even after death (as a narrated presence), the person was a subject with the potential to engage in the act of completing and augmenting him- or herself. Take just one, very mundane demonstration of the point:

> In February 1970, we were sitting in a domestic courtyard in Mafikeng, capital of the Tshidi-Rolong chiefdom, with the family of a ward headman, Mhengwa Letsholo. An elderly female neighbor, obviously well past childbearing age, walked across the public meeting space just beyond the homestead wall. "There goes Mme-Seleka," said the headman's wife, gesturing her way. "Mme-" denotes "mother of," although its connotative fan is rather broad. Trying to place her in social space, one of us asked whether she had sons or daughters. "Not yet," said the headman, "No, not yet." At face value, this seemed a facetious answer. There was no doubt that, given her age, Mme-Seleka was not about to fall pregnant. But it made perfect sense. For one thing, there were conventional means—such as the levirate and sororate—by which offspring might be "born" legally to a person who could not physically produce them. But there was another, less pragmatic dimension to Mhengwa's response: to answer in the absolute negative would have been to consign the woman's active life to the past tense, to pronounce her socially dead. As long as she was a sentient being, as long as she was still in the process of becoming, some form of maternity was always possible. "Not yet" implies the continuous present, just as "no" puts closure to something that once may have been but now but no longer is.

The only time that people stopped becoming was when they fell victim to witchcraft or were "eaten" by someone more powerful. In the former case, they were either immobilized by illness or mysteriously rendered inert, their capacity for productive activity negated (cf. Munn 1986). In the latter, which implied feminization, they were reduced to dependency and eventually lost all self-determination; typically, they ceased to toil on their own account, working instead at the behest of their masters and patrons. "Absorbed by another personality" was the way in which one early 19th-century missionary-ethnographer described this state of arrested becoming (Willoughby 1932:227). A second observer, J. Tom Brown (1926:137–38), wrote an unusually vivid description of men who, having been thus consumed, suffered an eclipse of their personhood:

> When a man's relatives notice that his whole nature is changed, that the light of the mind is darkened and character has deteriorated so that it may be said that the real manhood is dead, though the body still lives; when they realize that ... the human is alienated from ... his kith and kin, they apply to him a name (sebibi or sehihi), which signifies that though the body

lives and moves it is only a grave, a place where something has died or been killed. The essential manhood is dead. It is no uncommon thing to hear a person spoken of as being dead when he stands before you visibly alive. When this takes place it always means that there has been an overshadowing of the true relationships of life ...

*Sefifi* [*sehihi*], the term for this state of non-being, is the same as that for "death pollution." Interestingly, it describes a condition strikingly similar to the figure of the zombie, which has recently appeared in the South African countryside as part of a moral panic about joblessness in the postcolony (Comaroff and Comaroff 1999a). It speaks of an erasure of self-determination, of a body usurped, of an empty shell who toils mindlessly for others, of a slippage into the passive, past tense. But how, by contrast, do sentient social actors construct themselves? Wherein lies their mode of producing personhood?

### On Producing Personhood

The production of personhood here, we reiterate, was an irreducibly social process; this despite—or, perhaps, because of—the fact that, given the workings of the Southern Tswana social universe, initiative lay with individuals for "building themselves up." The epistemic emphasis on self-construction was embodied, metonymically and metapragmatically, in the idea of *tiro,* labor.[12] *Go dira,* in the vernacular, meant "to make," "to do," or "to cause to happen." It covered a wide spectrum of activities, from cultivation, cooking, and creating a family to pastoralism, politics, and the performance of ritual ( J. Comaroff 1985; Comaroff and Comaroff 1991:140ff ). *Tiro* was, still is, generally translated as "[a] work" (Brown 1895:308), and accented the *act* of fabrication. It yielded value in the form of persons, things, and relations, although it might be undone by sorcery and other malign forces (see below). But *tiro* was not an abstract quality, a commodity to be bought or sold. It could not exist as alienable labor power. Southern Tswana often said that, in the past, even the energies of a serf were not to be exchanged, let alone purchased. They were only available to his or her master by virtue of a *relationship* of interdependence; hints, here, of Hegel. Work, in short, was the positive, relational aspect of human social activity, of the making of self and others in the course of everyday life.

Not only were social beings made and remade by *tiro,* but the product—namely, personhood—was inseparable from the process of production itself. As Alverson (1978:132) has noted, "An individual not only produce[d] for himself, but actually produce[d] his entitlement to be a social person." This was captured in the various inflections of *go dira.* Its simple reflexive form, *go itira,* "to contrive oneself" or "to pose as," carried ambiguous moral implications.

It spoke of antisocial, egocentric self-enhancement; hence the common usage *go itira motho* (lit. "to make oneself, physically and socially, a distinct person") connoted "to be proud" or "haughty." *Go itira* contrasted with *go itirela,* the reflexive extension of *direla* ("work for"), which translated as "to make (work, do) for oneself" in an affirmative sense. For Tswana in Botswana during the 1970s, according to Alverson (1978:134), *itirela* still referred to the accretion of riches in family and social relations, in cattle and clients, in position and possessions; all of which was also held to contribute to the common good. The creation of these forms of value was dubbed "great work," the effect of which was to extend the self through ties of interdependence, often by means of objects. Thus the significance of property, most notably beasts, was that it both indexed *and* capitalized leverage over people. By extension, power was taken here to be a measure of command within a complex, labile field of material and signal exchanges. Far from being understood in terms of individual autonomy or self-sufficiency, its signature was control over the social production of reality itself.

The concept of self-construction—of *tiro,* "work," and *itirela,* "to make [for] oneself"—then, projected a world in which the "building up" of persons in relation to each other, the accumulation of wealth and rank, and the sustenance of a strong, centralized polity (*morafe*) were indivisible aspects of everyday practice. The object of that practice, minimally, was to avoid social death, to continue producing oneself by producing people and things. Maximally, it was to do "great works." But just as individuals were presumed to be unequal in their capacity to construct themselves, so not everyone was able to toil in the same kinds of way. Above all, male labor differed from female labor. Before the introduction of the plough—and after it, save for wealthy cultivators—women were associated primarily with agriculture, domesticity, and reproduction. The racial capitalism of the colonial state, and especially of the apartheid regime, played into this by coercing men into migrant wage employment away from home; their wives and daughters remained in the countryside. In addition to subsistence farming, these women were the source of the most basic value of all, human life. But their fertility also yielded polluting heat (*bothitho*) that could spoil the physical and social enterprises of their husbands, fathers, and brothers; even Christian converts evinced concern at this danger. Thus they were said to need physical confinement, denied an active role in the public sphere, and kept away from cattle, the most prized form of capital. Men, by contrast, were cool (*tshididi*), more self-controlled. They had the corporeal qualities necessary for raising stock, for effective social production, and for the management of the commonweal. While wives did hold fields on their own account, had their own granaries, and exercised some control over the disposal of their harvest, their "works"—the fruits of their labor pains and labor power (cf. Jeffery *et al.* 1989)—provided the material base, the mundane commodities, on which male politics, law, and ritual depended. The point was made repeatedly in Tswana poetics. For example, the origin myth of the male initiation, the most comprehensive of their *rites de passage,* told how society was born when the raw fertility of females was domesticated by men and put to collective ends.

## *Personhood, Negation, and Self-Defense*

The ongoing process of self-construction was, as we said above, under constant threat of countervailing forces; forces inherent in the social world itself. Because men, especially agnatic rivals, sought to "eat" one another, and because sorcery was an ever-present danger, work also involved protecting one's self and one's dependents from "being undone." *Dirologa,* the reversive extension of *dira,* described this mode of destruction. People took great pains to fortify their homesteads and fields against attack—and sometimes to attack their adversaries, real or imagined, before being hit themselves. Nor was this true only of "traditionalists." In the 1930s, Christian elites, deeply committed to "private interest and competition," were observed, by a Tswana anthropologist, to deploy magical means to doctor their crops and cattle in order to safeguard them;[13] also, to "get ahead." We observed the same thing, sometimes fused with Christian ritual, in the 1970s.

Of all the available preventive measures against being undone, however, the most fundamental, and the most effective, lay in the fabrication of personhood itself. In anticipation of the postmodern stress on multiple, fractal subjectivities and in a manner evocative of the partible *persona* described for Melanesia (see n.3), Southern Tswana were careful to fragment and refract the self in presenting its exteriors to the world. This derived from an ethnotheory of power/knowledge based on two foundational, if unspoken, axioms. *First,* because that self was not confined to the corporeal body—it ranged over the sociophysical space-time occupied by the sum total of its relations, presences, enterprises—anything that acted on its traces might affect it for good or ill; which is why human beings could be attacked through their footprints, immobilized by curses, enabled by ancestral invocation, undermined or strengthened by magical operations on their persons, their houses, their clothes, or their animals ( J. Comaroff 1985). *Second,* to the degree that anyone was "known" to others, she or he became vulnerable to their machinations, to being consumed by them. Conversely, empowerment, protective or predatory, lay in the capacity to conceal: to conceal purposes, possessions, propensities, practices—and, even more subtly, to conceal concealment, to hide the fact that anything at all was being hidden.

Put the two axioms together and the corollary is obvious: it made sense only to present partial, refractory aspects of one's person—of one's property, projects, interests, affect—to the various others who shared the same coordinates of the life-world. Hence the people with whom an individual worked, or engaged in economic enterprises, were shown a single facet; political allies saw another; those with whom s/he prayed or played, yet another; and so on. Clearly, given the nature of everyday existence here, and the local predilection for gossip and scandal, there were inevitable overlaps. Boundaries were breached, what was masked occasionally became transparent. Still, the effort to sustain the partibility of personhood, thus to empower the self and its undertakings, was a fundamental premise of being-through-becoming. So much so that it went utterly unremarked. But it was revealed, metapragmatically, at the one moment in the life cycle at which the coherence of biography was enacted: death. Echoes, *here,* of Sartrean existentialism.

The integration of the fractal human subject occurred toward the end of his or her funeral. In a public ceremony known as *tatolo,* people arose to narrate that part of the career of the deceased of which they, in particular, knew. And so, piece by piece, a composite portrait emerged, a life took shape from its shards. In the 1970s, we were told more than once that *tatolo* was the most engaging part of a burial—not least to mourning relatives, for whom the synoptic accounting was sometimes as much of a surprise as it was to relative strangers. In a universe in which social knowledge was a matter of insatiable interest and informational value, it is no wonder that *tatolo* held such fascination. It represented an existential *denouement,* the summation of a biography that had, until now, been an inscrutable work in progress. And was about to move onto an altogether different, even less scrutable plane. In the case of persons of power, the fascination grew exponentially: *tatolo* stood to reveal their ways and means, their ethical disposition, their secrets of being-and-becoming, in this complex, labyrinthine social world.

## CONCLUSION: THE DIALECTICS OF ENCOUNTER

The Southern Tswana conception of personhood, in sum, was part and parcel of a distinct, historically wrought universe of meaning and action, an Afromodernist universe in which labor, the self, and the social were mutually constituting. Shades, here, of Marx. This conception was at once different and yet similar to its idealized European counterpart. The latter had come to be represented, ideologically, in the liberal language of possessive individualism (Macpherson 1962), a language alien to vernacular African experience—especially because it appeared to background the social, to relegate it to mere "context." But, *pace* the conventions of Western knowledge, the antinomy between Euro-individualism and African communitarianism, past and present, is profoundly misleading. For one thing, as anthropologists never tire of pointing out, personhood, however it may be culturally formulated, is *always* a social creation—just as it is *always* fashioned by the exigencies of history. This is as true in Europe and the USA as it is in Africa or Asia; as true of the 18th as it is of the 21st century. And it remains true under epochal conditions in which the very existence of society is called into question.

Similarly the stress on the social and communitarian foundations of African personhood. Nowhere in Africa were ideas of individuality ever absent (Lienhardt 1985). Individual*ism,* another creature entirely, might not have been at home here before the postcolonial age; not, at least, outside of Protestant elites. But, each in its own way, African societies *did,* in times past, have a place for individuality, personal agency, property, privacy, biography, signature, and authored action upon the world. What differed was their particular substance, the manner of their ontological embeddedness in the social, their ideological formulation. All of which ought to underscore, yet again, why crude contrasts between European and African selfhood—or the reduction of either to essentializing, stereotypic adjectives of difference—make little sense. And why sociological and semantic similarities may be obscured by dissimilarities in languages of representation.

Michael Welker has offered the term "autoplexy" to signify the mode of personhood we describe for the late colonial Tswana world.[14] It is a mode of personhood, as he glosses it, that involved "playing with" a multiplicity of shifting roles and identities to secure freedom of action and social position. This form of play in a fluid, intricate field of relations, Welker concludes, produced something analogous in Africa to the autonomous individual of the post-enlightenment Western imagination. Perhaps. The more fundamental point, however, is that the idea of "autoplexy," and the analysis to which it applies, seeks to pay due regard to the nuances of African ideas of personhood. Also to treat them as parallel to, and commensurate with, their European counterpart: as their coeval rather than their benighted precursor.

We have situated this account in the late colonial period, not in "traditional" Africa. As we intimated at the outset, no such thing exists, least of all in respect of the signs and practices of personhood. Among Southern Tswana, those signs and practices altered a great deal over the long run. In part, this was due to the encounter with Protestant missionaries, who bore with them into the South African interior a strong commitment to liberal individualism and rights-bearing selfhood. The Protestants essayed contradictory perceptions of Tswana subjectivity. On one hand, "the natives" were described as "primitive communists," savages with no individuality or sense of self. Yet they were constantly accused of brute "selfishness" and "greed," even of a lack of "natural affection" for others (see, e.g., Dachs 1972:695). All of which made it necessary to instill in them a capacity for self-possession and an appreciation of refined individualism. For their part, Southern Tswana found the Europeans—whose idea of labor lacked the grammatical range and subtle semantic inflections of *tiro*—to be perverse in their insistence on private property and individual rights. To translate the discourse of toil into the vernacular, the Christians put *itira,* "to contrive oneself" (in the morally ambiguous, self-seeking sense of the term), over *itirela,* "to make oneself" (in a positive, socially accountable manner). What is more, they stressed the value of contracts, titles, and deeds, a mode of textualizing relations that, to the Africans, appeared to make humans into fragile "paper persons." It also disembedded exchange from its social referents and rendered visible what ought to be concealed, thus opening people up to being "eaten" more easily than before. To wit, the reduction of material transactions to these instruments of legality was referred to, by Tswana in the 1880s, as "the English mode of warfare" (Mackenzie 1887,1:80).

As this suggests, the dialectics of encounter were far from straightforward. For all the differences between European and Tswana sensibilities, Euro-Christian concepts of self and virtuous labor had strong resonances with indigenous notions of "great work" and being-as-becoming. As a consequence, the transcultural discourse of personhood here bore within it a number of legible, transitive signs; signs that pointed toward an ideological conjuncture for those who drew near to the church, adopted the practices of bourgeois civility, and entered the black elites spawned by colonial political economy. It also set in train a long conversation among Southern Tswana themselves about selfhood and civilization (see, e.g., Molema 1920; Plaatje 1996), one modulated by processes of class formation and social distinction. While some found the liberal individualism of *sekgoa* ("European ways") highly appealing and took on its terms, others repudiated it, even while being affected by it. Yet others forged various sorts of synthesis out of the antinomy.

They still do.

The conversation continues today across the northern reaches of the South African countryside, albeit in altered circumstances. Indeed, it is has become ever more fervent as anxieties about the future—about its social, material, ethical, and cultural dimensions—take on epidemic proportions amidst rising inequality, poverty, pathology, generational conflict, political alienation. With gathering talk of the need of Afromodern solutions to local problems, and of the ideal of *ubuntu,* an authentically African sense of the human, populist critique is to be heard, sometimes in soft whispers, sometimes in loud clamors, of the rampant excesses of Western ways of being-in-the-world. And of those people, black and white, who indulge in them.

At the same time, in the global north, the growing fixation in the present on perpetual "personal growth," expressed in various of its "new wave" disciplines, would translate easily into the long-standing Tswana argot of *go itira,* of the work of self-produced "becoming." In this respect, Euro-America *does* seem to be edging toward Africa. So do its theorists, especially those who have ridden the Lacanian wave into the age of the posts-, those who vex themselves about the fractal nature of the human subject, its polymorphy and multiplicities. As though *this* were a Euro-American invention. Had Euro-theory known a little more of Africa, past and present, perhaps the idea of a more complex notion of human personhood, one grounded in a multidimensional space-time, might have commended itself a long time ago.

# CHAPTER 3

# Liberalism, Policulturalism, and ID-ology

*Thoughts on Citizenship and Difference*

Herewith two fragments from the discourses of the recent South African past.

> ... we Blacks (most of us) execrate ethnicity with all our being.
> *Desmond Tutu, 1981*[1]
> *Future Archbishop of Cape Town*

For the Anglican cleric, in the late apartheid years, "native" cultural identities were little more than an excrescence of colonial racism.

> Our duty is to identify and define the main currents of [African] tradition and to incorporate [them] in the modern, technically advanced political entities that we are seeking to construct.
> *Penuell Maduna, 1999*[2]
> *Minister of Justice and Constitutional Development*

For the cabinet minister, the products of those very identities are a necessary element in the making of the postcolonial nation-state.

The difference? Twenty years or so in the history of difference.

\*   \*   \*

If Kymlicka and Norman (2000:1) are correct, recent debate in Euro-American political philosophy has been preoccupied by two, typically unconnected, issues: "minority rights–multiculturalism" and the nature of democratic citizenship. This seems unsurprising in an intellectual endeavor devoted largely to the study of Western politics; after all, the triumphal rise of neoliberal capitalism, new patterns of mass migration, and emergent ethnic and religious movements have all put pressure on the nation-state in its modernist form. But how salient are these issues outside of Euro-America? How significant are they in everyday *realpolitik* across the planet? On the face of it, they might appear not to be especially pressing in post-apartheid South Africa. Why not? Because this country, lately freed from the ethnically coded rule of a racist colonial state, has fashioned for itself a Constitution founded on the most comprehensive, most liberal, most enlightened notions of democratic pluralism. Not only is that Constitution unusually attentive to universal enfranchisement and human rights. Like many other recent constitutions in the global south, it is also quite explicit in its accommodation of the cultural claims of minorities. Indeed, if its own rhetorical construction were a description of its political sociology, South Africa—deeply committed to the rule of law, to the monopoly of the state over the legitimate means of violence, to a conception of citizenship that both transcends and tolerates diversity—would seem to inhabit the very ideal of the Euro-nation in its 21st-century guise. On one hand, it embodies all the principles on which that nation was founded (cf. Hobsbawm 1992:3–4); on the other, it has set about confronting the realities of difference in precisely the manner that many philosophers of "minority rights–multiculturalism" have proposed.

And yet, almost from the start, a "crisis of culture," a counter-politics of ethnic assertion against the jurisdiction of the state, has rumbled beneath the surfaces of the new polity, threatening to disrupt the founding premises of its Bill of Rights. This has entailed more than just a quest for the recognition of distinctive identities, languages, and life-ways, a quest that has become familiar elsewhere in recent years (Taylor 1992). It has also raised fundamental questions of sovereignty: the sovereignty of African traditional governance, in which ethnic subjects claim, and are claimed by, another species of authority. This authority, as we shall see, does not live easily with the hegemony of the liberal modernist state, although that state has always invoked it as its suppressed underside. The kingdom of custom sanctions alternative orders of law and justice, of the use of force, of responsibilities and entitlements, even of tribute and taxation. The generic citizen of postcolonial South Africa may be the rights-bearing individual inscribed in the new Constitution; also the rights-bearing individual—typically urban, cosmopolitan—presumed in much mass-mediated discourse. By contrast, ethno-polities and traditional leadership[3] speak the language of subjects and collective being (cf. Mamdani 1996). For most South Africans, it is the coexistence of the two tropes, of citizen and subject, that configures the practical terms of national belonging. But that coexistence, despite the Bill of Rights, does not always reduce to an easy, "flexible" accommodation (cf. Ong 1999): life as national citizen and life as ethnic subject are as likely to run up against one another—often in contradictory ways—thus making political personhood a fractured, fractal experience. It is when they do that the real sociology of citizenship in the "new" South Africa is most put to the test of democratic pluralism: citizenship not as it is envisaged in a political philosophy of the normative future, but citizenship in the concrete politics of a lived present.

The question of the postcolonial political subject, then, is not merely relevant to the construction of the "new" South Africa. It is crucial. But what light might this history-in-the-making shed on philosophical debates about citizenship and difference *sui generis?* How might it inflect a discourse that is heavily prescriptive and, as a matter of course, continues to frame the problem of political personhood, *tout court,* in Euromodernist terms? True, it has become a progressive commonplace to insist that "multiculturalism" has to be interrogated in its empirical particularity, that it takes diverse, labile forms, that liberal democracies ought to—some would say, can—be capacious enough to accommodate it (Modood 2000; Levy 2000; Kymlicka and Norman 2000). Still, while this may complicate matters productively, it leaves untheorized the most critical issue of all. What happens when a liberal democracy encounters a politics of difference that it cannot embrace ethically or ideologically within its definition of the commonweal, a politics of difference not satisfied with recognition, tolerance, or even a measure of entitlement—a politics of difference that appeals to the law or to violence to pursue its ends, among them the very terms of its citizenship? Which, to be sure, is occurring more and more across the world in the early years of the new century.

This last problem presupposes others: Why has the matter of citizenship come to capture the imagination, popular as well as academic, at this particular time, a time when the modernist nation-state, and the modes of representational politics that it has long presumed, are profoundly in question? Like "civil society" (cf. Comaroff and Comaroff 1999b), which has enjoyed a similar renaissance of attention since the late 1980s, the manner in which the concept is deployed is often as vacuous as it is appealing. Indeed, there seems to be a roughly proportional relationship between its vacuity and its mass appeal. Why, more and more, are contests over fractal identities and the terms of national belonging fought out by means of legalities? Might it be here, and in other sites of contestation, rather than in the realm of normative theory-making or policy prescription, that we may discern the emergence of pragmatic resolutions to the paradoxes of citizenship in polities founded on endemic, irreducible difference?

It is these concerns, these questions, that frame our narrative here. Also the argument we seek to make. Briefly stated, it is that, in postcolonies, which are endemically heterogeneous, citizenship always exists in an immanent tension with policulturalism; note the term, we shall explain it below. As a result, it is a terrain on which increasingly irreconcilable, fractal forms of subjectivity, embodied in self-defined aggregates of persons, may seek to open up possibilities for social action, possibilities in pursuit of interests, ideals, passions, principles. It is on this terrain that the modernist sense of ideology gives way to ID-ology, the quest for a collective good, and often goods, authorized by a shared identity. And, in the process, both the liberal modernist polity and the kingdom of custom are transformed. The term, ID-ology, is not ours: it derives from public discourse in South Africa itself. Argue Rapule Tabane and Ferial Haffajee in a newspaper report,[4] the Age of Ideology, "of genuinely competing ideas," is over, killed off by a mix of world-historical and local conditions. In its place has arisen a depoliticizing kind of "mongrel politics" in which party platforms tend to converge, in which charismatics crystallize their popularity into "customized political brands," in which differences are confined largely to the implementation of policy and the distribution of material advantage. In the upshot—this is us now, not Tabane and Haffajee—political belonging, and the contradictions implicit in it, become, above all else, a site of ID-ology, a site in which various sorts of identity struggle to express themselves in the politics of everyday life. And new forms of practical governance take shape.

A final note here, one that reiterates the central thesis of this volume. While we phrase our argument with respect to South Africa—and, more generally, to postcolonies—what we shall have to say applies, increasingly, to the nation-state form. And hence, increasingly, to Euro-America. Why? Because one of the *social* effects of neoliberal capitalism, and of the kinds of human flow that it generates, is to make polities, with few exceptions, ever more diverse, ever more heterodox, ever more prone to a praxis of difference that, in the end, is likely to run up against the limits of liberal citizenship; all the more so with the steady evacuation, across much of the world, of a politics of ideological contestation (see below). Not everywhere in the same ways, of course. But in some or other way. Which is why the postcolony is so often a harbinger of histories yet to happen.

First, though, to histories that have happened. And are happening.

## CONSTITUTING THE PROBLEM, PROBLEMATIZING THE CONSTITUTION

### *The Rule of Law and Dangerous Cultural Practices*

The postcolonial state in South Africa, under the African National Congress (ANC), has had no option but to take cultural difference—and especially cultural practices deemed "dangerous"—very seriously indeed. This, as we have intimated, is because it has been confronted, repeatedly, by social practices that fly in the face of its Constitution. Thus the police have been called upon to deal with, among other things, urban vigilante activities conducted in the name of Muslim morality;[5] "alternative" justice ostensibly exercised under the terms of African customary law;[6] bloody culture wars in the countryside; and witchcraft-related killings—so many, in fact, that an occult-related crimes unit was established in the 1990s to deal with them. And the Constitutional Court has had to deliberate, for example, on a claim, made in the name of Rastafarian belief, to recognize the use of prohibited drugs for ritual purposes;[7] it has also had to address such things as "customary" inheritance and succession, which run up against the gender equality clause in the founding law of the land (see below). For its part, the executive has had to respond to constant demands to permit "traditional" practices that have been illicit since colonial times. To wit, a number of Witchcraft Summits have been held since 1994 to discuss rural unrest, and the lethal forms of cultural policing occasioned by it, arising out of high incidences of *muti* (medicine) murders (Comaroff and Comaroff 1999a); one such meeting, in September 1999, was attended by prominent politicians, lawyers, and public intellectuals, including the then deputy president, Thabo Mbeki.[8] This amount of attention lavished on the issue is unsurprising. Not only do violent witch-purgings call into question the terms of national law and order. They do so by means taken to be irrational, even savage, according to the canons of enlightenment reason. As colonial rulers long ago realized, to condone them, even tacitly, is to grant them a measure of legitimacy.

But herein lies a paradox for the liberal modernist state in postcolonial, poli-ethnic times. In an epoch in which cultural rights have come increasingly to substitute for political and economic enfranchisement, no government— least of all one representing African empowerment—can afford to ignore the passions that inflame such forms of collective action, especially on the part of the majority that it strives to represent.[9] In this respect, dramatic acts like witch-burning are merely an extreme instance of the challenge posed everywhere to the sovereignty of the state, and to the laws of the nation, under the sign of ethnic particularity, of religion or regionalism, of the primordial politics of tradition. The African National Congress, to be sure, has been unable to resist, remove, or repudiate the affective appeal of cultural difference. Not only is it invoked in the name of ethnonationalism, most assertively by the Congress of Traditional Leaders of South Africa (CONTRALESA), the Zulu-centric Inkatha Freedom Party, and separatist fractions of the Afrikaner right. It is keenly felt by many ordinary South Africans, for whom "customary" attachments remain strong. As a result, its mass following notwithstanding, the ANC has had to revise the "post-ethnic" universalism to which most of its leadership[10] was once fervently committed. Always ambivalent, at best, toward anything associated with "tribalism," the liberation movements tended,

during the struggle years and after (cf. Lijphart 1995:281), to dismiss culture
and custom as instruments of colonial overrule—and to see chieftaincy as
highly autocratic.[11] This even as they sought to recruit sympathetic chiefs to
their cause. Recall here Desmond Tutu's outburst against ethnicity. Some
senior ANC cadres were still openly dismissive of indigenous authority in the
late 1990s, Barbara Oomen (2005:3 *et passim*) reminds us; former President
Thabo Mbeki's support for it always seemed more strategic than intrinsic.
As that support suggests, however, the regime has made audible its public
recognition of the kingdom of custom as part of the country's "unique mode
of governance," citing Section 12 of the Constitution as proof of its commitment; all of which follows what Kymlicka and Norman (2000:4) term "the
clear trend throughout the Western democracies towards greater recognition
of minority rights." This *volte face* was particularly noticeable before the 1999
election. Since then, party representatives have taken every opportunity—at
events such as royal funerals in the countryside, for instance—to persuade
powerful chiefs that they, and the cultural bases of their authority, have a
secure future in government.

The ambiguity persists, however. When the Local Government Municipal Structures Act (no.117) was passed in 1999, it made provision for the
division of the entire country, including chiefly domains, into municipalities.
Where their realms fell into these municipalities, traditional leaders were
permitted only 10 percent representation; the Act has been amended, but the
role of the chiefs remains tightly restricted. Said to be "above party politics,"
they are expected to confine themselves to, among other things, ceremonial
activities of various kinds, the administration of customary law, and the co-
ordination of cultural activities, including first fruits, rainmaking, and other
ancestral rites. In addition, they are expected to "perform such functions as
may be delegated ... by a municipal council," to "carry out all orders given
... by competent authorities," and to facilitate things like "the gathering of
firewood."[12] Hardly the stuff, this, of plenipotentiaries. In fact, as critics have
been quick to say, there is now "considerable confusion as to what exactly
the[ir] constitutional recognition implies."[13] Predictably, many of these rulers, seeing themselves as all-powerful in their realms, feel betrayed. This was
dramatically evident at a conference, organized by the Ministry of Provincial
and Local Government in August 2000,[14] to discuss "traditional leadership
and institutions" with a view to producing a white paper.[15]Assembled royals,
led by prominent members of CONTRALESA, declined to take part. Demanding that the Constitution be amended to recognize their sovereignty,
they refused to talk to anyone other than the state president. Since then they
have ridden a roller coaster. There have been times when they were sure that
government had been persuaded to do their bidding. And there have been
other times when they have declared—perhaps tactically, in order to rally

their followers—that they had "reached the end of the road," that "there was never an intention to accommodate [their authority in] the making of the 'new' South Africa."[16] Such statements typically draw denials from the ANC—which, in turn, adds fuel to the ongoing battle over the future of the kingdom of custom.

In playing the heady game of cultural politics, then, the ANC has conjured up a force that it is unable fully to control, a force that vitiates the very conception of nationhood on which the authority of the state rests. In theory, of course, it is just such contradictions that the Constitution—tacking, as it does, between an emphasis on universal human rights, vested in individuals, and the recognition of cultural pluralism—was designed to mediate. Public debate in South Africa, however, has already drawn attention to "major tensions" between those of its provisions that structure a system of democratically elected representatives and those that ascribe legitimacy to the kingdom of custom.[17] Let us pause briefly to take a look at how the Constitution itself treats the matter. This, in turn, will provide a frame for what we have to say about the pragmatics of citizenship as a terrain on which political subjects construct various sorts of ID-ology.

## *The Constitution of Dissent*

The Constitution of the Republic of South Africa, adopted in 1996,[18] has been accorded hallowed status in the formation of the postcolonial polity. Translated into all official languages under the legend One *law* for One *nation*—the italics are in the original—the text saturates the discursive fabric of everyday life across the country. Yet, almost from the start, as we shall see, there have been doubts about its ability to constitute either *One* Nation or *One* Law; these italics are ours. Even its comprehensibility has been questioned: in 1999, a mass-circulation black newspaper in Johannesburg, for example, referred to it as a Tower of Babel, pointing out that its vernacular versions are utterly opaque—and, hence, babble to those whom it was meant to enfranchise.[19]

Culture is dealt with primarily in two sections of Chapter 2 of the Constitution, its Bill of Rights. Section 30, *Language and Culture,* states that "everyone has the right to use the language and to participate in the cultural life of their choice"; Section 31, *Cultural, Religious, and Linguistic Communities,* adds that nobody belonging to any such community may

> be denied the right, with other members of that community, (a) to enjoy their culture, practise their religion and use their language; and (b) to form, join and maintain cultural, religious and linguistic associations and other organs of civil society.

But, in both cases, there is a clear constraint: these rights "may not be exercised in a manner inconsistent with any [other] provision of the Bill of Rights." In other words, precedence is given to those provisions that protect the dignity, equality, and freedoms—of which a very broad range is stipulated—of all persons, without prejudice or discrimination. Even when the Constitution, in Section 36, acknowledges that some constraints on those freedoms are "reasonable and justifiable in an open society," it stresses that any such constraint is to remain bound by the Bill of Rights; as we shall see, protagonists of the sovereignty of popular tradition and traditional authority have sought support for their arguments in this "justifiable" and "democratic" limitation of the universal rights of citizenship. Customary authority is not embraced in Chapter 2. It appears in Chapter 12, which states, in rather bland, general terms, that the Constitution recognizes "the institution, status and role of traditional leadership, according to customary law"—but, again, subject to the Bill of Rights and any relevant statutory law. In sum, the subservience of cultural particularity and the kingdom of custom to the "One *law* for One *nation*" seems unambiguous.

But is it? The South African Bill of Rights has been lauded, as we have said, precisely because it does seem to acknowledge, within limits, the entitlement of persons bound by culture, religion, and language to be governed by their own customs. True, the collective subject invoked here is not a group *per se;* the Constitution is famously silent on group rights. That subject is an aggregate of identity-bearing "persons." Nonetheless, the spirit of the law, especially as embodied in Sections 30 and 31, has justified claims to the effect that, in traditional communities where individual rights are alien, customary practice should prevail over the Eurocentric liberalism of the law; that, when a custom is backed by popular consensus and a clear and present collective interest, the cultural subject should take precedence over the national citizen. The Supreme Court of Appeal made a similar argument in 2000: in *Mthembu v Letsela,* it decided that women married under African customary law were subject to the rule of male primogeniture—and, thereby, excluded from inheritance of matrimonial property.[20] The court declared that the "interests of the community," as expressed in its "mores and fundamental assumptions," were of paramount importance in this matter. Here, in short, one of the highest tribunals in the land found against the Bill of Rights, as conventionally interpreted. Or, rather, the court found that there are situations in which culture ought to limit its provisions. The judgment drew criticism from some quarters, notably feminist. Not only did it prove that "the idea of equality before the law, regardless of sex or gender, is ... incompatible with certain aspects of customary law," wrote Khadija Magardie in a widely read national newspaper, but it was an "alarming precedent" for the triumph of "cultural relativism" over the Constitution.[21]

Magardie was correct. In this decision, the judiciary had given culture, and the prevailing practices of an ethnic community, priority over other provisions of the Constitution. But did it really mean that, thenceforth, cultural difference would amount to a limitation on the Bill of Rights? And what did it really prove about the (in)compatibility of custom with those other provisions? The evidence is inconclusive. In June 2003, for instance, application was made to the Judge President of the Western Cape High Court, John Hlophe, on behalf of two orphaned girls whose grandfather had inherited their father's home in Khayelitsha, on the outskirts of Cape Town, under the terms of customary law. The grandfather promptly stated his intention to evict the children and their mother, and sold the place in order to cover the expenses of his son's funeral. Lawyers for the girls sought an order to the effect that primogeniture under African law and custom, in this case, be "interpreted and developed in line with the constitution, particularly the right to dignity and the right to equality."[22] Or, if not, that it be declared unconstitutional. Clearly, they doubted that tradition could be rendered compatible with the Bill of Rights—and, if it could not, wished to establish the priority of the latter over the former. The defense, by contrast, asserted baldly that "customary law was recognized in South African law and protected by the constitution." Hlophe reserved judgment. In doing so, he repeated the vague and vacuous ANC mantra that tradition could, and should, be suitably updated. "We promise to develop the law as it should be developed in 2003," he said. Eventually this case, *Bhe v Magistrate, Khayelitsha,* would make its way to the Constitutional Court, which decided in favor of the two women.[23]

In 2000, three years before, we had put the question of compatibility to two constitutional court justices and received revealingly different answers. Albie Sachs, legal theorist of the liberation movement and a significant judicial force in the new dispensation, saw no necessary conflict between the Constitution and custom. The first always takes precedence over the second, he said. It provides the frame within which customary law, to the degree that it remains relevant to everyday life, might sustain itself in a liberal democracy. If conflict were to arise—as it did on the question of, say, the traditional right of males to inflict punitive beatings on members of their family—it was to be addressed by means of statutory law; *vide,* in this respect, the Domestic Violence Act of 1999. In a public speech on the topic, Sachs (n.d.:15–16) put the question in a more nuanced light. The Constitutional Court, he said, had left the "ever-developing specifics" of customary law to future deliberation and interpretation. This implied that its "liberation and transfiguration" would occur in "organic connection with the community." But its jurisdiction ought never to go far beyond the resolution of family and neighborhood disputes; even then, traditional authorities would have to act within the limits of the Bill of Rights. In short, there never was, nor is there now, a contradiction between culture and the Constitution. Ethnic subject and national citizen are one and the same legal person.

By contrast, Yvonne Mokgoro saw a palpable tension between the terms of the Constitution and the kind of law implemented in traditional tribunals, most notably in such matters as inheritance, succession, and domestic relations. In her view, the Constitutional Court operated at a great distance from law-as-lived—and from the policing of everyday life in the countryside. A good deal of local practice continued in defiance of the Bill of Rights, she observed; it was merely a matter of time before cases emerged that contested its Eurocentrism in the name of cultural difference. Meanwhile, these tensions were managed, day in and day out, in variously pragmatic ways, rendering real-law in the "new" South Africa more complex and diverse than most jurists acknowledged.[24]

Just how complex we shall soon see.

Before we address the real-life, pragmatically wrought tensions between the Constitution and the kingdom of custom, however, it is necessary to offer a few generic observations about *the* postcolonial nation-state. For it is only by means of a counterpoint between the general and the particular that we might make sense of the ways in which—here as elsewhere—the law of the land and the cultural lives of its inhabitants vex each other in arguments over sovereignty, citizenship, and the limits of liberal democracy.


## Reflections on the Postcolony

It became something of a commonplace in the early 1990s to observe that "postcoloniality" means disparate things to different people (cf. Darian-Smith 1996; McClintock 1992): that, while it denotes temporality, it refers to more than just the time "after colonialism" (Prakash 1995); that, in its positive voice, it evokes subaltern, "oppositional consciousness" (Klor De Alva 1995:245); that it "foregrounds a politics of . . . struggle" (Mishra and Hodge 1991:399). These sorts of statements have drawn their own criticism, but that is another matter. What is of concern here is that, in all the efforts to stress a kind of sensibility built into the postcolonial perspective, there has been a tendency to treat the postcolonial nation-state as something of a theoretical cypher on whose ground arguments about the past, about identity, citizenship, consciousness, and other things, may proceed unencumbered by the known facts of actual histories, economies, or societies.[25] Clearly, this is not the place in which to "theorize" postcoloniality, *sui generis,* even if it were possible to do so in the abstract. But, if sense is to be made of the emerging forms of government, politics, and popular subjectivity in post-apartheid South Africa, or anywhere else, a few general points are in order.

They have to do, by and large, with hyphe-nation, with the link between nation and state, state and nation. Some of them, perforce, reprise things we have discussed more fully in other places (e.g., 2000a; 2000b).

The modernist nation—as Benedict Anderson (1991), among others, has pointed out—was an imagined community defined, putatively, by its cultural homogeneity and its deep sense of "horizontal fraternity." This imagining, it is often noted, was more aspiration than achievement, and was often pursued by violent means. The European polity, after Westphalia, was always a work in progress: never a singular, definite article, it evinced a great deal of variation across time and space. Further, for all the idea that it was composed of rights-bearing persons equal before the law, it excluded many from its politics and its commonweal—and was, typically, inhospitable to difference. Nonetheless, the fiction of a unity of essence, affect, and interest, of common purpose and *civitas,* mandated the legitimacy of the state as sole guarantor of the individual entitlements and collective well-being of its citizens. Hence the hyphenation, the indivisibility of nation from state.

Much has been said in recent times of the so-called crisis of the modernist polity under the impact of global capitalism: of its shrinking sovereignty; of its loss of control over economic policy, cultural production, and the flow of people, currencies, and commodities; of a growing disjunction between nation and state (cf. Appadurai 1990). Whether or not *the* nation-state is alive and well, ailing, or metamorphosing—we prefer the third alternative ourselves—one thing is patent. The received notion of polities based on cultural homogeneity and a sense of horizontal fraternity, real or fictive, is rapidly giving way to imagined communities of difference, of multiculturalism, of ID-ology. This is true even in places as long antithetical to heterogeneity as the United Kingdom, which, despite occasional race wars on the streets of its northern towns, now projects itself, with apologies to Benetton, as United in its tolerance of Color and Culture. And in places like Botswana, long regarded, if not altogether accurately, as relatively homogeneous. To be sure, the rising incidence of cultural struggles and ethnopolitics since 1989 has called forth a torrent of scholarly argument. There is no need to retrace that argument here. For present purposes, we merely need to register the fact.

For most postcolonial nation-states the politics of difference is not new. Heterogeneity has been there from the first. Born of long histories of colonization, these polities typically entered the new world order with legacies of ethnic diversity invented or exacerbated in the cause of imperial governance. Colonial regimes, intent on the management of racial capitalism, never constituted nations in the Euromodernist sense of the term, even where they gave their "possessions" many of the ceremonial trappings of nationhood. In their wake, they tended to leave behind them not just an absence of infrastructure, but a heritage of fractious difference. This has been exacerbated, since *fin de siècle,* by some of the cultural and material corollaries of neoliberalism: the movement across the planet of ever more people in search of work and opportunities to trade; the transnational mass-mediation of signs, styles, and information; the rise of an electronic commons; the growing hegemony of the market and, with it, the distillation of culture into intellectual property, a commodity to be possessed, patented, exchanged for profit. In this world, freedom is reduced to choice: choice of commodities, of life-ways, and, most of all, of identities. In the upshot, the great irony, the great existential contradiction of our times, is that we seem to have entered an age in which identity has become, simultaneously, a matter of volition, of self-production through consumption *and* a matter of ineluctable essence, of genetics and biology.

As this suggests, postcolonies evince many features common to the modernist polities on which they have had, to a large degree, to model themselves. In coming to terms with the implications of global neoliberalism, they appear, in fact, to exaggerate those features. It is this that makes it seem as if, in their temporal aspect, they are running ahead of the unfolding history of the Euromodern nation-state; hence the subtitle of this volume. Our focus here is on just two of them, both corollaries of the founding of postcolonies not on homogeneity but on difference, not on deep horizontal fraternity but on a system of overrule that made "natives," perforce, into *both* identity-bearing subjects and, for some limited purposes, rights-bearing individuals.

The first corollary has directly to do with the refiguration of citizenship. The explosion of identity politics after 1989, especially in postcolonies, has manifested itself in more than just ethnicity. Difference is also vested, increasingly, in gender, sexuality, generation, race, religion, lifestyle, and social class. And in constellations of these things, sometimes deployed in contingent, strategic ways. While most human beings continue to live as citizens in nation-states, they tend only to be conditionally citizens of nation-states: their composite personae may include elements that disregard political borders and/ or mandate claims against the commonweal within them. In consequence, identity struggles of one kind or another appear immanent almost everywhere as selfhood is immersed into collective essence, innate substance, and primordial destiny. What is more, the assertion of autochthony—which elevates to a first principle the interests, "natural" rights, and moral connectedness that arise from rootedness in a place of birth—has become an ever more significant mode of exclusion within national polities; this, as Americans learned after 9/11, in proportion to the extent to which outsiders are held to undermine the Security of the Homeland or the Wealth of the Nation. It is, putatively, in the name of the latter that the state is becoming a metamanagement enterprise in the neoliberal world:[26] in the name of subjects who, even as they seek to be global citizens in a planetary economy of commodities and cultural flows, demand also to be shareholders in the polity-as-corporation. Herein, then, lies the complexity: the fractal nature of contemporary political personhood, the fact that it is overlaid and undercut by a politics of difference and identity, does not necessarily involve the negation of national belonging. Merely its uneasy, unresolved, ambiguous coexistence with other modes of being-in-the-world. It is this inherent ambiguity, we suggest, that makes the ostensible concreteness of concepts like "citizenship" and "community" so alluring.

Of the modes of being that constitute the 21st-century political subject, cultural attachments are often taken, popularly, to run deepest. In many postcolonies, they are also the most marked. As we have said, ethnicity, like all ascribed identities, represents itself as grounded at once in blood and sentiment, in a commonality of interest, and, by extension, in "natural" right. Add to this the fact that culture has increasingly come to be seen, and to be legally protected, as intellectual property (cf. Coombe 1998)—even more, as a naturally copyrighted collective possession—and what is the result? It is the dawn of the Age of Ethnicity, Inc. (Comaroff and Comaroff 2009). Observe, in this regard, that many ethnic groups have formally incorporated as limited companies; that a large number of others have established themselves as businesses to market their heritage, their landscape, their knowledge, their religious practices, their artifacts; that yet others have successfully sued for the unremunerated reproduction of their symbols, sacred and secular. Thus it is that identity, in the age of partible, conditional citizenship, is defined ever more by the capacity to possess and to consume;[27] that politics are treated ever more as a matter of individual or collective entitlement; that social being in general, and social wrongs in particular, are translated ever more into the language of rights.

Self-evidently, in this light, the term "multicultural(ism)" is insufficient to describe the fractious heterogeneity of postcolonies. Demeaned in popular usage, it evokes images of Disney's "Small World," of compendia of the Family of Man, of ritual calendars respectful of human diversity, and the like; in short, of benign indifference to difference. Neither as noun nor as adjective does it make clear the critical limits of liberal pluralism: that, notwithstanding the utopian visions of some humanist philosophers, the tolerance afforded to culture in modernist polities falls well short of allowing claims to autonomous political power or legal sovereignty. In postcolonies, in which ethnic assertion plays on the simultaneity of primordial connectedness, natural right, and corporate interest, the nation-state is less multicultural than it is policultural. The prefix, spelled "poli-," marks two things at once: plurality and its politicization. It does not denote merely appreciation on the part of the national majority for the customs, costumes, and cuisine of one or another minority from one or another elsewhere. It is a strong statement, an argument grounded in a cultural ontology, about the very nature of the pluri-nation, about its constitution and the terms of citizenship within it, about the spirit of its laws, about its governance and its hyphenation. As we have already seen, in South Africa this takes the form of an ongoing confrontation between Euromodern liberalism and variously expressed, variously formulated notions of "traditional" authority.

Talk of rights, of culture as intellectual property, of citizenship, constitutions, and contestation, brings us to the second corollary that flows from the heterogeneous social infrastructure of postcolonies. Whether weak or strong, intrusive or recessive, autocratic or populist, the regimes that rule them share one thing: they speak incessantly of and for themselves in the name of the state. Like those born of Euromodernity, postcolonial African states are statements (cf. Corrigan and Sayer 1985:30). They give voice to more or less authoritative worldviews, sometimes backed by military might, sometimes by carnivalesque ritual (Mbembe 1992b), sometimes by mass-mediated shows of rhetorical force. But their language is not arbitrary.[28] It is the language of the law. The modernist polity, of course, has always been rooted in a culture of legality. Its subject, Charles Taylor (1989:11–12) reminds us, was, from the first, an individual whose humanity and dignity were formulated in the argot of rights and legal privilege. The global spread of neoliberal capitalism has intensified the grounding of citizenship in the jural: this because of its contractarian conception of all relations, its celebration of "free" markets, and its commodification of virtually everything, all of which are heavily inscribed in the language of the law. It has also required that received modes of regulation be redesigned to deal with new forms of property, possession, consumption, exchange, and jurisdictional boundaries (cf. Jacobson 1996).

As we shall see, all of this reaches its apotheosis in postcolonies precisely because their hyphenation is so highly attenuated, because they are built on a foundation of putatively irreducible difference, because they are endemically policultural. In them, the ways and means of the law—constitutions and contracts, rights and remedies, statutory enactments and procedural rituals—are attributed an almost magical capacity to accomplish order, civility, justice, and empowerment. And to remove inequities of all kinds. Note, in this respect, how many new national constitutions have been promulgated since 1989: 105, and rising.[29] Note also the explosion across the planet of law-related NGOs—Legal Resource Centers, Lawyers for Human Rights, and the like—whose offices are now to be found in the most remote of African villages. During the 1990s there was even a "law train" that traveled around the countryside offering free legal advice; its volunteer lawyers took pains to encourage all citizens to pursue their rights, and to address wrongs, by legal means.[30]

But why the fetishism of the law? We have discussed this *in extenso* elsewhere (Comaroff and Comaroff 2006b; see also Chapter 6). For now, suffice it to say that the language of legality affords people in policultural nation-states an ostensibly neutral medium to make claims on each other and on the state, to enter into contractual relations, to transact unlike values, and to deal with conflicts arising out of them. In so doing, it produces an impression of consonance amidst contrast: of the existence of universal standards that, like money, facilitate the negotiation of incommensurables across otherwise intransitive boundaries. Hence its capacity, especially under conditions of social and ethical disarticulation, to make one thing out of many, to carve concrete realities out of fragile fictions. Hence, too, its hegemony, despite the fact that it is hardly a guarantor of equity. As an instrument of governance, it allows the state to represent itself as the custodian of civility against disorder—and, therefore, as mandated to conjure moral community by exercising a monopoly over the construction of a commonweal out of inimical diversities of interest (Harvey 1989:108). It is this, to return to our point of a moment ago, that is made manifest in the rash of new constitutions written over the past decade or so. Each domesticates the global-speak of universal human rights and the rule of law, an idiom that individuates the citizen and, by treating cultural identity as a private asset rather than a collective possession, seeks to transmute difference into likeness.

It is an open question whether these constitutions, this obsession with human rights—indeed, the language of legality itself—yield empowerment to those who previously lacked it. They do not, after all, guarantee the right to a living, only to possess, to signify, to consume, to choose. Nonetheless, the alchemy of the law, like all fetishes, lies in an enchanted displacement, one that resists easy demystification: the notion, not altogether unfounded, that legal instruments have the wherewithal to orchestrate social harmony and, thus, to manufacture something that was not there before. Its charm also lies in the fact that it obscures the most brutal of truths: that power produces rights, not rights power; that law is itself a product of the political, not a prime mover in constructing social worlds; that it, alone, is not what separates order from chaos or an equitable society from a state of savagery.

Put together the fetishism of the law and the policulturalism of the post-colony, and the product seems over-determined: a polity in which struggles over difference—in particular, struggles over the authority to police everyday life—tend to find their way into the legal domain. Often, indeed, into the dramaturgical setting of the courtroom. But here, surely, there ought to be a rude end to our South African story. To the extent that contestations over the right to police everyday life end up in the realm of the juridical, and to the extent that this realm is dominated by institutions of the state, what chance have claims made under the sign of culture and in the spirit of policulturalism against the hegemony of the Constitution, against the laws of the nation, against the ideological dominance of the universal rights-bearing citizen? This rephrases, in more general terms, a question we asked earlier. In a world regulated by Eurocentric jurisprudence, should we not expect that any assertion of Afromodernity, any argument for the sovereignty of the kingdom of custom, would have little prospect of prevailing? Would not the latter simply fade away of its own accord—or under the pressure of the former? American critical legal theory would probably concur, given its tendency to align the law with the power of the state. Others, like those who contend that multiculturalism is inimical to democracy, would hope that they were correct.[31] As we have implied, however, the matter is not so straightforward. For one thing, phrased thus, it presumes that law and culture—or, more accurately, European liberal legal universalism and appeals to Africanity—exist in a zero-sum equation. This Manichean opposition, it is true, may describe the way the issue is framed in South African popular discourse. But reality is much more complicated. The challenge is to make sense of the ways in which the forces of the African vernacular and those of liberal democracy are confronting one another at the present moment; how, in ongoing, often strident struggles, both are being transformed—thereby altering the very shape and substance of postcolonial politics, of citizenship, of democracy.

In order to do so, we appeal to a venerable anthropological device: an extended case. This case is paradigmatic of encounters, in the interstices of postcolonial constitutionalism, between the rule of law and the kingdom of custom. It concerns a battle, in the Northwest Province, over the alleged wrongs of a burial rite.

## From Customs of Death to the Death of Custom

### *Mogaga Meets the Human Rights Commission*

What happens when, as an anonymous local reporter wrote, there is a "head-on collision between the new South African Constitution and [the] age-old traditions, customs and cultures observed by millions of Blacks"?[32] The answer, in the case between Mrs. Kedibone Elizabeth Tumane, of Mononono village in the Northwest Province, and Chief Nyalala Pilane of the Bakgatla-Ba-Kgafela, under whose tribal authority the village falls, was a lengthy legal tussle, notable for the complex strategies—and the appeals to culture, the Constitution, democracy, and rights—on both sides. The dispute centered on Mrs. Tumane's refusal to perform a burial rite. At issue was a Tswana convention that requires a newly bereaved spouse to sprinkle a herb, *mogaga,* on her path when she walks abroad in public space. In theory, death pollution (*sefifi;* see Chapter 2) afflicts men as well as women (J. Comaroff 1980:643–44), but ritual prophylaxis is more stringently mandated for females, who are thought to be more open to contamination. In the past, the rite was usually observed for a year; some tribal authorities[33] continue to insist on regulating its performance in the cause of communal well-being. Mrs. Tumane, a staunch member of the Watchtower Movement, saw *mogaga* as contrary to the dictates of her faith. She claimed that, when she tried to leave home after her husband's interment, she had been prevented from doing so. What was more, members of the local community, deeming her behavior a deliberate breach of tradition, called for her banishment. After various efforts to settle the matter had failed, Mrs. Tumane endeavored to take Chief Pilane and his tribal authority to court. With the support of the South African Human Rights Commission (HRC),[34] she complained that her freedoms had been violated.

Some background here. Mortuary ritual has been a contentious issue among Tswana since time immemorial; early missionaries were quick to recognize that the space of death was a site of singular sensitivity (Comaroff and Comaroff 1997; cf. Durham and Klaits 2000). It still is. A survey in 2000 of chiefly court records in the Northwest revealed a score of cases brought against local people, mostly immigrants from other regions, who had refused to perform the proper mourning routines. These are matters of great moment because bereavement rites—the initial seclusion of surviving spouses, then the sprinkling of *mogaga* to cool their polluting footprints—are held to prevent the contagion of death from escaping abroad (J. Comaroff 1974:124f). In her affidavit to the High Court,[35] Mrs. Tumane affirmed that this is a widely shared belief. Its breach, she acknowledged, is said to threaten the lives of cattle or to withhold the rain. The growing impact of HIV/AIDS in the countryside has heightened such ritual anxieties: inadequately observed mourning practices are thought to play a role in rising mortality rates.

From this vantage, then, the performance of prescribed burial rites is not just a question of personal choice, or even of respect for custom. It is a matter, literally, of life and death for the community at large—and, therefore, the responsibility of its traditional authorities. But not everyone in the rural Northwest agrees. There has been opposition to these ritual demands, opposition most often mounted by women in the name of their right to freedom of belief. Thus, in June 1995, a group of "concerned" female cadres of the ANC and Pan-African Congress presented a memorandum to the Bafokeng chief, Lebone Molotlegi. It protested "the enforcement of traditional laws" in respect of burial that, it claimed, "deprived South Africans of their rights to full citizenship."[36] Citizenship, here, denotes a specific sort of political subjectivity: equal, rights-endowed membership within the liberal nation-state, not subjection to the kingdom of custom. There was precedent, in short, for Mrs. Tumane's application for an interdict to the High Court in Mafikeng in June 1998. She claimed that, because of her refusal to observe *mogaga,* a representative of the Kgatla tribal authority had ordered her to confine herself to her house and yard, forcing her to "live ... the life of an outcast."[37]

Mrs. Tumane emerges from the story as a woman of uncommon resolve. Our informants confirmed that prior religious tensions had sharpened local sensitivities to her ritual infringements and had heightened antagonism toward her.[38] Her eldest son, also a Jehovah's Witness—a second son in Mononono is not—had initially taken his mother's grievance to the regional ombudsman,[39] whose staff tried in vain to intervene with the tribal authority. The HRC was the next resort. Advocate Pansy Tlakula, then a Tswana-speaking commissioner with special responsibility for the Northwest Province, duly accompanied the complainant to a meeting with Chief Pilane. Tlakula had brought veteran politician Helen Suzman with her, suspecting that gender tensions might also be at work in the dispute. The battle between custom and human rights has often been reduced, in the heat of political argument, to a standoff between self-identifying "traditional" senior men and constitutionally empowered women and youth; that is, between "subjects" and "citizens."

In an affidavit sworn at Mononono, Mrs. Tumane noted that, at the meeting in June 1998, Pilane had agreed to end her confinement. By then, six months of seclusion had already elapsed; this, she added, was the prescribed length of time, according to a prior tribal authority ruling, for which the sprinkling of *mogaga* was now compulsory. The chief had consented then to call a gathering of the community, at which he undertook both to announce his decision to free her and to permit the HRC to inform people of existing constitutional provisions "relating to customary laws and practices."[40]

The promised gathering was duly held, although the HRC was not invited. But, rather than end Elizabeth Tumane's confinement, the "tribe" resolved that, because of her transgression, she should be banished from the village and the chiefdom. Pilane kept a low profile, allowing the ruler of a senior branch of the Kgatla in Botswana[41] to make a strong statement about the perils posed to tradition by the South African Constitution.[42] In challenging the sovereignty of the state and its One Law, customary authorities here presumed a political map that transcends national borders. For her part, Mrs. Tumane said that she had been threatened with assault at the meeting, the volatile crowd vowing that they were ready to expel her by force. "I really feared for my safety and that of my family," she attested.[43] Subsequent efforts by the HRC to remind the chief and the tribal authority of their earlier agreement elicited a letter from Pilane. He was not, he insisted, in a position to end the confinement. Mrs. Tumane was "being confined by her own custom," he wrote; this could not be changed without the "consent of the tribe,"[44] of which she herself was a member.[45] Her rights had been respected, he went on, save where they were in conflict with Section 36 of the Constitution, "which [wa]s applicable in all black South African communities." Section 36, recall, is the clause covering the limitation of rights. Here it was invoked to justify the suspension of a constitutional entitlement where it conflicted with a collectively endorsed custom.

Mrs. Tumane and the HRC countered that Pilane and the tribal authority *had* violated her constitutional rights: her right to equality (Section 9), dignity (Section 10), security of person (Section 12[1]), freedom of religion, belief, and opinion (Section 15), freedom of movement and residence (Section 21), choice of language and culture (Section 30), and just administrative action (Section 33). While the Kgatla were entitled to promote the religion and culture of their community, went the argument, they could do so only in a manner consistent with the Bill of Rights. An urgent court application was made and, on 20 July 1998, the Mmabatho High Court ruled it a violation of the Constitution to compel the performance of the *mogaga* rite. Pilane was ordered to lift Elizabeth Tumane's confinement immediately and to desist from threatening her in any way.

The order was an interim measure, pending a court hearing in November of that year. According to Advocate Tlakula, who litigated on behalf of the HRC, it had no appreciable effect on Mrs. Tumane's predicament. Meanwhile, the dispute became a *cause célèbre* in the Northwest. Reporters who traveled to Mononono to interview Mrs. Tumane wrote that she was relieved at the prospect of being released from "house arrest."[46] The case was also debated in the provincial House of Traditional Leaders, where the chiefs came into bitter confrontation with both the MEC[47] for local government, a senior ANC politician, and representatives of the HRC. They argued that the challenge to Chief Pilane was part of a general campaign to "violate" tradition in the name of the Constitution. Why were the customary rights of tribes not protected by that Constitution? Why were the rights of individuals put above those of indigenous peoples? Why was it that this case was being debated in the High Court rather than in the House of Traditional Leaders?[48]

In November, Pilane submitted a long answering affidavit[49] that repeated some of his earlier arguments. Beginning with a history of the Kgatla, it sought to establish that a chief "owed [his] position entirely to the support [he] had within [the tribe], inspired by its history, culture and traditions." Significant among those traditions were rituals of birth, marriage, and death; rituals, like the use of *mogaga,* that enjoyed "almost complete" observance among the Kgatla, irrespective of education or status. In words that might have been written by structural-functionalist anthropologists of the British School, the ruler declared: "Tradition is the glue that holds the tribe together, gives it a purpose, sustains its identity and allows for co-ordination and co-operation in ... efforts [toward upliftment]." While virtually all Kgatla regarded themselves as Christians, he went on, only a few, notably Jehovah's Witnesses, objected to performing the *mogaga* rite. Efforts to ascertain precisely which biblical injunction forbade the custom, so that "some compromise" could be reached, had been unsuccessful. So had attempts to get those churches that opposed it to produce their constitutions; a clear example, this, of the salience of constitutionalism, lower case, in post-apartheid South Africa (see above).[50] Pilane, here, gestures toward an accommodation between the Constitution and culture, an accommodation actively encouraged by the HRC, which advocates the "modernization and amendment" of traditional practices in line with the Bill of Rights. But again, the gesture remains entirely rhetorical: what a "compromise" might actually have meant in this case seems not to have been seriously considered by any of the parties.[51]

In addressing Elizabeth Tumane's claims in particular, however, Chief Pilane's affidavit abruptly changed direction, asserting that she had never been threatened or intimidated by his authority. *Mogaga,* he now insisted, was a "ritual voluntarily followed ... [T]here has been no compulsion." The complainant had, by her own choice, dissociated herself from the life of the village. This was her right. But, to the degree that she showed "contempt for tradition in the language of religious fervor and self-righteous indignation," her actions were "calculated to cause an affront to [local] dignity."[52] Mrs. Tumane was an "eccentric" who had *chosen* to marginalize herself; she was now feeling the hostility of "the tribe as a community." What is more, the effort of the HRC to turn a "non-issue" into a "human rights" case had backfired. The complainants had sought to demonize an unobjectionable rite in the hope of forcing it to "adapt" under the pretext that it infringed the Constitution. In joining the dispute, the HRC had made clear its contempt for the Kgatla and their customs.

Although the thrust of this affidavit was to deny that the *mogaga* rite was binding—or that Mrs. Tumane had actually been confined by it—Pilane's closing lines suggested otherwise. They reiterated that he was merely "chief by virtue of the decision ... of the tribe" and was, therefore, powerless to impose decisions that ran counter to the democratic voice of popular opinion. That opinion had been strongly in favor of punishing Mrs. Tumane. Rulers who had defied their people in the past, he reminded the court, had usually come to grief.

This was the last salvo fired by Chief Pilane in the conflict. It was definitive. On 25 February 1999, the High Court dismissed its *decree nisi* of the previous July on the ground that the disputed practice had been declared voluntary. By this time, anyway, the required period of mourning had long elapsed.

Advocate Tlakula told us that the HRC had indeed been interested in the constitutional issues raised by Mrs. Tumane's suit. In fact, the Commission regretted that Pilane had not stuck to his guns: that he had not made the strongest case for the sovereign cultural rights—or prescribed customary rites—of ethnic communities. Tlakula had anticipated that more emphasis would be put on the argument that Mrs. Tumane lived *voluntarily* among Kgatla and was thus bound by their life-ways. As she noted, there is precedent for the judiciary favoring tradition over human rights; the Supreme Court, remember, was to give priority to culture over gender equality in *Mthembu v Letsela*. Tlakula said that she had even toyed with the idea of passing on the record of an earlier case of this sort to Pilane's lawyers in the hope that they would mount the most forceful defense possible, thereby ensuring that the matter would be thrashed out in court. The HRC wanted very much to win a landmark ruling that would render it unconstitutional to force anyone to abide by a sectarian cultural practice. To be sure, even this would have been a limited victory. Tlakula had planned to base her counter-argument on Mrs. Tumane's right to freedom of association rather than her freedom of belief. She did not wish to pit "religion" against "culture," with all the complexities that this would inevitably have introduced. Above all—and here is clear evidence of how the politics of difference challenges the liberal rule of law—the Commission was anxious not to assert that "African culture was unconstitutional." It is one thing to outlaw compulsion, quite another to criminalize custom.

But the HRC lost its chance. Rightly or not, the chief's lawyers had told him that—in view of the weight accorded to the Bill of Rights in post-apartheid South Africa—he was bound to lose unless he declared that the *mogaga* rite was voluntary; a strategic retreat would, in any case, leave the legal status of custom advantageously murky. This tactical caution might have been justified, albeit for different reasons: Tlakula believed that Kgatla opinion was more divided than Pilane had allowed. Journalists, who interviewed local people, concurred:[53] Mrs. Tumane had been quietly abetted by many of her neighbors.

As is common in such cases, the public was invoked on all sides. Pilane had asserted, early on, that Elizabeth Tumane was confined by "her own custom," that it was beyond his power to release her from her duty to follow a popularly mandated tradition. While his disavowal of authority was somewhat disingenuous, the ruler's testimony rested on two broadly endorsed claims: first, that neglect of rites like *mogaga* is regarded by the majority of rural people as a clear and present danger to their physical and moral well-being; and, second, that the obligation to perform this particular rite had been legitimately affirmed by a *democratic* process, the Kgatla nation (*setshaba*) having voiced unanimous support for it in a public setting. In its discussion of the case, the House of Traditional Leaders in the Northwest Province had explicitly demanded more recognition for the legitimacy of collectively affirmed traditions and modes of governance. In so doing, it echoed a widespread sentiment in the countryside about the need to "Africanize" democracy by rescuing it from Eurocentric preoccupations with electoral processes and individual rights.

As we have seen, the chief opted for strategic compromise in his final affidavit. But, in his substantive statements, he returned repeatedly to the affront implied by cases like this to the integrity of Kgatla culture. Tellingly, his argument for the sovereignty—some would say fetishism—of custom reproduced the language of the Constitution. It was framed in terms of rights, freedom, dignity, and democracy. However, this language was used to evoke a very different vision of persons, polities, and politics, one that distinguishes ethnic subjects from national citizens; this in spite, or maybe because, of the fact that the two visions serve to define and limit one another—and that, in practice, neither is as distinct from the other as is often made out in the heat of dispute.

Little wonder, then, that the *"mogaga* case," as it became known in the Northwest, exemplifies the entrenched contradiction between the One Law of the nation and the kingdom of custom. Significantly, the conflict had no decisive outcome. The antinomy to which it spoke remains unresolved. And unresolvable. Mrs. Tumane lives on in Mononono—released, in the end, not by the court but by the passage of time. Other widows since have either performed the rite or desisted less visibly. The dispute, and many others like it, make three things clear. The first is the growing relevance, in this postcolonial democracy, of ethnically based arguments about rights and entitlements, arguments that frame local struggles against the authority of the state not merely in cultural terms, but with reference to a form of policulturalism that is making itself felt ever more globally. The second is the likelihood that, whatever pragmatic outcomes might be reached, these arguments will persist in pitting individual against collective rights, liberal universalism against culture, citizens against subjects. If anything, *pace* the utopian impulses of liberal multiculturalism, they are liable to reproduce rather than resolve the paradox of pluralism endemic to 21st-century nationhood. The third is the mounting tendency for stand-offs between the kingdom of custom and the Constitution to be pursued by legal means, whether in quarrels over rights among groups or in challenges to the sovereignty of the nation-state and its One Law.[54]

## INCLUSIONS, EXCLUSIONS, CONCLUSIONS

The *mogaga* case, in sum, is not in the least exceptional. It is paradigmatic of the way in which a politics of difference runs up against the limits of liberalism. Similar conflicts are occurring more and more frequently across South Africa over initiation ritual and occult beliefs, inheritance and succession, corporal punishment, landholding, and many things besides. Taken together, they point to the fact that a vernacular praxis is beginning to emerge. In the face of the confrontation between the Constitution and culture, and the values for which they stand, those who seek to assert the sovereignty of things African have arrived at a series of strategic positions. These are founded on the conviction that, in spite of a rhetoric of recognition for tradition, in spite of talk about its "liberation" by accommodation to the common law, the postcolonial state, even more than its colonial forebear, means to reduce the kingdom of custom to a shadow of its former self: in the argot of neoliberal social management, to make chiefs into lower-order service providers in the dispute processing and rural development sectors. Also in the sphere of ceremonial, although—as revealed by the *mogaga* case, which was concerned with the limitation of chiefly rights in the rites business—"ceremony" tends to be treated nowadays as little more than powerless pomp. The counter-tactics to which this has given rise range from (i) a politics of avoidance, through (ii) open confrontation, to (iii) overt hybridization.[55] The first was the strategy used, in the end, by Pilane in order to prevent the court from outlawing *mogaga*—thus allowing his people to insist on its performance in the future. The second, less common, has been resorted to by some traditional leaders in the effort to force the HRC to prosecute them for making cultural conventions compulsory, or for otherwise flouting the law of the land, thereby to challenge the ANC to put its tolerance to the test. The third has involved exertions on the part of other rulers to alter those conventions, by "tribal" legislation, just enough to render them acceptable under the Constitution. This tactic is less of a departure from the past than it may seem. African traditional codes have never been unchanging. Rather, as in the Euro-American sense of customary law, they have grown out of an evanescent history of practice—much in the manner espoused for the future by Justice Sachs (see above).[56]

Elsewhere we explore the implications of these and other means of acting on the conflict between liberal governance and the call of custom. What concerns us here are the implications for citizenship, political being, and democracy that flow from contradictions inherent in the scaffolding of postcolonial polities at this historical moment—contradictions observable in nation-states almost everywhere, if in locally modulated form. These contradictions stem, we argue, from disjunctures of hyphenation between the liberal modernist state and the policultural nation, disjunctures that have not been adequately addressed or redressed in contemporary normative philosophy or social policy.

Our objective, in sum, has been to explain why, despite strenuous and thoughtful efforts to resolve it, the antinomy between liberal universalism and policulturalism persists, why it resists even the best-intentioned, most capacious politics of tolerance. In so doing, we have sought to show how struggles over culture in post-apartheid South Africa have emerged from a concrete, ongoing history of difference, a history that has edged uneasily from Tutu's excoriation of ethnicity to Maduna's plea for the necessity of its accommodation. It is a history that sheds light on the generic vicissitudes of the life and times of the nation-state in the early years of the new century. For, as they face the forces of global modernity, postcolonial societies—like "late" liberal polities elsewhere, but more so, and sooner—are increasingly confronted by the challenge posed to the hegemony of their One Law under the sign of cultural identity; a challenge that has always lain, dormant for the most part, below the homogeneous surfaces of the nation-state form. Given the irreducible, steadily growing heterodoxy of these polities, and the shift in the substance of their politics *sui generis* from ideology to ID-ology, assertions of policulturalism within them are not to be satisfied by the mere recognition of difference or its by tolerant inclusion within the juridical institutions of the nation. To the contrary, these assertions, by their very nature, contest the sovereignty of the liberal democratic state, its constituent forms of politics and citizenship, its monopoly over the law and the means of violence. They are born of, and constantly proclaim, the *limits* of liberalism: the limited ability, in South Africa and elsewhere, of the democratic state to produce a unified nation amidst the intensifying flow of signs, goods, and people across its borders; the limited capacity of its authoritative discourse to frame an ideology to counter ID-ology and the centrifugal claims of diversity; the limited power of its Constitution to make actual the entitlements it guarantees; the limited facility of its instruments of governance to reconcile the equality it promises its citizens with the stark disparities of life in the postcolony.

It is these limits that reproduce the tensions between the philosophical tenets of universalism and the practical realities of difference, between the abstract language of individual rights and the vernacular sentiments of collective identity, between the truth-claims of citizenship and the true-life experience of ethnic subjecthood; the tensions, that is, that shape the everyday politics of culture and erupt intermittently into dramatic confrontations like the one between Mrs. Tumane and the Kgatla tribal authority. The fact that such conflicts are litigated, that this case brought against the kingdom of custom was framed in terms of the plaintiff's rights to citizenship, is no accident. The growing salience of the law—in fact, the legalization of politics *tout court*—is, for reasons that we have made plain and will return to in Chapter 6, an integral feature of the neoliberal moment. Even in contesting the sovereignty of the state, traditional authorities have no choice but to engage it in jural terms: in the idiom of rights, constitutionalism, and due process. But, in arguing both with and through the law, advocates of difference are having an impact on its ways and meanings—by, among other things, forcing it to fashion a jurisprudence that can deal with culture without criminalizing it.

It is in such cases, too, that the shape of a new popular politics is discernible, a politics that is catching flame as older struggles—under the signs of class, race, and partisan ideology—fade away. This may not be the kind of politics, the sort of dialectic, that critical theorists might have chosen. It does not, after all, address directly some of the more profound moral and material forces shaping the lives of contemporary South Africans. Or others elsewhere. But it *is* a politics nonetheless, a politics that is yielding new styles of activism, new forms of subjectivity, and new sites of history-in-the-making. In postcolonies and in the world at large.

# CHAPTER 4

# Nations With/Out Borders

*The Politics of Being and the Problem of Belonging*

ANTHROPOLOGISTS ARE FOND OF STORIES AND RIDDLES. THE stranger, the more puzzling the better. So let us first pose a riddle, then tell a story.

The riddle: What might the Nuer, a remote tribe in the Southern Sudan, have to do with Carl Schmitt, the noted German philosopher, notorious apologist for Nazism, and, of late, one of the most quoted social theorists in the English-speaking world? For their part, the Nuer are famous among anthropologists, not least because, in the 1940s, they were held to pose an epistemic challenge to received Western political theory (Fortes and Evans-Pritchard 1940:4). This was largely owed to the fact that they had a political system without government. According to Evans-Pritchard (1940a, 1940b), their storied ethnographer, they lived in "ordered anarchy": a state-of-being without a state to rule over them. In this respect, they were the archetype of so-called acephalous African political systems, systems that were later to be evoked, by Michael Barkun (1968) and others, in accounting for the segmentary oppositions on which the fragile coherence of the Cold War world system sustained itself. *Contra* Hobbes, order here did not congeal in offices or institutions, in courts or constabularies, in finite territories or fixed geographical borders. It inhered, rather, in virtual grammars of action encoded in the idiom of kinship: in an immanent sociologic of fission and fusion, of relative social distance, that brought people together or forced them apart in situations of conflict. Thus, if a homicide occurred within the tribe, it was dealt with by established means of self-help and retribution. If it occurred beyond its margins, what followed was warfare between polities. Practically speaking, though, those boundaries between inside and out were renegotiated, dialectically—they were objectified and made real—in the process of dealing with the very transgressions that breached them. The Nuer polity, then, was a field of *potential* action, conjured by the need to distinguish between allies and antagonists, law and war.

This is where Carl Schmitt comes in. In the *Concept of the Political* (1996), Schmitt portrays politics, Nuer-like, as a pragmatic matter of the will to make life-or-death distinctions between friend and enemy. In other words, as a matter of making order by drawing lines. Of inscribing the political in collective identities, at once physical and metaphysical, carved as much out of the logic of who we are *not* as who we are; indeed, of entailing the one in the other, and both in the affective, sublime act of arriving at unequivocal oppositions when they count. Like those, for example, between theologico-civilizations caught up in an apocalyptic clash between the good and the bad in the ugly days after 9/11; days in which the planet was terrified by uncertainty because it was so uncertain about terror—terror that ambiguated formerly clear axes of global geopolitics; days in which "US" came to spell not just the United States but "us." As Evans-Pritchard might have said of the Nuer, in an orderly world, in a world of absolutes, everything is relative since all things are relatives. Except those who are not, who fall beyond the law, beyond the ethical margin, and who, therefore, are enemies to be excised, outlawed, or, *in extremis,* unsacrificially disposed of (cf. Agamben 1998). Order, in short, is wrought from disorder, political existence from anarchy, by virtue of drawing the line. It is at that line that the riddle is resolved: that line where the Nuer and Schmitt meet, there to agree on the inscription of the normative in a grammar of difference, made manifest by enacting boundaries at once existential, ethical, and legal—and, as we shall see, immanently violent.

## The Fire, Last Time

So much for the riddle, to which we shall return. Now for the story. It is about a fire, about aliens, about a nation in the making, and about its borders, both internal and external. It is a tale we have told before, but one we feel compelled to revisit in light of recent events.

The story raises a host of questions: What might disasters—natural and otherwise—tell us about the architecture of 21st-century nation-states? How might the sudden flash of catastrophe illuminate the meaning of borders and the politics of belonging? And to what extent are those two things, borders and belonging, morphing—along with the substance of citizenship, sovereignty, and national integrity—in this, the neoliberal age, one often associated with states of emergency? These questions have a number of deeper historical implications hidden in them. But we are running ahead of ourselves. Let us title our tale . . .

## Apocalypse, African Style

The millennium passed in South Africa without incident; this despite public fears, before the event, of murderous violence and mass destruction. Then, two weeks later, Cape Town caught fire. On a hot, dry Saturday, the veld flared up in a number of places across the greater metropolitan area. High winds carried walls of flame up its mountain spine, threatening historic homes and squatter settlements alike. As the bush continued to burn, helicopters dumped ton after ton of water on it. Round-the-clock reports told horrific tales of beasts grilled alive, of churches incinerated, of vineyards razed. The city sweltered beneath a blanket of smoke as ash rained down on its boulevards and beaches.

In total, 9,000 hectares burned. The mountains smoldered sullenly for weeks. So did the tempers of the populace. Blame flew in many directions, none of them politically random. Fire is endemic to the region. But, being of calamitous proportions, this one raised fears about the very survival of the natural kingdom at the Cape. Its livid scars evoked elemental anxieties, saturating public discourse as it called forth an almost obsessive desire to construe it as an apocalyptic omen, an indictment, a call to arms. The divinations that ensued—in the streets, the media, the halls of government—laid bare the complex *social* ecology whence the conflagration itself had sprung, casting a sharp light on the state of a nation then not yet six years old.

Apocalypse, we noted at the time, eventually dissolves into history. Therein, to borrow Mike Davis's (1995) felicitous phrase, lies the "dialectic of ordinary disaster." Thus, while early discussion of the fire was wild and contested, it reduced, in time, to a dominant interpretation, one that, while not universal, drew enough consensus to authorize strong state action and broad civic collaboration. Here, clearly, was an ideology in the making. As such, it played upon an implicit landscape of affect and anxiety, inclusion and intrusion, prosperity and loss. Via a clutch of charged references, it linked the fire to other public concerns at the heart of contemporary nationhood, concerns about citizenship and identity, about organic society and common humanity, about boundaries and their violation. But its efficacy in this respect rested, first, on producing a plausible explanation for the extent of the blaze.

Initially, carelessness or arson was suspected, the latter pointing to a campaign of urban terror attributed to "Muslim fundamentalism" that had gripped the Cape long before 9/11.[1] Then the discourse abruptly changed direction, alighting on an etiology that took hold with unusual force: whatever had sparked it, the catastrophic scale of the fire was blamed on alien plants, plants that burn more readily and fiercely than does native vegetation. Outrage against those plants grew quickly. Landowners who had allowed them to spread were denounced for putting the population, and its "natural heritage," at risk.[2]

Note: "natural heritage." Heritage has become a construct to conjure with as global markets and mass migration erode the distinctive wealth of nations, forcing them to redefine their sense of patrimony. And its material worth. A past mayor of Cape Town, for example, was wont to describe Table Mountain as a "national asset" whose value is "measured by every visitor it attracts."[3] Not coincidentally, South Africa was then engaged in a bid to have the Cape Peninsula declared a World Heritage Site in recognition of its unparalleled biodiversity. This heritage is embodied, above all, in *fynbos* (Afrikaans, "fine bush").[4] These small-leaved evergreens that cover the mountainous uplands and coastal forelands of the region have come to epitomize its organic integrity and its fragile, wealth-producing beauties. And, as it has, local people have voiced the anxiety that its riches are gravely endangered by alien vegetation, whose colonizing effect is to reduce local ecologies to "impenetrable monotony" (Hall 1979:134).

The blaze brought this to a head. Efforts by botanists to cool the hysteria—to insist that fire in *fynbos* is not abnormal—had no effect. A cartoonist, Chip Snaddon, casting his ironic eye on the mood of millennial anxiety, drew a flying saucer above Cape Town. Peering down at the city as it sank into a globally warmed sea, its mountain covered by foreign flora, a little space traveler exclaimed, "Glork plik zoot urgle." Translation: "They seem to have a problem with aliens" (Figure 1).[5]

The satirist touched a raw nerve. The obsession with alien plants gestured toward a scarcely submerged sense of civic terror and incendiary panic. But what exactly was at stake in this mass-mediated chain of consciousness, this litany of alien nature? What does it tell us about contemporary efforts to conjure up the nation and its patrimony, about insecure identities and uncertain entitlements? Observers elsewhere have noted that an impassioned sense of autochthony, of birthright—to which alienness is the negative counterpoint—has edged aside other images of belonging since the last years of the 20th century; also, that a fetishism of origins seems to be growing up the world over in opposition to the effects of neoliberal *laissez-faire*.[6] But why? Why, at this juncture in the history of the modernist polity have boundaries and their transgression, not a new concern after all, become such an urgent issue? Could it be that the public angst here over invasive flora speaks to an existential conundrum presently making itself felt with new intensity at the very heart of nationhood everywhere: In what *does* national integrity consist? What might polity and society *mean,* what moral and material entitlements

# Chip **SNADDON**

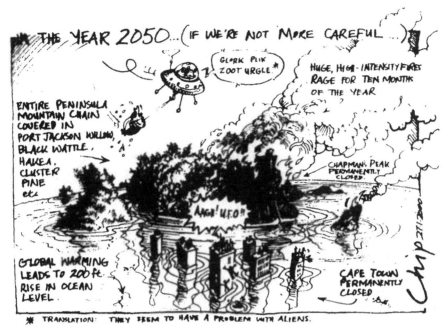

"They Seem to Have a Problem with Aliens," Chip Snaddon, *Cape Argus,* 27 January 2000, p.23.

might it entail, at a time when global capitalism and its cultural mediations appear almost everywhere to be breaching sovereign borders, almost everywhere to be displacing politics-as-usual?

In order to address these questions—in order to make sense both of our narrative of catastrophe and of the more general matter of why it is that aliens of all sorts have become such a burning preoccupation—we must take a brief detour. It takes us into the interiors of "the" late modernist nation-state.

## THE NATION-STATE IN PERSPECTIVE, RETROSPECTIVELY

As we have noted, Euro-nations might have been founded on the fiction of cultural homogeneity, but since the late 20th century, polities everywhere have had increasingly to come to terms with difference. Historical circumstance has pushed them toward an ever more heterodox nationhood (see Chapter 3). Hence the growing concern, scholarly and lay alike, with citizenship, sovereignty, multiculturalism, minority rights, and the limits of liberalism.

Hence, too, the xenophobia that haunts heterodoxy almost everywhere. Of which more later.

The move toward heterodoxy is itself part of a more embracing world-historical process, one in which 1989 figures centrally. That year, symbolically if not substantively, heralded the *political* coming of age, across the planet, of neoliberal capitalism. While its economic roots lie much deeper, this, in retrospect, is often taken to have been the juncture at which the old international order gave way to a more fluid, market-driven, electronically articulated universe: a universe in which *supra*national institutions burgeon; in which space and time are recalibrated; in which geography is rewritten in four dimensions; in which a new global jurisprudence displaces its internationalist predecessor, partially overlaying the sovereignty of national legal systems; in which transnational identities, diasporic connections, and the mobility of human populations transgress old frontiers; in which "society" is declared dead, to be replaced by "the network" and "the community" as dominant metaphors of social connectedness; in which governance is reduced to a promiscuous combination of service delivery, security provision, and fiduciary oversight; in which liberty is distilled to its postmodern essence, the right to choose identities, subjectivities, commodities, sexualities, localities, and almost everything else. A universe, also, in which older institutional and instrumental forms of power—refigured, now, primarily as biopower—disperse themselves everywhere and anywhere and nowhere tangible at all: into transnational corporations and NGOs, into shadowy, privatized parastatal cabals, into syndicated crime and organized religion, and into unholy fusions of all of these things.

In the upshot, "the" state is held to be in constant crisis in many parts of the world: its legitimacy is tested by fiscal mismanagement, debt, deficit, poverty, corruption; its executive control is perpetually pushed to the limit; and, most of all, its hyphenation—the articulation, that is, of state to nation, nation to state (see Chapter 3)—is widely under challenge. This is especially so in postcolonial polities, whose ruling regimes often rely on theatrical means to produce governmental power, to call forth national unity, and to persuade citizens of the reality of both (Mbembe 1992a; Worby 1998). They are not alone in this, of course. Resort to mass-mediated ritual excess, not least ritual orchestrated in the name of security, features prominently right now in the politics of state in many places.

As we noted in the last chapter, this broad historical transformation has any number of corollaries. Here, we focus on just three of them. Forgive us a little repetition in the cause of continuity and comprehensibility.

The *first* is the reconfiguration of the modernist subject-citizen. One corollary of the growing heterodoxy of the nation-state has been the burgeoning of identity politics. Not just ethnic and cultural politics. Also the politics of, among other things, gender, sexuality, age, race, religiosity, and style. The multiplication of such bases of attachment puts ever more stress on hyphenation. The corollary? The more diverse nation-states become, the higher the level of abstraction at which *the* nation-state exists, the more those vested in its existence seek to shore up its integrity. And to divine, diffuse, and disarm anything that appears to endanger it. Part of this process, of bolstering the nation against assertive claims in the name of identity, is to appeal to the primacy of autochthony: to the unambiguous loyalties, the interests and affect, that flow from *place of birth*. Nor is this just a tactic, one that appeals to those in the business of government. It resonates with deeply felt populist fears—and with the proclivity of citizens of all stripes to deflect shared anxieties onto outsiders.

Autochthony is implicit in many forms of identity, of course. It also attaches to places within places, parts within wholes. But, as a *national* claim against aliens, its mobilization appears to be growing in direct proportion to the sundered hyphenation of the sovereign polity, to its popularly perceived porousness and impotence in the face of exogenous forces. Citizens *in* many contemporary states, whether or not they see themselves primarily as citizens of those states, seem able to re-imagine nationhood in such a way as to embrace the ineluctability of internal difference: "multiculturalism," "rainbow nation," and terms like them provide a ready argot of accommodation, even amid political conflict. However, when it comes to the limits of that difference, autochthony constitutes an ultimate line, the *fons et origo* of fealty, affect, attachment. Whatever other identities the citizen-subject of the 21st century may bear, s/he is unavoidably either an autochthon or an alien. Nor only s/he. It, too. Nonhumans, also, may be autochthons or aliens.

The *second* transformation of the modernist polity concerns the regulation of borders—and, hence, the limits of sovereignty. Much of the debate nowadays over the sovereignty of the nation-state hinges upon the contention that governments can no longer plausibly claim to control the mobility of currencies and commercial instruments, of labor and commodities, of flora and fauna, of information, illegal substances, and unwanted aliens. Nor can they always control enclaved zones, the frontiers *within* their realms, those under the sway of organized crime, religious movements, corporations, and the like; all of which has led many contemporary nation-states to resemble patchworks of sovereignties, laterally arranged in space, with tenuous corridors between them, all surrounded by terrains of ungovernability (Comaroff and Comaroff 2006b). National frontiers have always been more or less porous, of course. But technologies of space-time compression *do* appear to have effected a sea change in patterns and rates of global flow—of the concrete and the virtual, of humans, objects, signs, currencies, communications. Which is why so many states act as if they were constantly subject both to invasion from the outside and to the seeping away of what, like offshore commerce, jobs, and human capital, ought properly to remain within. South Africa, for instance, laments the pull of overseas markets on some of its more productive citizens[7]—while anguishing, xenophobically, over the inflow of migrants. And Western Europe, despite its so-called demographic winter, agonizes over the specter of a future Muslim majority. More immediately, it worries about the ubiquitous presence of racially marked others of various provenance.

Our object, though, is not just to remark on the heightened concern with borders and their transgression. It is also to observe that this concern is the product of a paradox. Under current global conditions, given the logic of the neoliberal capitalist economy, states find themselves in a double bind. In order to garner the value spun off by that economy, they require at once to open up their frontiers *and* to secure them: on one hand, to deregulate the movement of currencies, goods, people, and services, thus to facilitate the inflow of wealth; on the other, to establish enclaved zones of competitive advantage so as to attract transnational manufacture and media, investment, information technology, and the "right" kind of migrants—tourists, corporate personnel, NGOs, and laborers who will work cheaply and tractably, without the entitlements of citizenship. In this way, the nation-state is made, in aspiration if not always in reality, into a business both in itself and in the business of attracting business; in sum, part franchise, part licensing authority. This in the interest of its "stakeholders" who desire simultaneously to be *global citizens* and also *corporate national subjects* with all the benefits that accrue to membership of a sovereign nation. The implication is plain enough. The border is a double bind because the commonweal appears to demand, but is threatened by, *both* openness and closure. No wonder the anxiety, the avid public debate in so many places, about what should or should not be allowed entry, what is or is not in the collective interest. And who ought to share it. Hence the arguments, too, between those who would globalize capital by erasing all barriers and patriots protective of the national good.

The *third* salient feature of the predicament of the nation-state is the decentering of politics into other domains: into the law, technology, ritual, the media, and, above all, the market. Prior to the global economic crisis of 2008, in fact, it had become commonplace in many circles to speak of "the end of politics" and the "retreat of the social" (Kapferer 2005): of a world in which interpersonal relations dissolve into the natural, the biological, the contractual; a world in which "the community" is both the site and the product of the purposive enterprise of empowered moral subjects; a world in which public life is reduced to struggles, often fought by means of lawfare, over "special" interests and issues, among them, the environment, abortion, health care, child welfare, domestic abuse, gender inequality, human rights, crime, and capital punishment. Under these conditions, urgent questions of the moment, often addressed with reference to technical imperatives, become the stuff of collective action, cutting across older lines of ideological and social commitment. Each takes the limelight as it flares into public awareness and then burns down, its embers consigned to the recesses of collective consciousness—only to flame up again if kindled by contingent conditions or vocal coalitions. Or both.

Our evocation of the imagery of fire returns us to South Africa, but to a South Africa now situated, if all too summarily, in a history of the present that involves altered forms of citizenship, an obsession with boundaries, aliens and autochthony, and various displacements of the terms of modernist politics as we have come to know it.

## NATURING THE NATION

*A Lesson from Fynbos*

The full impact of the fire in January 2000 flowed from the capacity of the burning bush, of the flowers and flames, to signify. To signify charged political anxieties, many of them unameable in everyday discourse. To signify the aspiration that, from the ashes, might arise a distinctly national, post-apartheid South African sense of community, nationality, inclusion. The question, patently, is how? How *did* those flowers and flames come to mean so much? And what inchoate terrors did they portend?

First, the flora. Flowers have long served as national emblems. The Giant Protea, which typifies *fynbos,* has been South Africa's for many years. It stands in a totemic relationship to the nation; a relationship, that is, of people to nature, place to species, in which the latter enriches the former—so long as it is venerated and not wantonly consumed. But it is also a fetish, a natural displacement of emotively charged identities rooted in acts of national assertion.

It was not always so. The use of *fynbos* for the indigenous plants of the southern Cape is recent. It was only at the end of the 1960s that the term, and the particular range of associations to which it now refers, became established in either popular or botanical parlance.[8] This was precisely the time when international demand for local flora took off, and a national association was formed to market it; *fynbos* export is now a huge industry. It was also the point at which statesmen began explicitly to dub these flora a "natural asset"—and at which botanists asserted, urgently, that they were a fragile species worthy of conservation as a "unique biome type" (Kruger 1977).[9] Not long before then, in 1953, an authority on the subject actually described *fynbos* as an invader that threatened the local grassveld (Acocks 1953:14,17). What is now said of aliens was being said, a half-century ago, of this "South Africa treasure," this passionately protected icon of national, natural rootedness.

But it is not just as fragile natural heritage that *fynbos* has captured the imagination of the South African public. It is also as a protagonist locked in mortal struggle with foreign flora that threaten to take over its habitat and choke off its means of survival. A parenthetic note here. Similar anxieties about plant invaders have manifested themselves in other nations as well: nations, tellingly, where human in-migration from less prosperous places is a mass concern—the USA, for example, and Australia, where, ironically, South African flora are demonized (Wace 1988; Carr *et al.* 1986). In Britain there has been discussion for some years now about removing huge expanses of alien rhododendrons, once very popular, from National Trust properties.

There was a time when there was great enthusiasm for non-indigenous vegetation. In the high colonial age, British rulers encouraged the import of exotics into their overseas "possessions" for what seemed, at the time, to be good, modern ecological reasons (Hall 1979). It took quite a while for those desirable imports to become invasive aliens, pests, even green cancers (National Botanical Gardens 1959). And it was only in the 1990s that aliens came to be held publicly accountable for the fragility of Cape flora. This is abundantly clear from the way in which attitudes to fire in the *fynbos* shifted over that decade, culminating in the catastrophe of January 2000.

As we have said, fire is endemic to the Cape. Expert opinion acknowledges that the conservation of biodiversity actually depends on natural conflagration. What is more, in the past, foreign plants were only one of many factors held to produce fires of distinct kinds; in fact, an authoritative report on the topic published as late as 1979 (Kruger 1979) does not even list them as a concern. Neither, remember, did public blame in 2000 alight immediately upon them—although when it did, they became a burning preoccupation. Literally. Fire, after all, is an elemental source of energy, heat, and light. And a close-to-hand means of destruction, terror, purification. It smolders in the colonial memory as a quotidian instrument of revenge on the material trappings of domination. "With our boxes of matches," Winnie Mandela declared, "we shall liberate this country."[10]

But what does fire have to do with aliens?

Until the fall of apartheid, the term "alien" had archaic connotations in South Africa, being enshrined in laws aimed at barring Jewish entry in the 1930s. Those laws remained in place until amended in the 1990s,[11] when immigrants became a fraught issue in a society that, to the eyes of many of its citizens, seethed with a surplus of the unemployed and unruly, the criminal and the contagious. It was at the same time that foreign plants became both the subject of a popular sense of crisis and an object of national renewal (Hall 1979:138). The most striking symptom of this was the Working for Water Programme, launched in 1995. Part of the post-apartheid Reconstruction and Development Plan, the scheme, a flagship project to create jobs and combat poverty, centered on routing out alien vegetation. Unemployed women and youth, ex-offenders, even the homeless, would be rehabilitated by joining eradication teams. Alien nature, in other words, was to be the raw material of communal rebirth.

The blaze in Cape Town gave yet further impetus to this. As public feeling focused on the foreign "scourge," the state seemed intent on coaxing "a spirit of community" from the ashes.[12] Ever more overt official connections were made between the war against those aliens and the prosperity of the nation.[13] The most portentous of them issued forth from the presidency itself. "Alien plants," said Thabo Mbeki, its incumbent at the time, "stand in the way of the African renaissance."[14]

## FOREIGN OBJECTS: THE POLITICS OF ESTRANGEMENT IN THE POSTCOLONY

And so, in rhetoric that mirrored and magnified the public mood, invading plants became embroiled in the state of the nation. But this does not yet answer the question we posed a moment ago: To what anxieties, interests, and historical conditions did the allegory of alien nature speak? What underlay the ideological inflation that began with the burning bush, went on to inflame patriotic passions, and flared so fiercely as to endanger the African renaissance? An answer is to be found in a cluster of implicit associations and organic intuitions that, as they surfaced, gave insight into the infrastructure of a popular consciousness then under construction; into the way in which processes of naturalization made it possible to speak the unspeakable, to assail the unassailable, thus to deal with the challenges and contradictions inherent in making a nation under post-1989 conditions. These are conditions of which we spoke earlier: the changing meaning of citizenship and belonging, borders at once open and closed, people unavoidably on the move, irreducible social and cultural heterodoxy, the displacement of politics, and a shrinking commonweal.

Take this satirical comment by a well-known South African journalist:[15]

Doubtless there are gardening writers who would not think twice about sounding off in blissful praise of something as innocent ... as the jacaranda tree ... But ... you may be nothing more than ... a racist. Subliminally that is[16] ... Behind its blossoms and its splendid boughs, the jacaranda is nothing but a water-hogging ... weed-spreading alien.

Once, the jacaranda had been described as "almost South Africa's national tree" (Moll and Moll 1994:49). Now, in a bizarre drama in which flora signify what politics struggles to name, it had become an object of estrangement, even racialization. Some went so far as to speak of the "ethnic cleansing" of the countryside;[17] this in a land obsessed with who is or is not a citizen, with constitutional rights and wrongs, with routing out all vestiges of racism. But it was a wry letter from a West African scholar to the *Mail & Guardian*, the country's most distinguished weekly newspaper, that made the political subtext most brutally plain.[18]

> It is alien-bashing time again. As an alien … I am particularly prickly about criticisms of aliens even if they are plants … But before the Department of Home Affairs is dragooned into investigating the residence permits of these plants I, as a concerned fellow alien, wish to remind one and all that plants such as maize … soybean, sunflower … originated outside of the continent of Africa. In any case, did the fire causing alien plants cross the borders and establish plantations … by themselves?

For this human alien, ecology had become the site of a distressingly familiar crusade: the demonization of migrants by the state and its citizenry alike. How long, we wondered, as we witnessed the rising temperature of this rhetoric, before a metaphorical spark (Coetzee 2008:23) would leap the species barrier and alight on the human objects toward whom it had long been reaching?

It has been noted that the migrant is the specter on whose wretched fate the triumphal neoliberal politics of the "new" Europe has been founded.[19] In South Africa, too, a phobia about foreigners, above all foreigners from elsewhere in Africa, has been the offspring of the fledgling democracy, waxing, paradoxically, alongside appeals to *ubuntu*, a common African humanity. In the 1990s, that phobia congealed into an active antipathy to what is perceived as a shadowy alien nation of "*illegal* immigrants"; the qualifier, "illegal," has become inseparable from the sign, just as, in the plant world, *invasive* has become locked, adjectivally, to alien. Popularly held to be "economic vultures"[20] who usurp jobs and resources, and who bring with them crime and disease, these anti-citizens are accused—in uncanny analogy with non-indigenous flora—of spreading uncontrollably. And of siphoning off the wealth of the nation (Sinclair 1996:14f; Reitzes 1994:7).

Aliens, then, are a distinctive species in the popular imagination. In a disturbing parody of the past, they are profiled by color and culture, thence to be excluded from the moral community. Once singled out, "illegals" are seldom differentiated from *bona fide* immigrants.[21] All are dubbed *makwerekwere*, a disparaging term for people who cannot speak properly. Not surprisingly, they live in terror that their accents will be detected.

The fear is well-founded. With the relaxation of controls over immigrant labor, South Africa—the "America of Africa" (see Chapter 1)—has become the destination of choice for many people from the north; estimates, which have fluctuated wildly, ran as high as 9.5m, 4.1m of them allegedly illegal, in 1995 (Crush 1999:3).[22] This influx has occurred amidst transformations in the domestic economy that have altered relations of labor to capital, leading to a radically downsized job market in which over 80 percent of employers opt for "non-standard" labor (Adam *et al.* 1998:209), much of it done by lowly paid, non-unionized "illegals," whom farmers and industrialists claim are essential to their survival in competitive global markets (Reitzes 1994:7). Small wonder, then, that routing *the* alien, who has come to embody a serious threat to local work and welfare, began to emerge as a persuasive mode of confronting economic dispossession, reversing job loss, regaining a sense of organic community.

And so the stage was set. In 2008, amidst sharply increasing unemployment, rising food prices, and growing discontent about the lack of housing and services, violent attacks were unleashed against foreigners, first around Johannesburg and then across the land. "Troops called in as SA Burns,"[23] screamed the local press, while media across the world bore graphic images of property torched and bodies set aflame. Fire and aliens again. In a manner that evoked the necklacing and witch-burnings of the 1990s, but throbbed with the macho populism that surrounds ANC leader and national president Jacob Zuma, young men armed with pangas and sticks took to the streets to purge their neighborhoods of foreigners.[24] These strangers were dragged from their homes amidst frenzied accusations that they had stolen jobs, undercut the minimum wage, usurped scarce housing, fostered crime, and spread AIDS. The ethnic profile of the victims showed some predictability: Zimbabweans who had fled their troubled homeland in large numbers were the most likely victims nationwide. But the identity of scapegoats also varied with local sociology. In some parts of the Cape, Somali shopkeepers were targeted. On the East Rand it was Tonga-speaking "Shangaans" (Vachangana) from Mozambique—long a major presence in a mining industry then rapidly shedding its workforce—who most embodied the protean scourge of otherness. In each case, the designated alien served as foil for a desperate struggle to forge a sense of citizenship from the ashes, a citizenship long promised, still denied.

Through all of this, the state has remained an ambiguous actor. On one hand, its representatives have joined outraged voices at home and abroad in condemning the attacks and in insisting on respect for universal human rights. On the other, the forces of law and order were slow to respond to the ethnonationalist violence in 2008, as they had often been before that. Furthermore, while it engaged in pious condemnation of "savage" xenophobes, allegedly abetted by criminal gangs and/or an insurgent "third force"[25]—again, echoes of the apartheid years—government was conspicuously silent on the desperate social conditions and sense of neglect that set the scene for this brutal drama.

At times, the regime has also contributed to the national mood of xenophobia by permitting its enforcement agencies, their effectiveness ever more in question, to wage "war" on foreigners by means of high-profile raids on immigrant neighborhoods. These tactics have been accompanied by official promises, loudly declared in the media, of a "US-style bid to rid SA of illegal aliens."[26] At the country's largest deportation facility, the privately owned Lindela Repatriation Centre, foreign nationals have been harshly beaten, their human rights seriously violated, their property looted.[27] The state has made little visible effort to regulate the facility, despite two investigations into it during the late 1990s by the South African Human Rights Commission (2000).

Reference here to the "US style" of alien management is telling. In the USA, too, shows of decisive action in the face of the "immigrant problem" exist alongside an almost farcical legal paralysis on the issue at a national level. Here, too, a history of official double-speak makes plain the paradox of porous borders. It highlights the contradiction between sovereignty and deregulation, neoconservatism and neoliberalism, national protectionism and global free trade, the homeland as fortress and the transnational flow of labor. In the US, too, spectacles of enforcement make futile attempts to redress the anomaly of strangers who have become essential to domestic reproduction: strangers who have both intimate local knowledge and foreign loyalties, real or imagined, raising specters of crime and terror; who are simultaneously indispensable and disposable, visible and invisible, human and degraded; who reside ambiguously inside, yet beyond the law. In June 2007, for example, "dozens of armed immigration agents, supported by police in riot gear," stormed a meatpacking plant in Greeley, Colorado, one of five simultaneous, well-publicized raids on similar facilities across the nation.[28] Termed "Operation Wagon Train," these raids were hailed by US Homeland Security and Immigration and Customs Enforcement—ICE by name and by nature—as a "major blow" in its "war against illegal immigration." Many of the deported workers were back within a week. Their labor, like that of an estimated twelve million other undocumented workers, is indispensable to American industry, agriculture, and the service sector. The impasse here, plainly, is very similar to the one we witnessed in South Africa, although in the US it is exacerbated by the tension between transnational agreements like NAFTA, which open up frontiers to capital, industry, and labor, and local politicians, who seek to criminalize foreign workers and keep them imprisoned inside the "developing world." In North America, observes Gary Younge, the political border is no longer coterminous with the physical borders of the nation-state. The former, the *de facto* border, is now more a matter of "economic expediency and political opportunism than either law or order." And it crisscrosses the country, deploying ethnic and racial profiles in order to secure the homeland by dividing nationals from aliens wherever they rub up against each other.

Shades, here, of the politics of contingency we identified, at the outset, as characteristic of Nuer sociology and Schmittian philosophy. Among the Nuer, recall, the objectification of boundaries between inside and out, law and war, "occurred in the process of dealing with the very transgressions that breached them." For Schmitt, the essential political gesture lay in drawing the line, indeed in making life-and-death distinctions, between friend and enemy. This is exactly what happens when aliens in South Africa are either flushed out by the police, with little attention to their legal rights—or worse yet, attacked by angry mobs of local people. Also what happens in the USA, where would-be illegal migrants may be apprehended not only at points of entry into the country, but anywhere that their difference from nationals comes to light, anywhere that lines may be crossed, anywhere that they may be espied and reported by citizens. "Operation Wagon Train" is no arbitrary turn of phrase. Its cavalier reference to the conquest of the West—a process, incidentally, that made America's first autochthons into aliens—reveals a deeper truth. It returns the US to a language of state-making as a species of colonial heroics, in which, as one anti-immigrant group put it, "citizen control" is to be reestablished. Seen in this light, armed raids on migrant enclaves might not seal the border. But they do create an "impression of effectiveness" on the part of the state in a political context in which illusion has become, perforce, its own reality. Here, in short, is an instance of the kind of symbolic activity of which we spoke earlier: the mass-mediated ritual excess, directed at producing state power and hyphenation, that features so prominently in efforts to secure sovereignty in a neoliberal age.

## ENDS AND MEANINGS

Geschiere and Nyamnjoh (2000) have noted the growing stress in Africa on the exclusion of the stranger, not least in reaction to the social and economic uncertainties, and the destabilization of borders, set in motion by rising global flows of labor, capital, commodities, and persons. This is true of post-apartheid South Africa, where outrage against aliens has provided a versatile call to arms, forcing a new line of separation that unifies a home-grown population otherwise divided by class, color, culture, and much else; not fully or finally, of course, but nonetheless visibly and volubly. Nor, as we have intimated, is South Africa alone in this. Similar processes are evident more or less everywhere that the nation-state is perceived to be plagued by conditions that threaten to dissolve its borders, opening them up to unwanted aliens of all sorts, undermining the coordinates of moral and material community—and making them seem more like contested colonial frontiers than the secure margins of the modernist polity.

The increasing ambiguation of those borders, we have noted, arises from the embrace of the nation-state in a global economy whose ways and means have transformed not just received patterns of production and consumption, but also the articulation of labor to capital, the movement of persons and commodities, the nature of sovereignty and civic identity, geographies of space and time, order and security, war and law, and the like. Because of their particular histories, postcolonies like South Africa manifest these things in especially acute form. But, in many respects, they are merely condensed, hyper-extended prefigurations of what is becoming visible elsewhere. Which returns us to one of the central theses of *Theory from the South*. As northern governments resort to the language of wagon trains and frontiers, as journalists talk of an "apartheid planet,"[29] as the post–Cold War world gives way to a state of "ordered anarchy," we may be forgiven for thinking that the colonial societies of the south, and the postcolonies that have grown out of them, may be seen less as historical inversions of Euro-America than foreshadowings of what, in a postmodern world, it might become. Or is becoming.

This speculation is not idle. European colonial regimes managed the political and economic contradictions inherent in industrial capitalism by means of a politics of spatial separation. The segregation of metropole and colony not only obscured their material and cultural interdependence. It also served to keep well apart the humanitarian, modernizing, rule-governed, freedom-seeking face of liberal democracy from the exclusionary, violently secured forms of subjection, extraction, and devastation that were its underside. Colonies were zones of occupation in which the European civilizing mission was countered by the dictates of control and profit—and by the need to secure the contested frontiers held to stand between order and chaos. Defending those boundaries in the name of progress often warranted the suspension of enlightened ways and means, even in the face of resistance and humanitarian outrage.

The long process of decolonization that set the stage for a new Age of Empire has disrupted this spatial logic. The Cold War era might have marked time between the two imperial epochs, but it came undone when economies were deregulated and capital moved offshore, escaping state oversight, globalizing the division of labor, deterritorializing sovereignty and jurisdiction, scrambling received relations between politics and production, leaving discarded people and landscapes in their wake. As multinational corporations relocated many of their factories to distant sites of cheap labor, fresh forms of enclaved colonial extraction were invented, extraction with minimal costs, *sans* state apparatuses, safety restrictions, or civilizing missions. At the same time, workers who could move from blighted postcolonies sought to find opportunities for themselves in post-Fordist, northern economies. In the process, the structural and spatial separations of metropole and colony began to erode. And as they did, migrant communities, camps for illegal aliens, inner-city wastelands, zones of occupation, and burning *banlieues* brought colonial conditions into the heart of Euro-American polities—there to call forth modes of governance that, once again, draw the line between friend and enemy, law and war. Reciprocally, states in the south and east have taken on many of the features of the north, from the growing preoccupation with democracy and the law, to inventive forays into modern urbanism, heavy industry, electronic communications, global finance, commodity design, and so on.

In the face of all this, received models of society and politics have undergone revision in Euro-America, among scholars and statesmen and ordinary citizens alike. The image is fading of an organic society, *à la* Comte and Durkheim, in which divisions of class and culture were contained, ideally at least, within national boundaries; in which, also, the pathological, criminal classes were believed, through welfare and reform, to be recoverable "citizens-in-waiting." On the rise is a rather different archetype: that of the state as citadel; of its territory as embattled homeland; of prisons as sites not of recuperation but of the warehousing of those deemed disposable, or exploitable at rock-bottom rates; of borders as elusive lines to be drawn and redrawn within the polity and beyond against the endless threat of others who challenge its moral and corporeal integrity, enemies who take the form of aliens, migrants, terrorists, home-grown saboteurs, felons, the indigent poor. This, once more, is the world of Carl Schmitt, in which politics is not about democratic participation and redistribution but about securing the frontier between autochthon and intruder, good and evil, citizenship and subjection. It is also the world of the Nuer, with their constantly shifting lines between inside and out, kin and stranger. Is it to be wondered, then, that conditions that nurture phobias of alien nature and campaigns of ethnic cleansing should also have generated a new, rapidly growing global industry, the so-called homeland security sector? This industry, after all, makes and markets "high-tech fences, unmanned drones, biometric ID's, video and audio surveillance gear, air passenger profiling and prisoner interrogation systems" that, ostensibly, allow us "to enjoy relative safety amid constant war"?[30] All this may seem a world away from allegories of alien plants and natural autochthony. But the link between them is patent. Both speak to efforts to bring to order the real or imagined anarchy of our late modern age. Or, to be more precise, to make sense of, and to act upon, some of the contradictions and contingencies, the uncertainties and insecurities, the ambiguities and ambivalences brought about by a deep historical disjuncture: the disjuncture, that is, between the modernist world as we knew it and the world now taking shape all around.

# CHAPTER 5

# Figuring Democracy

*An Anthropological Take on African Political Modernities*

## I.

12:01 a.m., 25 April 1994. Wale Street, Cape Town, South Africa: The last strains of the anthem of the ancien régime—part requiem, part death-rattle—drift off into the night. A local choir, carefully rehearsed for the occasion, begins to belt out the new national song, with its familiar, once-banned libretto of liberation, its hymn-notic harmony of hope. The old flag, long an emblem of colonialism and apartheid, is folded away for the last time. Its replacement, a brash, multicolored icon of consensus, is raised. The symbolism, by intent, is too obvious to miss. Calico curtains ring down and up as the world's latest Midnight's Child, the "new" South Africa, is born.[1]

PERHAPS IT WAS SACRILEGIOUS, AT THAT PRECISE MOMENT, THAT moment of unreserved optimism, to recall Malcolm Bradbury's *Doctor Criminale*. In this novel about a postmodern philosopher, a fictional fusion of Foucault and Derrida, the Hungarian ex-wife of the hero, one Gertla Riviero, reflects upon the recent transition to democracy and free-market economics throughout much of the contemporary world (1992:276):

109

"Democracy, the free market," she muses, "do you really think they can save us? ... Marxism [was] a great idea, democracy [is] just a small idea. It promises hope, and it gives you [Kentucky] Fried Chicken."

Ms. Riviero's commentary is sad, cynical, salutary. Especially so when read in the cooling afterglow of post-election South Africa. Especially so as we call to mind the queues that waited for hours outside polling stations in those last heady days of April 1994, some in almost sacral silence, some in carnivalesque revelry. Those snaking, eternal queues reminded us of the interminable lines that graced McDonald's in Moscow a few years back as people voted with their feet not merely for hamburgers or cheeseburgers, but for a market economy and capitalist consumerism. The association may seem irreverent. Yet Gertla Riviero's question carries an obvious, ominous punch, precisely because it calls into doubt our taken-for-granted narrative of democratization, a heroic liberal myth that links the conventional practices of modernist politics to the prospect of material and social salvation. So, too, if in a different way, does the image of patient, passive people standing in millennial lines to choose either cheap food or political candidates; all the more so as we recall Bayart's (1993) discomforting aphorism for African public life, to wit, "the Politics of the Belly."

Let us pursue this question, and follow these lines, for a while. They lead us into an unexpected encounter with very different philosophies of governmentality, democracy, and modernity.

## II.

It became commonplace during the 1990s, especially in Europe and North America, to ascribe the *fin de siècle* push for democracy in many parts of the world to the end of the Cold War and the triumph of the free market over communism. In fact, as many have pointed out, this view was flawed from the first. Apart from all else, the push began well before 1989. But no matter: the association is itself a symptom, often misrecognized, of something much longer in the making, namely, a fundamental reconstruction of the modernist world order. We have ourselves suggested before that the events of 1989 were evidence of an unfolding Age of Revolution, an epochal process akin to the one that began in 1789—the European Age of Revolution, that is, which gave us modernity, the seeds of the nation-state form, industrial capitalism, the second colonialism, and much besides (J.L. Comaroff 1995). The present revolution has been marked, in particular, by the rise of a planetary political economy in which sites of production and consumption are widely dispersed; in which social class is rendered barely visible by being scattered promiscuously across the earth; in which finance takes precedence over fabrication, flexibility over fixity, the short run over the long; in which the state outsources many of its received operations, not least those involving the exercise of violence; in which the nation is confronted by the irreducible fact of increasing demographic heterogeneity; in which governance is represented primarily in the argot of technical oversight; in which politics, more a matter of ID-ology than ideology (see Chapter 3), is increasingly focused on the simultaneous calculi of right, interest, and entitlement, often pursued by judicial means.

For many, these things are cause for despondency. Let us return to Doctor Criminale, Bradbury's figurative philosopher. Ours, he says (1992:330), is

> the media age, the age of simulation ... The age of no ideology, only hyperreality ... Too little reality, also too much. Everywhere, wild fantasies, everyone wants a violent illusion. Life is a movie, death a plot ending, no stories are real. And even the philosophers think in unrealities, [as] they describe a world of no ethics, no humanism, no self.

In this new Age of Revolution, fear of the atomic bomb subsides. But *anomic* bombs explode all over the place. People across the globe—alienated, disempowered, dispossessed—commit extraordinary acts of violence in the name of ethnic and national aspiration. The "me" generation folds into the "we" generation. And the end of politics, at least politics as anything more than the pursuit of brute interest, appears visible on the horizon.

The scenario, like Doctor Criminale himself, might be fantastic. It is, however, becoming ever less fictional, ever more recognizable.

But how is this darkly pessimistic view of the contemporary world to be reconciled with the rise of late 20th-century democratic movements in so many far-flung places? Were those movements not a positive, liberatory sign of the times in that premillennial moment, that Great Time of Signs? And how, in particular, ought we understand them in Africa, long seen in the West as the continent-least-likely-to-democratize-itself?

It is difficult to gainsay those who draw connections between the recent rise of democracy and the triumph of consumer capitalism—even if the line of causality that joins them is at once complicated and the subject of ongoing debate. Capitalism, to be sure, does not require democracy; it has done perfectly well under authoritarian regimes in the past, and continues to do so in many parts of the late modern world. But those nation-states that seek to democratize themselves appear, these days, to require at least the figment of a free market. An elective (or is it electoral?) affinity connects the ballot box to business. Nor is it a passive affinity (cf. Young 1993:299f). US overseas aid has become largely conditional on the establishment of "democratic institutions."

For which read "regular elections." To wit, in 1996, Robert Mugabe—then still a leader of some standing, now a discredited dictator who takes every opportunity to excoriate the West—drew a direct connection between ballot box, business, and foreign involvement in African politics: "Western countries," he said, push "multi-party [systems] for Africa" because it enables them to "buy influence" and "manipulate parties" into creating congenial economic environments.[2]

The contemporary Western concern with the democratization of the global south, however, is not reducible to utility alone, important though that may be. It has roots in the hegemonic, indeed ontological, association throughout the global north of freedom and self-expression with choice. Democracy has become to *homo politicus* what shopping has long been to *homo economicus:* a sacred, cosmic fusion of free will and righteous human satisfaction. They are, so to speak, two sides of the same coin, two regimes of consumption underpinned by the same mode of ideological and material and production.

> On 1 May, at 11:48 p.m., during the counting of votes after the first free election in South Africa, SATV Channel 2 broke into its local news coverage to broadcast a meta-advertisement, an advertisement for advertising. "ADVERTISING," blared the message on the primal screen, "THE RIGHT TO CHOOSE."

It is no coincidence, then, as several theorists have observed, that democracy has increasingly been reduced, in practice, from the substantive to the procedural (e.g., Farer 1989; Barsh 1992); that, purged of any ideological density, it has come to connote little more than the periodic exercise of preference, the satisfying of desire, the physics of pure interest. To wit, it does not take a political theorist, or the fictional Ms. Riviero, to make the point that, understood thus, democracy *is* a small idea, one that *is* more likely to bring with it Kentucky Fried Chicken and McDonald's than an amelioration of the human condition. We might go yet further: to argue that processes of democratization bespeak a historical paradox, namely, that "the people" are being empowered in the politics of state at the very moment when, as we have noted, the politics that count are moving elsewhere—to global processes and institutions, into the corporate world and nongovernmental organizations, the media and the law, new social movements, "grassroots" coalitions, and other domains of civil society.

To phrase all this in the interrogative voice, is it possible that Doctor Criminale is correct: that democratization is a product of the death of politics, of its dispersal to everywhere and anywhere and nowhere in particular? Is democracy rising because it has become politically beside the point?

> An echo here from home. Speaking of democracy in a workshop at the University of Chicago many years ago, Wayne Booth—author, tellingly, of *The Rhetoric of Fiction* (1961) and *The Rhetoric of Irony* (1974)—observed that freedom of speech is guaranteed in America only to the extent that no one is listening; that, while everybody has a right to talk, nobody has an obligation to pay attention; that democracy disempowers by encouraging a cacophony in which voices cancel each other out.

Put these two things together—the reduction of the Idea of Democracy to the exercise of choice and the decentering, de-institutionalization of politics—and what do we get? For one thing, some of the concerns that many Africans, academics and intellectuals and every-persons alike, raise about the export of modernist European models to the global south: that they are founded on an "extremely narrow" conception of public life, one that places too much emphasis on "votes and free-market economics"[3] and too little on the realization of universal human rights, civil liberties, the commonweal, and transparent, accountable government—all of which, according to recent survey research, tend to be embraced in popular African definitions of democracy (cf. Bratton 2002:5), definitions that also take on heavy local inflictions across the continent. Given that the meaning of the term is hardly unambiguous or uncontested in the global north, as Mahmood Mamdani (1986, 1990, 1992) has noted—we paraphrase him heavily here—how much more murky does it become in Africa, whose vast array of dynamic, evanescent cultures have their own theories and practices of politics, of personhood, of power, of representation? As this suggests, the cultural transitivity of the concept cannot simply be presumed, as it so often is by comparative political scientists. The more general implication? That the common presumption in the West according to which Africa ought to adopt the liberal modernist Euro-American model (see, e.g., Bratton and Mattes 2001), an ideology floating free of its social and historical moorings, leaves Africans with a unenviable dilemma: to opt for either (i) a highly *un*-African political order, wherein the body politic is composed of autonomous, individualized, rights-bearing citizens whose primary political being is congealed in the exercise of the ballot;[4] or (ii) an "indigenous" alternative, usually characterized as anti-modern, ethnically based, patriarchal, traditionalist, customary, communalist, clientalist, and authoritarian—and/or, more insidiously yet, populist. What kind of choice is this? Even more fundamentally, what, in its *own* terms, might democracy actually mean in Africa?

Mikael Karlstrom (1996:485) observed in the mid-1990s that, notwith-standing the burgeoning literature on democracy in contemporary Africa, surprisingly little heed had been paid to this last question. As long as it is not adequately addressed, he added, we have little hope of grasping postcolonial politics at all, little hope of making sense of such things as, say, the Ugandan insistence that political parties are inimical to representative government. But there is yet another corollary here. Some African counter-discourses on democratization, as we have already intimated, are grounded in a vernacular political anthropology that offers a substantive critique of conventional Western political theory and practice. By confronting this narrative we stand not merely to understand African politics better than we do now—to understand what lies beyond the "politics of the belly," beneath the "banality of power ... in the postcolony."[5] We might also arrive at a more reflexive, critical ap-preciation of our own received political forms.

On the Lévi-Straussian principle that one good case may illuminate an entire world, let us offer an exemplary instance to make our argument. Our choice will be surprising, perhaps. We do *not* take a country in which repre-sentative government or electoral politics have been repudiated, subverted, or misappropriated. Such examples are either too easy or too stereotypic to be useful. Rather, we take Botswana, the African nation-state most widely regarded as a "model" democracy[6]—and the closest, by common agreement, to the Western ideal. This very similarity, at least in appearances, will serve to underscore a brace of revealing differences.

## III.

Consider the following facts. In October 1974, Botswana held its third na-tional elections, in which the ruling Botswana Democratic Party (BDP) won an emphatic 85 percent majority of the seats in the national assembly.[7] Both before and after the ballot there was a great deal of public discussion, seem-ingly spontaneous and unprovoked, of the advantages to be gained from the introduction of a one-party state. Many people clearly favored a move away from the existing British-style multiparty system; so much so, in fact, that the president at the time, Sir Seretse Khama, felt compelled to comment repeatedly on the subject, to refuse even to ponder the possibility—and to encourage people both to vote and to consider the merits of *all* parties. His public state-ments were featured prominently in the *Botswana Daily News* at the time.[8]

In hindsight, and from the vantage of the global north, this expression of popular support for a one-party system would seem odd. First, it did *not* come primarily from BDP voters. Adversaries of the government were among its more enthusiastic protagonists; to wit, *Puo Phaa,* official organ of the opposition Botswana National Front—which was led by Bathoen Gaesitsiwe, the ex-ruler of a large chiefdom—urged the formation of a "national government, fusing all political groupings into a single administration."[9] Second, it was *not* engineered by a cadre of bosses or captains in the name of a mass ruling party. At the time, as Colclough and McCarthy (1980:41) note, the BDP was anything but that: "indeed it scarcely exist[ed] between elections." Third, in refusing insistently to change existing electoral arrangements, much to the delight of South Africa and other Western powers,[10] the Khama regime was aware that the BDP was passing up its best chance to gain a legitimate monopoly of the organs of state. Fourth, and most puzzling of all, demands for a one-party system were typically justified on the ground that it would foster both better government *and* more participatory democracy.

These demands resonated with informal views we encountered in rural Botswana at the time, especially in the south.[11] As we shall see, they were consistent with the way in which village populations tended to participate in electoral processes. What is more, they echoed opinions we had heard before. During the previous general election, in 1969, we had been delivered a memorable lesson in comparative political anthropology by a local teacher, an organic intellectual from the edge of the Kalahari. This man, who described himself as "neither a radical nor a traditionalist," had argued that one-party systems were the "only true social democracies." With due respect for old European verities, he added politely, the very idea of a multiparty democracy is a contradiction in terms. It abases politics, shrinking them to nothing more than an occasional act of choice. And, by erasing all real government accountability between elections, it licenses the *in*difference of regimes in power both to popular participation and to public criticism—thereby alienating the citizenry at large from the everyday functioning of the state. President Khama seems to have been aware that views of this ilk had been gaining currency among people in the countryside. Speaking before the 1974 election at Oodi, a small town near the capital, he went to great lengths, in defending multiparty democracy, to stress that "the Government's intention was not to fetter or discourage ... criticism." That, he said, would be "against our Setswana tradition."[12] Of which more later.

How, then, do we *explain* such manifestations of antagonism against multiparty democracy, especially where it seems to have taken root so successfully? Why did it appear to these people as an oxymoron, as *antithetical* to participatory politics, even as an elaborate Western mystification? What accounts for the positive light in which a one-party system came to be regarded here? And to historicize these questions, one or two more: Was this outburst of *vox populi* merely a passing moment in the history of the public sphere in Botswana, its civil society crying out, ever so briefly, against the postcolonial state? Or did it speak to something more enduring. If so, what?

And how? After all, foreign observers have been quick to comment on the non-involvement—"apathy" or, worse yet, "ignorance" are the words commonly used—of the electorate in matters affecting national politics in the 1970s and 1980s.

In order to address these issues, we begin by turning to so-called traditional Setswana political theory and practice, a vernacular theory and practice that, albeit contested and constantly transforming itself, persisted through the colonial epoch; then to its conjuncture with the postcolonial politics of the nation-state. For it is here, we believe, that the answers lie. Observe, in all this, that we have three subtexts, three not-so-hidden agendas. One is to show that African political anthropology, despite repeated criticisms of theoretical aridity, has something yet to add to the analysis of world-historical phenomena. The second grows out of an old axiom. Long ago, Fortes and Evans-Pritchard (1940:4) said that Western political philosophy, because of its lack of comparative perspective, has had nothing useful to say to political anthropology. We seek to turn this on its side: to argue that a political philosophy found in another social world may be the basis of a critical anthropology of our own. The third is to provide a corrective to the persisting tendency in the global north to reduce Africa to adjectives—communalist, clientalist, patriarchal, and the like—thus to reproduce tired racist archetypes. And, worse yet, to mistake those archetypes for empirical descriptions in which to ground political theory.

## IV.

Botswana, until 1966 the Bechuanaland Protectorate, is usually said to be made up of eight distinct chiefdoms ("tribes"). These, prior to incorporation within the British Empire in 1885 and with modifications during the colonial period, were the major, but *not* the only,[13] political communities into which indigenous populations were grouped.[14] Although the system of local government has changed over the years, and chiefs have been denuded of much of their authority,[15] the eight chiefdoms still exist. Some of the larger ones are today (more or less) coterminous with the jurisdictions of districts and their councils. Moreover, while its urban centers have grown enormously, Botswana is stereotypically seen as a predominantly rural nation: much of its citizenry was raised in, and sustains active links with, "villages."

While chiefdoms varied in size and in the minutiae of their institutional arrangements, the dominant features of their political organization, cultures, and ideology were broadly shared. These have been thoroughly documented;[16] although there does remain some controversy about the politics of succession to high office[17]—and an unfortunate tendency among Western social scientists to typify the public sphere in Tswana communities, often glossed as the "*kgotla* system" (see below), in rather too simple terms.[18] For present purposes, the briefest of summaries will do.

From the earliest documentary accounts we have of centralized "Bechuana" polities, dating from the first half of the 19th century, three things are clear.[19] The first is that the chief*ship* was seen to be the *axis mundi* of the social world. It was, as one Tshidi-Rolong elder said to us in 1969, like the *pinnegare,* the central pole, of houses of old. Everything—the fertility of the earth and the abundance of the rains, security from attack and success in war, the passing of the seasons and "giving of the seed-time," material wealth and spiritual well-being, the crafting of legislation and courts that judged fairly—all these things, and much besides, turned around the apical office. Its holder, in principle at least, personified his people, signified their sovereignty and subjectivity, embodied their essence. He was known by an honorific whose form was the metonymic singular of the name of his "nation" (*morafe*): Mokwena, the ruler of the Bakwena (*mo-,* singular; *ba-,* plural), Mongwaketse, the ruler of the Bangwaketse, and so on.

But, second, a clear line was drawn between chiefship (*bogosi*) and chief (*kgosi*), office and incumbent. The former stood for the very existence of the polity. It was the public sphere incarnate, the *morafe* made manifest and represented back to itself as a political principle. The authority vested in it—albeit historically shifting over the long run—was taken, at any moment in time, to be beyond question. The latter, by contrast, was merely human. He might be more or less effective a ruler, more or less influential, more or less adept at mobilizing the political capital available to him. Early European visitors to the Tswana were impressed by the charisma and command of some "kings" who, it is said, struck awe into their followers and whose slightest whim elicited the strictest compliance. But they were also fascinated by the frankly critical way in which most sovereigns were addressed at their own courts. And by the fact that their power was often constrained by the sheer unwillingness of their subjects to do their bidding.[20] Elsewhere (e.g., J.L. Comaroff 1975, 1978; see n.17) we have shown that a chief who lost all legitimacy, who was said publicly to be "not fit to rule" (Campbell 1822,2:157), was likely to find his genealogical status successfully contested by a rival. This in spite of the prevailing rules of ascription according to which sovereigns held office by virtue of birth, not election. It was always possible to unfix the fixities, to unscrew the inscrutabilities, of ascribed rank by reconstruing the relations that gave rise to it.

The third thing of note is that great store was placed here on what might be glossed as "good government." Substantively speaking, chiefs were responsible for all aspects—political, judicial, administrative, material, spiritual—of collective well-being; that is, for everything in the public domain. This, furthermore, is to be understood in historical terms: sovereign responsibility embraced the fluid realities of time, space, and situation. Where transformed conditions demanded, say, that the colonial state be dealt with in a particular fashion, or that dams and storage depots be built for purposes of agrarian development, rulers were held to account for the discharge of these functions. But, and this is the crucial point, the ideology of good government paid less attention to the *content* of public affairs than to the *means* by which they were managed.

Tswana ideas about the proper means of governance were elaborate, nuanced, and enduring; we heard any number of discourses on the topic in the 1970s. Above all, they stressed (i) the participatory, consultative aspect of the public sphere, in which there was, ostensibly, "perfect freedom of debate" (Philip 1828,1:133), and in which all male citizens (more recently, all adults)[21] were entitled to a voice—just as they had the right to be represented by headmen on chiefly councils; (ii) the proportional relationship between the performance of any ruler (assessed against the canons of good government) and his legitimacy (as indexed in his recognized capacity to wield control over people, policy, and public life); and (iii) the fusion of what, in Western social science, is nowadays distinguished as civil society and the state.

In sum, chiefs were expected to rule "with" the people. *Kgosi ke kgosi ka morafe,* went the most quoted adage in the Tswana political lexicon, "a chief is chief by the nation." What this meant, in practice, is that sovereigns were expected to surround themselves with advisors to guide the everyday life of the polity, men for whose advice and actions they were held responsible; to hold regular meetings of councils of headmen and other chiefly conclaves; to summon public assemblies of various kinds from which emerged policy that reflected popular views and attended to the commonweal; to ensure that the hierarchy of courts over which they presided did not favor the rich over the poor, royals over commoners, or men over women (even though the latter, as "jural minors," had to be represented by male kin); to be open always to approach by their subjects, whose physical welfare they were also obliged to heed, redistributing food and other requisites in times of need.

In Southern Tswana chiefdoms, in fact, past rulers were—in some places they still are—recalled by the legislation they introduced (cf. Schapera 1943) and by the wisdom of those whom they recruited as advisors. They are also remembered by their capacity to bring rain, itself a sure spiritual gauge of political mastery; but that is another story. Ultimately, in this respect, chiefly success was numbered in observable achievements: "improvements," in the Protestant-saturated language of modernist governance. But delivering improvements, in turn, hinged on the public cooperation that a ruler could command. Which, tautologically, depended on the degree to which he was seen to measure up to the ideals of good government. Note, by way of example, the following text, which we published more than thirty years ago (J.L. Comaroff 1975:145). It comes from a speech made by a local elder statesmen in February 1970 at the installation of Besele, the new ruler of the southernmost chiefdom of Barolong:

> A chief can only be judged by what he does ... If you treat [people] with respect, they will treat you with respect. If you shun them, they will shun you. And if you frighten them they will run away ... We will be watching to see whether you are going to make improvements. Chiefship is not an easy job. A chief never sleeps. A chief does not discriminate. Batswana say that a chief is chief because of the nation. If we cannot see you in the court [*kgotla*] we shall draw away from you. And if we do will you still call yourself chief?

In analyzing this text when we first published it, we noted, in particular, how it underscored the significance attributed, in the local political *imaginaire,* (i) to the Hegelian interdependency between ruler and subject; (ii) to the measurability of chiefly success in terms of practical, palpable accomplishment ("what he does, his industry ... [his] improvements"); and (iii) to the possibility that an authoritarian or an inattentive sovereign may be repudiated ["shunned"], even removed ("if we [draw ourselves away from you, will you still [be able to] call yourself chief?"), notwithstanding the ideology of ascription in terms of which succession to high office is represented (see above; also n.17).

This, self-evidently, implied the existence of a model of incumbency, a paradigm of political legitimation in terms of which the actions of rulers were evaluated and their authority negotiated; by which, that is, the equation of performance to power was given practical, realized form. At the core of this equation was a simple socio-logarithm: the willingness of political subjects to comply with the commands of a chief was held to depend on the degree to which he could demonstrate, in public, that he had properly discharged the obligations of his office.

It follows—*pace* received wisdom that goes back to *African Political Systems* (1940) and persists in some quarters—that the rights and duties of Tswana (and, for that matter, other African) sovereigns were never immutable, never fixed by "tradition." To the contrary. Their authority varied widely. As we have already said, some appeared, alike to their subjects and to outsiders, as mighty kings. Having established their legitimacy, they could exercise almost dictatorial power. Others found it hard to impose their wills, or their executive decisions, at all. Most, however, traversed the line between these extremes during their reigns.[22] To be sure, many of the scholarly arguments that surround the analysis of Tswana politics, past and present, flow from an inattention to precisely this capacity for transformation over time and space.

How, then, did the model of incumbency, the equation of performance to power, work out in everyday practice? The answer to this question begins with the fact that, whatever their formal agendas, public meetings were also forums in which chiefly regimes were subjected to debate and evaluation. The process was founded on a crucial assumption: that there existed, tacit but nonetheless well understood, an incremental scale of sovereign authority; that, as the legitimacy of a ruler increased, the more inclusive (and exclusive) became his recognized right to regulate the various ways and means, the instruments and institutions, of governance[23]—expanding, potentially at least, until it embraced virtually all aspects of social life. Thus, for example, before the passage of the Tribal Land Act (1968), a strong chief enjoyed, among other things, sole control over the distribution of fields, pasturage, and residential plots—either allocating them himself or appointing surrogates to do so—and a monopoly over the creation of new political constituencies (wards, sections, villages, provinces), along with the offices that ruled over them. He also could expect to be obeyed when he summoned labor for communal works and improvement projects, to receive sundry forms of tribute, to minister over the timing of the ritual and agricultural cycles, and to have his legislative initiatives, executive orders, and legal judgments implemented with dispatch.[24]

Conversely, a ruler who lost his legitimacy, a process that occurred slowly rather than suddenly, found it ever more difficult to exert control as, cumulatively, he forfeited the various rights of office. The exact composition of this scale of rights differed from chiefdom to chiefdom. But it appears to have existed in some form everywhere; again, with contrasting degrees of explicitness. In Barolong, for instance, the first thing a chief would lose was his sway over the activities of voluntary associations, which were likely to listen to him politely and then ignore him utterly; thence he would forgo his monopoly over the allocation of land, this usually being effected by public demand that a committee be appointed to "help" him make decisions. Next went the presumption that judgments and sentences handed down in his court would be executed without question. This was followed by the erosion of other capacities and entitlements: to call people to labor on public works, to enact legislation, to establish new constituencies or regulate space and time, to demand tribute, finally even to summon meetings.

But this leaves one part of the question unanswered. By what rhetorical means and concrete measures was the indigenous equation of performance to power *actually* resolved? How was the legitimacy of a reigning chief—the substance and scope of his command over the public sphere—*actually* negotiated? How, in short, did sovereign authority *actually* come to expand or contract?

Through *mahoko,* words. Words spoken in *kgotla,* in the public sphere, which were assumed to have great pragmatic power to affect the world; words spoken in the genre of political oratory, a genre not specifically named in Setswana but one for which Tswana are justly famed. Theirs is a rich aural culture, in which the aesthetics of utterance are potent indeed. And in which the negotiation of chiefly legitimacy takes on a very particular form.

Before saying more about that genre, however, a point of clarification. The *kgotla* might have been where chiefly authority was negotiated, but the *production* of that authority, and the power that lay behind it, was an altogether more complex matter. To hold that legitimacy was determined by the unconstrained consent of the governed, that it was decided purely by argument in town meetings, or that rulers bore passive witness to their own evaluation—all of which is implicit in the vernacular model of incumbency—is to simplify reality. Public debate, always the object of careful strategy and management, was a site of struggle, not a neutral enactment of *vox populi*. The distribution of support to which it gave voice depended, in major measure, on prior power relations, relations forged in offstage dealings of various kinds. The discourse of chiefly evaluation provided a medium by which the invisible calculi of patronage and influence congealed into social "facts," namely collectively recognized lines of alliance and antagonism. There is a tautology here, of course: civic discussion was taken both to reflect *and* to determine sovereign legitimacy. But the tautology is more apparent than real. Verbal exchanges in *kgotla* made manifest, and so converted into the currency of politics, all the transactions that occurred, dispersed and individuated, across the axes of everyday life.

Tacit in all this is a political dynamic of some moment for the more general question at hand. Inasmuch as discourses of chiefly evaluation expressed alliances and antagonisms, support and opposition for the ruler—inasmuch, that is, as they were a partisan theater of the political—they tended to be articulated around identifiable *factions*. The existence of (usually a pair of) such factions was endemic in local public life. (The reasons for this are too complex to go into here. They flow from the fissiparous character of Tswana polities of the past, which were often wracked by rivalries over the chiefship. These invariably pitted the reigning sovereign against an agnatic adversary, thus dividing the *morafe* into two blocs, each around its royal leader.) One of the factions was always composed of "king's men," core supporters from among whom the personnel of his regime were drawn; 19th-century missionaries, tellingly, sometimes referred to them as "the chief's party." The other, which might be more or less articulate(d), bounded, and assertive, depending on circumstance, typically clustered around senior royal patrikin who were, potentially and often in practice, the ruler's primary adversaries for position and property. Again, all this has been well documented. The point, as far as we are concerned, was the taken-for-granted, almost inevitable presence of factional alignments in local politics. For out of these blocs came the primary players, the *dramatis personae,* of the public sphere—as well, significantly, as the political and dialogical motivation that gave shape to discourses of chiefly evaluation.

The aesthetics of public discourses about governance and chiefly performance—the poetic play, that is, of form and substance—held the key to their politics. The latter derived from the juxtaposition, in "parliamentary" speeches, of two kinds of utterance; two styles, whose difference was closely connected to the vernacular distinction drawn between office and incumbent. One style (elsewhere we have referred to it as a "formal code"; J.L. Comaroff 1975) spoke of the ideals of good government, and of the regnant ideology of chiefship, largely in idiomatic form; phrases like *kgosi ke kgosi ka morafe* (see above), *batho ga se ba melamu, ba bokwa ka lotlhare* ("people are not ruled with clubs, they are waved with winnowing fans"), and others specified expectations of office-holders. These utterances relied heavily on formulaic speech and were rarely phrased in the first person singular, their author usually being the collective "we" ("We Barolong say that ..."; "It is our way/custom ..."; "Our fathers taught that ..."). What is more, because they invoked shared values, they presupposed the consensual agreement of speaker and audience.

Strikingly different from these formulaic utterances, the second kind addressed the performance of the chief. Phrased always in the first person singular ("I must speak my mind, Chief! ..."; "I have heard what others say. It is my view that ..."), statements made in this register were not formulaic at all. Typically frank and forthright, sometimes even brutally censorious, they tended to be syntactically more elaborate, to deploy a wider vocabulary, to rely more on evidentiary argument than on shared assumptions, and to be voiced with a view to their persuasive force. These statements were made in a spirit of political argumentation. In observing such speech acts, we were also struck by the fact that, in contrast to more formal utterances—which, at best, were heard in polite silence—they were typically listened to in rapt attention.

These two styles were deployed in careful counterpoint to one another during the course of most political speeches. For their part, "king's men" sought to convince the public at large of the *convergence* between the ideals of good government and the reigning incumbent's record of actions and accomplishments; this by iterating the first, in formulaic speech, as a point of reference, a template almost, against which to mount first-person polemics, propositional claims, and political arguments. Conversely, opposition factions would try to force the greatest plausible *divergence* between the mantras of good government and the material performance of the office-holder, at least as they construed it in their narratives of failure.

For chiefly protagonists, it follows that the greater the degree of convergence they could establish in the public eye between ideal and performance, the broader the claims they could make for expanding the authority of the ruler. Ultimate success, in theory, was when office and office-holder became as one, when statements in the formulaic mode about the first might be said to apply to the second; in practice, this condition of absolutism was never reached in Tswana polities, there being counter-forces that put constraints on the accumulation of sovereign power beyond a certain point. The inverse is also true. For opposition blocs, final victory occurred when the divergence between the ideal of good government and the performance of an office-holder became so great—and, concomitantly, sovereign authority so truncated—that the ruler was no longer a "real chief." Whereupon, as we implied earlier, he could well be deposed.

Participation in discourses of chiefly evaluation was not confined to those who identified with one or other faction, although the close supporters and active antagonists of a ruler were likely to be most vocal; also the most caught up in the political tactics and intrigues that often lay behind, and broke through to the surface, in the dramaturgy of public dialogue. The un-aligned, however, did not merely add their voices to the debate. They acted, at once, in the manner of a chorus and a jury, echoing or disagreeing with the arguments of those more partisan, commenting on their plausibility and persuasiveness, and suggesting implications that might follow for the standing of the chief. From these interventions a measure of consensus was likely to emerge as speakers began slowly to draw closer in their views; this measure serving to confirm, expand, or re-delimit the state of sovereign authority for the time being.

In sum, the *kgotla* was more than a forum for the discussion of social policy, although it certainly was that, too. Nor was it just an African analogue of the classical *polis* (see n.18). It was also (i) a context for ongoing discourse about governance and sovereign authority—and, simultaneously, (ii) a space of contestation in which the powers of a living ruler were negotiated and given social currency. Its primary constituencies were factions rather than political parties, one a chiefly bloc and the other an opposition. These constituencies, patently, did not differentiate themselves according to ideology or matters of principle. Their arguments, recall, were about the *means* of government, not its content. In striking contrast to Western nation-states, where policy is seen from within to be the provenance of partisan politics, here it was taken to be a product of public discourse.

There is much more to the subtleties and the substance of Tswana political culture, past and present. Also to the workings of its public sphere. Enough has been said, however, to allow us to revisit, and to make sense of, contemporary discourses of democracy and the postcolonial politics of this nation-state.

Two brief, final observations before we do.

One is that there has been a revisionist tendency, in some circles, to portray the *kgotla* system as an altogether more repressive, more authoritarian institution than we and others allow. Good (1992:70; cf. Parson 1984:6f), for instance, says that "the *kgotla* essentially operated to facilitate social control by the leadership," the implication being that it had less to do with the politics of public deliberation than with the sheer exercise of power by ruling cadres (cf. van Binsbergen 1995). This might have been true, some of the time, of some of the stronger, more centralized chiefly regimes—such as that of the Ngwato, the largest of all "tribal" polities in Botswana and the one usually treated as paradigmatic. But, as a general statement about the Tswana public sphere, the claim does not bear scrutiny. The documentary record shows that the *kgotla* was always a site of active political contestation in which, far from merely being exercised, sovereign authority had to be negotiated. And could be forfeited as well as fortified, withdrawn as well as won.

The other point is that, in the passage from the past to the postcolonial, the *kgotla* has remained a crucial element in the political *imaginaire* of Botswana. This is in spite of its roots in the "village." Or its "traditionalist" connotations. Since independence, in fact, public forums, called "freedom squares," have been created all over the country, including in urban contexts. The resonance with an older vernacular public sphere could not be more obvious. Furthermore, as we shall see in a moment, national politicians have found themselves drawn back to the *kgotla* even in the course, and cause, of distinctly nonparochial political processes. In short, what we speak of here is far from a quaint anachronism, a romantic remnant of days gone by. It describes a cultural context, and a set of discursive practices, that are very much of the continuing present.

## V.

Let us return, then, to postcolonial politics and discourses of democracy.

In 1965, some months before Botswana became independent, national elections were held for the first time. Here, as in many other parts of Africa, decolonization—in the formal, political sense of that term—was fairly rapid. Three years earlier, the Botswana Democratic Party (BDP) had been established under the leadership of Seretse Khama and "other bourgeois nationalists" (Good 1992:72) drawn largely from a cattle-owning elite with strong connections to the countryside. From the start, the BDP promised to relegate chiefship and "tribalism" to the peripheries of postcolonial governance. It pledged itself to the evolution of a secular liberal nation-state, European in style; to the growth of a secure capitalist economy based on a mix of agrarian and industrial development, conventionally conceived; to a politics of moderation, the rule of law, and broad principles of social justice.

From the start, too, as Picard (1987) notes, the BDP groomed itself to be a "government party." Enjoying strong support from the colonial administration, it acquired "a monopoly of the resources and apparatus of the state" (Good 1992:72). Other parties were formed as well, some of them earlier. But they never approached the levels of organization, the material and cultural capital, or the broad-based following of the BDP. The latter was helped by the fact that its members of parliament and district councillors "frequently [had] close kin ties with the traditional aristocracy" (Colclough and McCarthy 1980:41). Although the party set out to marginalize chiefs, and to distance post-independence Botswana from its indigenous political cultures, there is no question that Seretse's own popular status at the grassroots was due, in part, to his royal rank—which had been dramatically underscored by imperial intervention. Heir to the Ngwato chiefship, he had famously been forced, by Her Majesty's Government, to renounce his rights to office as a condition of return from an involuntary exile occasioned by his marriage to a white woman.

That first election, as we said above, yielded an overwhelming victory for the BDP. What was most notable about it, though, was the very high turnout: 74 percent of all those registered. This was in spite of the fact that, in some parts of the country, voter education had been severely limited. Moreover, because distances to polling places were often large and transport was not always available, it was physically difficult for many actually to cast a ballot. Nor was the organization of the election entirely problem-free. All of this made the high rate of participation altogether remarkable—and interesting, too, in light of accusations, voiced in the media and by foreign observers in the 1980s, that a disturbing proportion of the populace of Botswana evinced indifference to, or ignorance of, the democratic process. It is even more striking in light of what was to happen later.

What, then, did happen later?

Several things, of which four stand out. The *first* was a radical drop in voter turnout in subsequent elections, down, for example, to 31 percent in 1974. There is one conspicuous exception, however: 1984, the national ballot after Seretse Khama's death, when his successor, Quett Masire, had to go to the country as its new president-in-waiting. And go to the country he did. Literally. He went from *kgotla* to *kgotla* in an effort to persuade people to vote, to prove his willingness to listen to their demands, and to assure them that he would govern them well (Shepherd 1984:28.) An explanation for these patterns of voter turnout? According to Holm (1987:124), "a segment of the public" thought that, "as has always been the case with a chief, there is no need to reelect the President. Thus they do not go to the polls until a new President is chosen." He is correct to draw the parallel, although we would take it further. As incumbents of apical offices, chiefs and presidents were subject to similar ideologies of governance (cf. Charlton 1993:331): both were expected to demonstrate their acumen and accomplishments in office; neither could assume their legitimacy; each was held to account for his actions, for the wisdom of his advisors, for the performance of his regime; and each had to subject himself to evaluation—all of which Masire appears to have appreciated. But, as long as they ruled "with the people," and delivered the fruits of good government, there was no particular need to vote for or against them; under which conditions, ironically, as Colclough and McCarthy (1980:44) conclude, "declining turnout [may] be taken as a mark of approval." Indeed, Holm (*op. cit.*) implies, it is only when a new incumbent has to be designated, for reasons of death or deposition, that there is a felt need for an expression of *mass* public opinion. Then, too, the process runs in close parallel. In each instance, a candidate is identified by a ruling cadre (the majority party in the case of the president, powerful royal factions in the chiefdoms), and is presented to the polity for its consideration. Hence the high turnouts in 1965 and 1984. And the indifference on most other occasions.[25] In such circumstances, procedural democracy—defined (i) by elections whose primary justification is the abstract passage of time, (ii) by an ethos of choice and change, and (iii) by mass public participation—seems a somewhat curious creature. Of which more in a moment.

In this respect, *second,* another statistic is noteworthy. In the 1970s and 1980s, it was said that only a small proportion of the populace "knew" their parliamentary representatives, except where they were major public figures. Struck by this at the time, we did a preliminary survey, asking the question of 105 people in five southern villages. Around 55 percent said that they had no idea of the person concerned. Another 30 percent could give a name, but nothing else. Just under 15 percent answered in the affirmative. Yet more remarkable was the fact that over a quarter offered, unsolicited, that it made little real difference: that BDP members of parliament were the advisors and councillors of the president and that he was responsible both for appointing them and for their actions. Echoes, again, of a model of governance whose genealogy stretches deep into *setswana,* "Tswana ways." In point of fact, politicians have become less anonymous in recent years. Still, one part of the idea, that a leader is responsible for the personnel of his/her regime, remains firmly intact.

*Third,* notwithstanding low voter turnout and the relative anonymity of political representatives, election meetings held by the BDP tended to draw crowds in the countryside. Among the opposition parties, in contrast, only those visited by important personages—an ex-chief back home, a charismatic figure with a big following, and the like—were well attended. We sat at many with only the candidate and a few of his friends. At BDP meetings, too, local people expected the president or a "close advisor" (i.e., a cabinet minister) to present themselves. Constituency politicians, those parliamentarians whom they "did not know," were not good enough. After all, and this is the point, these meetings were knowingly modeled on the *kgotla,* that space of intersection between civil society and the state, between the public sphere and the politics of incumbency. Their object was not just to discuss matters of social concern, to play at popular, consultative democracy. It was also to evaluate the performance of the president and his party. And to hold him accountable for the extent to which the BDP had met the demands of good government. In this light, it seems injudicious to conclude, as van Binsbergen (1995:25–28) does, that the appeal to the "*kgotla* system," dubbed a "neotraditional facade," is merely a cynical effort by an authoritarian "state elite" to subjugate, appropriate, and manipulate local institutions. This was *not* the spirit in which Masire went to the country in 1984, nor the tenor of the BDP meetings that we attended over the years. Perhaps, though, it is the trend of the present and future. But that is another story.

In both their poetics and their politics, BDP election meetings evoked earlier discourses of chiefly authority. Speakers tended to line up into blocs of pro- and antagonists—the former being local party members, the latter, a coalition of dissent—surrounded by an unaligned public. Most of them spelled out the requirements of good government, typically in formulaic terms and in the authorial name of the transcendent "we" of nationhood and/or *setswana.* And then they offered their appraisals, often in starkly frank, pragmatic prose, always in the first person singular. In so doing, depending on their political positioning, they either proclaimed a convergence or a divergence between ideal and reality. Supporters, in particular, told a teleological tale of improvement. They spoke of the very successful "*material* performance of the post-independence state" (van Binsbergen 1995:27); also, usually, of the disbursement of resources "to all parts of the country equally" and the absence of clientelism (Charlton 1993:341). Others disputed just these things. The specifics of their counter-arguments were contingent on place and circumstance, but they were frequently couched in accusations that government had "forgotten them." (A popular pun in the south played on the name of the capital, Gaborone, named for the local chiefly dynasty; BDP critics called it *ga re bone,* "it does not see us.") On both sides of the debate, however, there was the tacit assumption, utopian perhaps, that the BDP could only expect to enjoy legitimacy and the cooperation of the populace to the degree that it established the quality of its governance.

This is not to say that the electoral process mimicked the workings of the *kgotla,* past or present. The politics of the nation-state were *not* those of the chiefship writ large, nor are they today. Nonetheless, they did converge in two things. One was a deep aversion to autocracy at all levels of governance; hence Khama's insistence that to "fetter criticism" is "against ... Setswana tradition." The other was the unspoken conviction, widely distributed across the various publics of Botswana, that substantive democracy depended on the simultaneity of (i) discourses of policy, seen here, as we said, to be the product of deliberative processes, not of partisan interest; and (ii) discourses of accountability, in which the proportionate relationship between performance and power was negotiated. The outcome of that negotiation, expressed in a quantum of sovereign authority, might have been heavily influenced by offstage dealings, by the capillary workings of the state, and by the social capital mobilized by ruling elites. And it might have been perverted by the covert forms of authoritarianism of which van Binsbergen speaks. But, for now, what is significant is this: underlying all public spheres was a civic culture that specified the means of producing a certain kind of participatory politics, a politics grounded in an articulate, popular ideology of good government.

In this civic culture, it will be clear, elections were important to the degree that they opened up a space, periodically at least, for *substantive* democracy. On the other hand, voting—*procedural* democracy—was much less salient, save at moments of crisis. Which is why people in the countryside would attend protracted political meetings and then often not cast a ballot, or do so more to express their dis/approval for the governing party than to exercise choice. Thus, for example, in 1974, the Botswana National Front (BNF) candidate from Barolong, O.B. Marumolwa, voted for the BDP—*against* himself. After hearing the president and a cabinet minister speak at several meetings, and give account of their performance, he declared that they should remain in office. "You do not just remove a ruler," added Marumolwa, himself of royal descent.

This brings us, *fourth,* to the curious character of political parties here. Recall Colclough and McCarthy's (1980:41) comment that the BDP was "not a mass party" at all; that it barely existed between elections; that it was, more than anything else, an immanent reservoir of support centered on the president and his cabinet. Nor, for their part, have any of the minority parties been an enduringly significant presence in the public domain. Even at their most active, these parties have served less as coherent ideological alternatives to the BDP than as a critical opposition, pure and simple. Some of them have been odd ideological hybrids. The BNF, for one, grafted a "traditionalist" wing, headed by a former chief, onto a "radical" one, led by a left-wing Euro-intellectual. Custom and communism partying together is hardly what Weber had in mind in his classic typification of this species of voluntary association. In fact, both the BDP and BNF seem to have behaved more like the factional blocs we encountered in *kgotla*. This impression is reinforced by their conduct in the national assembly (Colcough and McCarthy 1980:46):

> [T]he daily business of the National Assembly is conducted in a manner closer to the best of the African one-party states than to the Westminster model. The alignment is not so much the government benches against the opposition as Ministers against the backbenchers. Sometimes, indeed, opposition members are seen to support the Government when its own backbenchers are critical. Thus the role of the National Assembly, like that of the traditional Kgotla, is to audit proposals made by those in authority: to approve them and occasionally reject them. The Ministers respect this function of the assembly.

Talk here, once more, of a one-party state, and its juxtaposition to the workings of the *kgotla,* brings us full circle to the problem with which we began, and to the *denouement* of our argument.

## VI.

Put together these various points and it will be clear what the call in the 1970s for a one-party state was all about. It was an argument, in effect, against *procedural* democracy. Against democracy as the mere exercise of electoral options. Against the idea that freedom may be equated with choice. Against democracy, to return to Gertla Riviero, as a small idea, the kind of European export that promises the world and delivers Kentucky Fried Chicken. Given their own conception of participatory politics, their own ideologies of sovereign authority, legitimacy, and accountability, it is obvious why so many citizens of Botswana were alienated by the Western model, at least as presented to them. And why, by threatening to confine mass public involvement to a fleeting season every five years, it opened up a chasm between the state and civil society. For some, the very fact that the BDP leadership was so keen to sustain a Euro-styled multiparty system was itself an indictment.

More positively, the agitation for one-party government—toward which, interestingly, the national assembly was then moving in its own routine procedures—was a demand for a (re)turn to *substantive* democracy, to a civic culture in which participatory politics would be the stuff of everyday life. And in which the ruling regime was authorized to act for the nation in proportion to its warranted performance in office. Put another way, it called for a vernacular, indigenously rooted version of the kind of liberal democracy that Euromodernity has long idealized but scarcely realized—let alone implanted successfully elsewhere, especially when other interests have intervened. In hindsight, the gesture might appear to have been utopian, quixotic even. It also dated to a particular moment in the early history of this postcolony. But it gave voice to a deeply felt critique of taken-for-granted European political practices and institutions.

That critique spoke of a specifically African alternative, one that demanded not less popular sovereignty but more, not less accountability but more, not just choice but a public culture of criticism. All of which, of course, the global north has been moving steadily *away* from in recent times; prescient here is Julius Nyerere's piquant comment, made already in the 1960s, to the effect that the United States has "only *one* political party, but ... [has] created *two* versions of [it]."[26] Euro-American heads of state tend these days to act with ever greater impunity, to claim ever wider executive authority, and to promise as little government as possible. Concomitantly, large numbers of their citizens appear willing to forgo freedoms, sovereignty, and the rule of law in the name of security and material well-being; *vide* the Patriot Act in the USA and the introduction of detention without trial in the UK, both post-9/11 measures that recalled the days of high apartheid in South Africa. Except in moments of rupture, moreover, levels of political involvement in the north seem steadily to wane, amidst accusations of epidemic apathy. In some European countries—Spain, Portugal, and Sweden being notable cases—an even smaller proportion of voters are currently able to name electoral candidates than was the case in Botswana in the first years of its independence (Norris 2004:230–48).[27] As citizens of that nation-state sought ways to move from procedural toward substantive politics, so the West seems intent to move in the opposite direction. In September 2009, a public intellectual and journalist in the USA, well known for his centrist political views, could quite plausibly title a widely syndicated essay on contemporary America, "One-Party Democracy."[28] Echoes of Nyerere, several decades on.

The process that we have described here, we reiterate, was firmly located in the social realities of Botswana at the time: in its comparative ethnic homogeneity, its small size, and its proximity to a particular historical past, all of which made the dream of a demos founded on popular sovereignty and direct state accountability appear eminently viable. These realities do not obtain everywhere. To the contrary: Botswana was, and is, relatively unique. And yet the vernacular political forms found there bear strong similarities to others in Africa (cf. Chabal 1986), some of them clearly visible, some submerged, some violently suppressed. This raises a familiar conundrum, if in unfamiliar terms: Why is it that, for the most part, democracy, however it may be defined, is so fragile across the continent? What is it that intervenes between the conditions of its possibility, which are patently present, and its practical realization? How is it that the possible is rendered, if not quite impossible, then so difficult to accomplish? Why, where democracy may be said to prevail in the nation-states of the global south, *does* it seem more procedural than substantive, more "thin" than "thick"? Could it be that Euro-America's contemporary move in the same direction, toward a thinned out version of representative government, provides a clue? That Africa has merely seen the emptying out of the large idea, its reduction to a small one, *before* the global north? That, in this regard, too, the latter is evolving toward the former? And for the same reason, namely, that politics itself is escaping the formal public sphere and the institutions of state more and more as it migrates elsewhere. Could the de-democratization of north and south simply be a devolutionary counterpoint coming to us *everywhere* as part of the neoliberal age—an age in which, Archbishop Ndungane of Cape Town recently argued,[29] citizens everywhere are valued purely as "voter fodder," in which "good government, transparency, accountability, integrity and honesty" are known largely by their absence? If so, does it not demand that we address this counterpoint in taking on the Big Question of Theory, ca. 2010: Wherein lies the future of politics and the public sphere, *sui generis,* as the new century unfolds? Is it, as we have begun to suggest in previous chapters, in new social and religious movements and other forms of mass action, in politics of life, their strident mobilization of "the street," their ever more assertive resort to lawfare, their deployment of the Internet, and all the other means of experimental insurgency that have emerged so powerfully in the south and appear to be migrating northward?

CHAPTER 6

# History On Trial

*Memory, Evidence, and the Forensic Production of the Past*

## AN UNTIMELY FRAGMENT

In South Africa, the end of apartheid brought with it any number of creative, often unorthodox, ways of engaging the past.1 Among the most majestic was the Truth and Reconciliation Commission, a passion play in which "We, the People" sought rebirth by together confronting painful memories, long repressed. Similar attempts to find renewal in the ritual revisitation of trauma are widespread in the political culture of our age. They express, simultaneously, homage to what has gone before and a desire to transcend it, a paradox evident in most epochal transitions, to be sure. But, these days, there is also something else at work: a detectable loss of faith in a telos of open-ended possibility (see Chapter 1). In this mood we seem especially anxious to repossess history—less, as some suggest, in a spirit of nostalgia than as a means of kick-starting the future, of vesting time itself with lost direction and purpose (cf. Hartog 2003).2

Take an example we have discussed before, a popular South African TV series from the immediate post-apartheid years, titled *Saints, Sinners and Settlers*. A mix of fact and fantasy, the series set out to reevaluate history through a sequence of criminal trials in which heroes and anti-heroes alike were called to give account of their actions—and were then held to judgment. The first episode was striking for its neoliberal *denouement*. It had two of the bitterest 19th-century colonial antagonists, the Zulu ruler Dingane and the white Voortrekker leader Piet Retief, meeting again in court; Retief is commonly believed to have been killed on Dingane's orders in an incident that, even now, divides white from black historical conscious-ness. In the final scene, the two men come to life again and are pictured standing together on the sublime coastline of KwaZulu-Natal. Retief makes a proposal to Dingane: that they bury the historical hatchet and go into partnership to develop a tourist resort on this very shore. Here, to be sure, is Truth and Reconciliation as farce. While promising to deliver a verdict on history, *Saints, Sinners and Settlers* is concerned, above all, to allow each protagonist his day in court. Each is asked to give his version of disputed events, to make a clean breast of his deeds. But the object of the exercise was less to resolve the conflict or amplify the record than to redeem a stake in the past—a past that, cleansed of strife, may profitably be recycled as heritage in the present.

Ours, it is often said, is a world in which life imitates TV. Sure enough, almost a decade after the series was first broadcast, the launch was announced of AmaZulu World, a 44 billion rand (c.$6.5b) historical theme park and mixed-use development on that same stretch of coast; this at the behest of the Zulu King Goodwill Zwelithini, official guardian of his people's patri-mony, with the backing of a group of corporate investors, both national and global. A giant statue of the Zulu warrior, King Shaka, was to be its signature feature, serving as a colossal brandmark of the enterprise. Swords might have become ploughshares, or corporate shares, for those in a position to flog the past-as-possession. But what of the losers? What of the 10,000 families of the Macambini community, for instance, whose eviction from what they hold to be *their* ancestral land was a precondition for work to begin on "Africa's first world-class internally branded entertainment … park"?[3] The legitimacy of their claims to a past has been overridden by claims of another kind: claims to the past as the stuff of profit, to what Palmié (n.d.:9), writing about the historiography of slavery, terms memory as "corporate property." For the dis-placed, alas, it is the same old history all over again, uncannily reminiscent of the apartheid era, when the ruling regime would forcibly remove people like them from their homes in the name of culture and tradition. And, more often than not, redistribute it to whites.

What sense are we to make, here, of the simultaneous celebration and silencing of the past? What are the costs of deregulating history, of transform-ing it into capital, in a context in which citizenship congeals ever more into identity-as-possession, where community building is becoming ever more synonymous with the market? And why is it that the courtroom has become the crucible in which particular memories become the stuff of recognition, entitlement, and claims on the future?

## The Right Time to Remember

Forgetfulness, Nietzsche (1957:6–8) insisted, is a necessary condition of all action. "We must know the right time to forget as well as the right time to remember," he wrote in *The Use and Abuse of History*, if historical awareness is not to be "the grave-digger of the present." Notoriously averse to history as the "science of progress," he insisted that the "unhistorical" was crucial to the health of individuals, communities, and "systems of culture." For him, viable agency depended on the "plastic power" of people and nations, a power to dissolve the "past and the strange" into the present and familiar, to heal wounds by forgetting "what [one cannot] subdue."

Nietzsche's defense of strategic amnesia is hardly unique. Many have followed Renan's (1882) original insight that the narratives that undergird the modern nation-state demand forgetting, thus to separate what Reinhart Koselleck (2002; cf. Anderson 1991) calls "collective expectations of the future" from particular, selective "experiences of the past"; to force a rupture, that is, between history and memory (Rubin n.d.). Yet, in a climate in which expectations of the infinite possibilities of that future have been thoroughly shaken, we seem to be imbued with an obligation to remember, to ground aspiration in modes of legitimation that reach backward, rather than forward in time. Techniques of recollection both organized and diffuse, public and private, proliferate on all sides. Today, *contra* Nietzsche, healing requires recovering the repressed, disinterring symptoms of injury, recounting the pain of old atrocities. Social reconstruction, be it of war-torn nations, defiled democracies, or brutalized subjects, is deeply vested in rituals of recollection, testimonies of suffering, public confessions of abuse—willful or otherwise. What is more, recollection is not simply a means of laying the past to rest. Popular *aides memoire*—archives, museums, monuments, murals, installations, statuary, even, as we have seen, theme parks—are designed to heed the command that "thou shalt not forget to remember" (Harries 2010:125–26). They urge us to dwell in what Lambek (1996; cf. Palmié n.d.:10) dubs a "past imperfect." Yet, while the explicit rationale of the lucrative memory industry is "Never Again," it serves also to anchor identity in heritage. And heritage, in turn, is closely tied to claims to recognition through genealogies of victimhood. Hence the rapidly growing number of holocaust and atrocity memorials that have been established across the world.

There is a paradox here, however. Amidst all the clamor of memory work, ours is also an era in which many have declared history to be dead, at least, history in its modernist sense, as national narrative and/or as scholarly discipline. Could it be that, notwithstanding all this memorialization, we are also becoming profoundly "unhistorical," if not perhaps quite in the positive sense that Nietzsche intended?

This paradox of presence and absence—of the abundance, even fetishism, of memory in precisely the contexts where history seems most threatened—is especially visible in those societies that have undergone transition from illiberal pasts. Take, for instance, a recent *Economist* report on the "end of history" in contemporary Eastern Europe.[4] The past two decades of post-Soviet nation-building, it says, have been a phase of "therapeutic historiography" in which communist propaganda has been replaced by various alternatives. But the exhilaration of the early years, in which old taboos were reassessed, has given way to complexity and diversity. History is being overtaken, as Fukuyama (1992) might have predicted, by the triumph of liberalism. "Power is up for grabs," the piece concludes. And, in any case, remaking Europe in the present is "more fun" than is quibbling about the past. The flood of indignant replies elicited by this report, most of them packed with thoroughly historical counter-evidence, belies the veracity of its claim.[5] But similar observations have been made about the loss of history in southern Africa, where an infatuation with memory goes along with the desire, most notably among the "born free" generation, to seize the present and be rid of the burden of the past.

Collective efforts to transcend that past, however, do not amount to the end of history. Neither did the putative triumph of free-market democracy. History no more disappears with forgetting than does an ostrich with its head in the sand; unless, of course, it is taken to be nothing more than historical consciousness, oblivious to its own social, cultural, and material embedding in the world. All the same, we would argue—at least for the likes of South Africa—that the present *is* being rendered "unhistorical" in significant respects. But this is less by way of forgetting than by dint of an *excess* of memory of a particular kind: the kind that makes it hard to recover any chronicle of a *shared* past. Or to arrive at a critical understanding of how its legacy ought to be read in the fractured outlines of the unfolding present.

For Nietzsche (1957:23), what impeded a critical understanding of this kind was the pathological modernist view of history as a rational science, a spectacle of universal becoming that smothers all personal being. Nowadays, the threat is of the opposite kind: a celebration of the past as privatized, subjective, democratized, as a species of recollection that lays partisan claim to events, genealogies, geographies, identities. As this implies, memory—despite the tendency to treat it as a direct, unmediated mode of knowing—is always a contextually shaped representation, always imbricated in the play of signs and power that underpins conventionalized efforts to produce value. In this, it is no different from history. At the same time, it has become a privileged medium for recuperating facts about the past, in particular about pasts honed by suffering and abuse. Memory emerges as if from a bedrock of universal humanity, speaking truth both to discredited modernist-nationalist chronicles and to cynical hegemonies. Purged by pain, it is apprehended as an act of witnessing—of giving testimony at the court of public assessment—in a process of history-making that is often framed, figuratively and ever more pragmatically, in the medium of legal adjudication.

Whether or not history as we know it is dying, it appears increasingly to be caught up in a "juridification of the past"; the process, that is, in which the rights and wrongs of historical acts and facts, and the claims arising out of them, are subjected to determination either by legal procedures or by their simulacra (J.L. Comaroff 2009). In Spain, for instance, "the return of memory" to the public sphere—held by social activists to be the *sine qua non* of "real" democracy—has been underwritten by a Law of Historical Memory (2007), an act authorizing the recognition of the experience of victims of violence on both sides of the Spanish Civil War.[6] The juridification of the past also reflects the growing global salience of mechanisms of restorative justice in contexts of political transition; hence the more than thirty national truth commissions established across the world over the past three decades (cf. Posel and Simpson 2002).

Quasi-judicial investigations into political violence are hardly new: the Carnegie Endowment for International Peace inquired into crimes against civilians during the 1912–13 Balkan Wars. But, as Grandin and Klubock (2007:1) point out, more recent truth commissions have their origins primarily in Latin America's so-called transition to democracy. Their political salience, they insist, is not so much to lay the foundations for constitutional rule as to "index the shift from the global crisis of the 1970s ... to the post–Cold War would-be *pax* neoliberal." Not vested with legal authority to indict and prosecute, at least for the most part, these commissions have nonetheless operated within the framework of national or international human rights law, making case-by-case decisions as would a panel of voting judges (p.2). But they have been less concerned to confront the violence and inequities of the past than to deploy the law, after Durkheim, as a means of realizing social solidarity through consensus, tolerance, and forgiveness. This in-built limitation has meant that mechanisms of transitional justice have quickly exhausted their capacity to consolidate the institutions of liberal jurisprudence in the regimes they have fostered. Indeed, for Grandin and Klubock (2007:1,3), their utility seems to have passed with the transitional moment itself. They were, in every sense, at cross-purposes with history, calling upon the past more to extract a national mythos than to probe the production of the present in all its complexity.

The point is well-taken. But the continuing appeal and zealous reworking of these mechanisms of transitional justice in diverse political contexts suggests that "transition," rather like crisis, is an imprecise analytical category, one not easily equated with a specifiable historical epoch—as, for example, "the transition" to neoliberalism. To be sure, truth and reconciliation commissions are implicated in the ongoing, late liberal present in complicated ways; they do much more than merely chart the passage from the *ancien régime.* In many contexts—like South Africa, Canada, and Colombia—they have been explicitly hailed as forums for rewriting national history, thus to replace authoritarian, partial accounts of times past with the fullness of collective recollection. In Colombia, the National Committee of Reparation and Reconciliation has a separate Historical Memory division charged with producing an authoritative, inclusive chronicle of the origins and evolution of the country's internal armed conflict. Guided by professional social scientists, its personnel traverse the land in their effort to assemble, firsthand, the searing testimonies of its ravaged citizens.[7]

Neither are these quasi-legal procedures the only, nor even the most explicit, means of juridifying memory. As we note in Chapters 1, 3, and 5, there is an ever more avid turn to lawfare by individuals and groups across the world, especially in the form of class action suits. Thus, in 2001, Kenyans injured by British Army munitions left behind after independence lodged a complaint that resulted in the award of significant damages; the London law firm that acted in the case went on to prepare another against the British government, this time on behalf of Mau Mau veterans tortured in detention camps in the 1950s.[8] We return, in a moment, to another, a South African instance of this species of litigation. Clearly, there is a significant move afoot to redefine colonialism itself as a culpable offense—thereby to reduce history to the language of torts, of plaintiffs and perpetrators, injuries and liabilities.

But what are the consequences of the coupling of law and history? Wherein lie the implications of arriving at authoritative accounts of the past by way of legal processes in which time and event, memory and evidence, agency and motivation are defined in juridical terms? What becomes of historiography when it is hitched directly to restorative justice, to forensic means of producing truth, to establishing guilt and amnesty, to repairing injury and restoring democracy?

## History Learned, History Lived

The tendency toward forensic history-making in South Africa needs to be viewed against the background of a crisis that has been facing the discipline of history in schools and universities over the past decade.[9] In 2001, then national Education Minister, Kader Asmal, launched the South African History Project, itself the fruit of an investigation into the so-called deterioration of history in the new nation, a decline with clear parallels elsewhere in the world.[10] During the immediate post-apartheid period, the subject, tainted as a tool of Afrikaner indoctrination, "virtually disappeared" from school curricula, having been subsumed in a bland *mélange* of "social studies."[11] In the upshot, debate about its relevance has taken on what has been described as "an increasingly desperate tone" (Cobley 2001:624). Terence Ranger has gone even further: "History is becoming today what Anthropology was in Africa in the 1950s," he observes, "the discipline that dare not speak its name."[12] The government might have given its imprimatur to public rituals of remembrance, but its critics accuse it of encouraging collective amnesia in the classroom.

In contrast to history-as-learned, history-as-lived thrives here in a vibrant array of popular genres and media. The transition to majority rule came amidst seismic shifts both in global geopolitics and in received modes of communication and representation. It also saw the deregulation of public cultural production. Released from the "totally heroic" stance that, for Njabulo Ndebele (1991:47), had typified history-making under apartheid, ordinary South Africans have avidly reclaimed access to the past, pressing it into the service of a host of identities and media, new and old, epic and banal. On the face of it, this seems a lively instance of Simon Schama's ideal of popular, "performative history,"[13] a genre that, while often scorned by Western scholars, has also had significant champions, from Herodotus to Benjamin. The genre has rich counterparts in the South African present: in assertively revived "traditional" rites of ancestral veneration, for instance, through which people of all stripes seek to connect with the dead in contexts of crisis or in important moments of passage (White 2004). Benjamin, says Schama, was acutely alive to the fact that those who seek to save history from the machinations of the powerful must capture memory where they can find it, not least in its fragmentary modern forms; "in the mesh of contemporary wiring," as it were. In like spirit, Schama insists that ours is not a time to "fetishize the meditative." We have to respond to history in its divers habitations, he urges, acknowledging its special gift for puncturing the pretension of theocracies. And for deflating claims to the effect that the present is an inevitable outcome of mythic determination.

Vernacular publics in contemporary South Africa certainly *do* evince a fascination with rediscovering the past wherever they might find it. Whether in print media, television drama, or radio talk shows, in Pentecostal churches or victim support groups, they express considerable faith in the healing power of confession. Pop singers disinter forgotten folk heroes. Publishers are inundated with personal memoirs. There is a delight in the emergence of truths long repressed, of a *vox populi* that wells up to fill the space left by discredited master narratives. Museums and archives are reconfigured to retrieve a suppressed multicultural record. Take the edgy, justly acclaimed District Six Museum in downtown Cape Town, in many ways an exemplary instance of reclamation and *re*-cognition through collective recall (Rassool and Prosalendis 2001). Documenting the triumphal return of a mixed-race population forcibly removed from the District in the late 1960s, it is quite literally a House of Memory, composed of an assemblage of aural recollections, personal documents, and prized objects. Its artifacts are arranged so as to speak eloquently of emblematic biographies, some of them placed in poignant reliquaries, or "memory boxes." In this, the museum enacts a new kind of pointillist history, a quotidian mosaic, a soundscape of multiple voicings. Its curators have been cogent critics of the crass commercialization of heritage against which its own, communally engaged project is positioned.

Walking through its affecting displays, however, one cannot help being overwhelmed by the chorus of testimony, the babel of passionate, partisan reminiscences that echo through the museum. But the very effectiveness of this clamor raises a more general question about the efflorescence of memory in the here and now. Amidst all the talking, who exactly is listening? And to what? The question runs far beyond District Six or South Africa. Academic historiography evinces a similar pluralization of voices, to the extent that many historians express a wariness of the very idea of the authoritative account in favor of an interest in "the production of history" itself (Cohen 1994), or the study of "micro" and "vernacular" histories, each valid in its time and place. This move toward production and pluralization has enriched the ethnohistorical record; it also illuminates the subtle mechanisms through which politics inflects the idiomatic rendering of past. But it is less concerned with the need to comprehend the larger, more or less systemic forces, forces at once material and semantic, that structure the world in which those diffused, vernacular histories themselves unfold.

In postcolonial, post-totalitarian contexts like South Africa, there is an understandable wariness, both popular and scholarly, of heroic national narratives; we have noted the tendency to remark, if not the death of history *tout court,* then the apparently infinite postponement of a new South African story.[14] The vernacularization of academic history, as we have already intimated, must be understood in this light. But it also risks reinforcing the diffusionary effects of political and economic liberalization on cultural production in general, which is writ large in the privatization of memory and the particularization of the past. These things cannot substitute for a shared responsibility to "recollect" in more holistic terms, to figure how the polyphonous histories of the present—not least the flight into memory itself—fit into larger structures of transformation: into trajectories that may not be adequately captured by older modernist narratives, but nonetheless demand that, as scholars of the south, we make sense of them. We are still challenged to connect the dots, to contemplate the logic that might link disparate events on the postcolonial South African scene, among them, the discordant incidents cited at the start of this chapter: the advent of AmaZulu World, symptom of a triumphal reclamation of the legacy of the past, and the threatened removal of the Macambini community, itself a condition of the former's possibility. By what larger mechanism did one party's redemption of the past become the other's undoing? Nor is this a unique occurrence. Forced removals of apartheid proportions have become a distressingly frequent downside of the new prosperity of this and other African postcolonies. What silences and erasures, exemplified by the fate of the Macambini and communities like them, lie barely detectable behind ebullient assertions of identity, epitomized by AmaZulu World? Having been privatized, having dissolved into a multitude of genealogies, having become the object of ongoing struggles for voice, is history disappearing into cacophony? Does democracy in its neoliberal form, by encouraging a strident politics of recognition based on parochial claims to the past, spell the end of *all* modernist history (cf. Joyce 1995)?

It is in light of these questions that we address and assess the growing importance of juridical history-making, of history produced, articulated, and authorized through the courts. In what follows we consider two instances of history-on-trial that have had a significant impact on public debate and political processes in South Africa. Both raise issues about state-making, citizenship, and the role of genealogies of injury in determining recognition and entitlement. The first is the already-noted, state-mandated Truth and Reconciliation Commission (TRC); the second, a class action being pursued in the Second Circuit Court in Manhattan by a self-declared group of "victims of apartheid" under the Alien Tort Claims Act. Both have attained the status of historical allegories, dramas that enact the metamorphosis of polity and people in the postcolonial moment. Both are based on evidence culled from personal experience of traumas past, evidence held not to be fully acknowledged in existing histories of colonial exploitation, racial discrimination, and violent suppression. Both are founded on a resolute faith in the moral and performative force of the law to compel transformation, to produce incontestable evidence, to set right from wrong—and, along the way, to offer a more authoritative, inclusive account of bygone times. And both have garnered international attention as precedent-setting, notwithstanding debate about the adequacy of reducing matters of such historical complexity to the terms of liberal jurisprudence. Critics have pointed to the restricted conventions of truth, testimony, and proof entailed in these procedures, to the narrow conceptualization of motive and intent they presume, and to their limited definitions of consequence and restitution (Mamdani 2000; Ross 2003:8f, 162–65; but cf. Fullard and Rousseau 2008, who disagree). It has also been claimed that, by failing to consider the broader socio-economic ramifications of apartheid as a *system* of domination, the TRC in particular has impeded debate about sustainable means of redressing its structural effects. Why, then, the enduring enthusiasm for legal mechanisms in acting upon, and reclaiming, history? How might their appeal be connected with the tendency to privatize the past? And what might all this have to do with the fetishism of memory as raw truth, as a distinctive possession, as the *sine qua non* of political subjectivity and identity?

Before we turn to the two cases, and return to the various questions we have posed thus far, a brief diversion is in order.

## HISTORY AS HERITAGE

While the processes at issue here are hardly limited to South Africa, Africa, or even the postcolonial world, it is in the latter that their lineaments appear most clearly to be drawn. Because liberation from apartheid in South Africa came together with global neoliberalization, its new leaders found themselves struggling to reconcile democracy long postponed with the spirit of *laissez-faire.* Hence the battle to establish sovereign governance under conditions that vest the wealth of nations in the transnational movement of labor and capital, goods and signs, thus to undermine local manufacture, local enterprise, local proletariats; hence the effort put into constructing a meaningful sense of national belonging; hence the energy exerted to forge moral and material "community" in circumstances that promote inequality, difference, and bitter controversies over identity-based claims on the past. Hence, also, the impossibility of accomplishing any of these things under prevailing conditions. All of which clearly have broad implications for the ways in which history is defined, construed, and deployed. For present purposes, however, we confine ourselves to just two of those conditions: the *changing basis of belonging* and the *legalization of politics.* We deal with them summarily here, since we have already encountered both in previous chapters. Again, we beg indulgence for a little repetition in the cause of narrative coherence and comprehensibility.

In Euromodern nation-states, at least in theory, belonging was a form of attachment vested in cultural homogeneity and civic equality, a form of universal citizenship held to transcend partisan ethnic identities. National historiography, many have argued, was instrumental in fostering these imagined communities, not least by dissolving parochial differences of culture and modes of memorialization into a single narrative of peoplehood. By contrast, most postcolonial polities have their origin in colonial states that were never unified nations, polities in which cultural diversity was cultivated as the basis of a politics of divide-and-rule and an economy founded on the racialization of labor. Of course, the conceit of the nation as imagined community was always, everywhere, more an aspiration than a reality, more a fiction than an accomplished fact. But it was harder still to make it plausible in postcolonial polities, where *Midnight's Children* (Rushdie 1981) inherited troublesome legacies of ethnic disparity and constitutional incoherence.

To those legacies have been added the cumulative effects of neoliberal deregulation that, especially since 1989, have not merely transformed the nature and geopolitics of national sovereignty, but have compounded the internal diversity of polities almost everywhere: the transnationalization of the division of labor; the migration of large populations of people in search of work and economic opportunity; the rise of an electronic commons and, concomitantly, the ever more rapid circulation of objects, images, information, and ideologies; the growing hegemony of the market and, with it, the spreading capillaries of capital in its myriad forms; and, most significant for present purposes, the burgeoning belief, sanctioned by a rising global legal order, that culture and history are intellectual property, assets to be possessed, patented, and protected as commodities. Freedom, in this market-driven world, amounts primarily to the right to choose: to choose, among other things, identities and allegiances—and also the modes of producing them.

Which is where the matter of citizenship—and, specifically, the changing bases of belonging—becomes salient. The implosion of identity politics since 1989, which has occurred in rough proportion to the erosion of the nation-state as a culturally homogeneous community, has expressed itself in a proliferation of claims to rights and resources made in the name of gender, generation, race, culture, religion, sexuality, and various displacements of class; also, in assemblages of these species of identification, some of which transcend national boundaries, mandating ever more strident demands within them against the common good. While most peoples of the south continue to live within nation-states, they do not necessarily or unambiguously recognize themselves as national citizens. Not only is the governmental reach of states uneven in many places, the landscape being a palimpsest of contested sovereignties and jurisdictions (Comaroff and Comaroff 2006b:35), but critical functions of governance, from policing to the delivery of services, have been outsourced to the private sector. Meanwhile, the state, drawn into the role of attracting investment and facilitating business, tends increasingly to treat its subjects as stakeholders in the polity-as-corporation, operating in an ever more competitive, deregulated global marketplace. In such circumstances, the calls of citizenship are compromised by the claims of other attachments and identities, or identities of otherness, both above and below the level of the nation-state.

Of those claims, ethnicity is often taken to be the most elemental. This is because it is grounded, existentially, in biogenetic kinship, in a common past, in shared cultural practices, and also in a voluntary act of attachment; in the essential components, that is, of "life itself." Concomitantly, genealogy, its common mode of reckoning and representation, partakes of a doubling: it charts a collective history *and* records membership in the materialities of blood, bodies, bones, and soil. In the age of the market, in which people become "entrepreneurs of themselves" (see Chapter 1), this doubling, in turn, conduces to a process of reduction: first from history to heritage, then from heritage to culture and, finally, from culture to intellectual property. To the degree that we now live in the era of Ethnicity, Inc., of Heritage PLC (Comaroff and Comaroff 2009; see Chapters 1 and 3), an era in which history-as-culture is a commodity to be branded and marketed, ethnic groups tend to define themselves as corporations, whose past, like its vernacular knowledge and practices, is a distinctive, alienable species of capital. Which accounts for why it is that, in a time of multiplying allegiances, history and identity are defined primarily in terms of rights to possess, transact, consume; why politics, in so many places, threatens to dissolve into what Tom Vanderbilt (1997:140) calls "a host of special-interest groups clamoring in the trading pits of pluralist relativism." In these respects, as we have long attested, postcolonies are not different in kind from the modernist nation-states upon which they have little option but to model themselves. They are rather speeded up, hyper-extended transformations of those nation-states; anticipations, if you will, of the history of Euro-politics running slightly ahead of itself.

This brings us to the other aspect of the postcolonial present with which we are concerned here: shifts in the nature of politics itself and, in particular, its migration into the law—a process that runs closely parallel, and is patently related, to the juridification of history. As we have already noted, global conditions have had a marked impact on liberal-modernist political life, especially in the south. To many, politics appears to have been depoliticized (see Chapter 4). Or rather, to have been deflected into other domains: into the market, the media, and technology, into shadowy public-private "partnerships" and religious theocracies, into criminal para-states and again, above all, into the law. In the upshot, there has been a strong tendency for parliamentary processes to be reduced to struggles over special interests and issues; just the sort of thing that Vanderbilt (*ibid.*) had in mind. It is not that the institutional *forms* of liberal democracy—parties, elections, unions, legislatures, and the like—have disappeared. But their significance has shifted in proportion to other, more compelling sites and operations of power, wealth, knowledge. In Africa, for instance, where structural adjustment labored to make democracy synonymous with privatization, with the increasing salience of NGOs, and with "reduced" government, there has arisen, in dialectical counterpoint, a wide range of social movements, coalitions, and mobilizations committed to a vital "politics of life"—to which we shall return in Chapter 8.

The interpolation of politics into the law is not without precedent, of course. The modern liberal state itself was founded on a juridical scaffolding. In colonial polities, moreover, where basic rights were often denied to "natives," the very suspension of the law for political ends—and the segregation of subject from citizen—was accomplished by legal means. Apartheid, Mahmood Mamdani (2000:181) points out, fetishized the judicial; he interprets the excessive legalism of the TRC, and its resultant inability to distinguish law from justice, as a consequence of this legacy. But, to anticipate what is to come in a moment, the journeyman jurisprudence of the commission was not only a product of the past. Like state-making processes elsewhere, it was also caught up in the cultural habitus of the neoliberal present, which rests heavily on the argot of rights, injuries, contracts, and courts. This is especially so in those postcolonial and post-totalitarian societies that try to reinvent themselves as liberal democracies, *ex nihilo,* in the absence of robust civil institutions. Here a great deal of reliance is placed on the capacity of jural instruments actually to *produce* civic order and social justice. Recall the large number of new constitutions promulgated since 1989—well over a hundred (J.L. Comaroff 2009)—and the popular reverence reserved for them in countries like South Africa, where the language of legality has become almost a *lingua franca.*

The creeping judicialization of politics should be understood, then, in relation to recent shifts in the construction of nation-states and their modes of governance. Not only are their bureaucratic, administrative, fiscal, and security operations increasingly outsourced and/or executed via contractually complicated public-private partnerships. Ruling regimes are also faced with the growing demand to commit themselves to the rule of law, to recognize rights to difference that transect older political cartographies and constituencies, and to answer to their citizens in their own or in international courts and tribunals. Under these conditions, the language of legality offers an ostensibly—note, *ostensibly*—neutral register for communication across lines of social and cultural cleavage, making it possible to equate unlike values, to authorize hybrid collaborations, and to adjudicate impossibly contradictory claims. The pragmatic promise of jural instruments is that they have the capacity to create equivalence amidst contrast, providing a currency that appears to allow for the transaction of incommensurable interests across otherwise intransitive borders. Thus it is that law offers a common denominator, and a means of imposing coherence, in socially and ethically incoherent circumstances. Therein, in part, lies its hegemony—although, in itself, it is anything but a guarantor of equality.

Put (i) the judicialization of politics together with (ii) an assertive politics of difference, add to them (iii) a turn to genealogical claims to identity and (iv) the erosion of the nation as homogenous imagined community, and the rising importance of the courts in history-making seems unsurprising. In prospect, the law promises to authenticate the terms of citizenship and political personhood—and to adjudicate among claims to rights and recognition, responsibilities and liabilities, rooted in the past.

# History On Trial

That promise—the promise of the law to set wrongs to rights—underpinned the South African Truth and Reconciliation Commission. Its unique blend of the jural, the memorial, the ritual, and the therapeutic yielded a model of transitional justice that has since gained global currency as a technique of post-conflict appeasement, especially where violent, authoritarian regimes give way to ones that seek recognition as legitimate democracies (Wilson 2001; Ross 2003). Like other commissions of its kind, the TRC was not, *sensu stricto,* a court of law. But it went to considerable lengths, as Richard Wilson (2001:59) notes, to "mimic the law," opting for a "legal-positivist" rather than a "sociological-historical" *modus operandi.* And it did make history, patently, in more senses than one. But it is telling that, unlike some of its counterparts elsewhere, it did not call upon professional historians, relying more on lawyers and statisticians (Harries 2010:127).[15] For, as Wilson (*ibid.*) goes on to add, its procedures were designed above all to translate diverse testimonial practices into concrete, verifiable evidence; that is, into data of a very particular sort (Ross 2003:79).

We have noted that the TRC has been censured for the limited scope of its investigative mandate. Colin Bundy (1999), for one, points to its calculated reduction of "the systematic discrimination and dehumanization" of a colonial order, centuries in the making, to a picture of "gross violations of human rights from 1960 to 1993." Others stress that its mandate precluded any consideration of the politico-economic architecture of apartheid, of its pervasive, terrifying violence, or of its collaboration with corporate capital, both local and global (Mamdani 2002; Ross 2003; Harries 2010). The commission focused explicitly on individual acts of torture, murder, and rape, on graphic evidence of bodily violation, and on the retrieval of the intentions of perpetrators, conceived in terms of narrowly defined "political objectives." For David Thelen (2002:182), the fact that its Amnesty Committee granted immunity only to those behaving out of loyalty to political or military organizations, be it those of the state or the liberation movements, arose from the belief that "the usual narratives of history—a struggle by institutions for power" could induce ordinary people to do otherwise unacceptable things. This, in turn, implies a faith that the truth-finding process might "disentangle" named persons from the institutions that had corrupted them, so that, in the words of the TRC report, they could "become human again," become members of a "normalized" society (Thelen 2002:185–86). The reclamation of their humanity, though, required "full disclosure of relevant facts" and, while there was no absence of debate about the nature of truth, method, or objectivity within the orbit of the commission (Posel and Simpson 2002:4), its deliberations presumed that those facts *could* be laid bare in all their completeness; this by way of the rigorous use of law-like procedures and the revelatory force of "memories of pain and suffering" (Ross 2003:79).

Positivist conventions of liberal jurisprudence are taken for granted here, conventions that presuppose the possibility of drawing clean distinctions between truth and deception, sincerity and cynicism, actual occurrences and acts of witnessing. Like other endeavors of the same sort, the TRC assumed a "mimetic relation" between memory and event (Das and Kleinman 2001:14; Ross 2003:77f). Even more, it attributed a unique revelatory power to recollection fueled by trauma, by memory so charged that, as veteran journalist Hugh Lewin put it, it needed neither interpretation nor explanation (Thelen 2002:163). Here, in prospect, was a means of separating the human subject from the ravages of history: out of the "unfolding open-endedness" of anguished recall, wrote Thelen (2002:164f), witnesses "struggled ... with the deepest recesses of their individuality and humanity," with the "fluid human wildness they had ... experienced." Regrettably, he concluded, the commission—like many scholars critical of its procedures—sought to "tame" this flow by imposing upon it a restrictive narrative structure (p.165). For Thelen, in short, the act of recollection, at its most passionate, spontaneous, and redemptive, is unlike other forms of communication: it eludes the logocentric effects of context and convention.

But memory everywhere is put into words according to particular genres of speech and self-presentation, genres parsed by received ideas of occasion and personal status, of gender, age, race, culture, whatever. Indeed, the evidence makes plain that the public enactment of recall to the TRC—what Buur (2001:163) has termed its "practices of everyday truth production"—was a complex, multiply mediated process, involving witness selection, briefing, coaching, and the shaping of testimony according to stylized protocols (Ross 2003:79).[16] What is more, the salience of cultural conventions was overtly invoked. In calling upon people to come forward and "tell their stories," for instance, the commission cast "story-telling" as a long-standing African tradition. In all this, the rationalization of memory, its reduction to a coherent narrative, was not merely inevitable. It was integral to the efforts of victims of apartheid to make their suffering the basis of claims for recognition: their recollections were rendered into texts that circulated beyond the contexts of their utterance as a species of political currency (cf. Silverstein 1998). They became more or less standardized objects that, like legal facts, could be judged, their truth-value consecrated, the culpability they disclosed made into a public good.

It is this currency, the coin of memory, that was supposed to fuel the process of reconciliation, animating the triangulation of truth, humanity, and forgiveness. Many observers have remarked that, in South Africa and beyond, the link between truth and reconciliation is taken to be self-evident:

"It is only on the basis of truth that true reconciliation can take place," wrote Desmond Tutu in the introduction to the TRC report.[17] His rhetoric of repetition here affirms that truth is a sublime force, waiting to be voiced in a language of confession that transcends history and its distortions. Public rites of recall are also understood as abreactions, in the psychoanalytic sense: as acts of collective catharsis that, by re-membering experience, purge it of its malignant excess (cf. Lévi-Strauss 1963). At work is an ideal of transcendent truth, a truth beyond human manipulation—itself a modernist conceit, to be sure. "Truth exists," Georges Braque (1971) once said. "Only falsehood has to be invented."

As all this suggests, the alchemy of reconciliation rests on the recuperation of the human subject as a remembering self, her humanity made authentic through suffering. Victims are prime vehicles of the truth, their degradation forcing a shared recognition of essential humanness, of the minimal conditions of species-being. Elsewhere in his introduction, Desmond Tutu makes reference to Ariel Dorfman's *Death and the Maiden*. In the drama, it is only when the rapist acknowledges the abuse, Tutu tells us, that his victim lets him go. "His admission restores her dignity and her identity. Her experience is confirmed as real and not illusory and her sense of self is affirmed."[18] As Hacking (1991:863) has observed, we are heirs to an Aristotelian tradition in which "personal identity is constituted by memory ... [a]nd any type of amnesia results in something being stolen from oneself." Yet the record makes plain that many survivors did *not* have their half-remembered, uncertain grasp of the past clarified, recorded, or legitimated by the TRC (Matshoba 2002:144). Their experience, it seems, did not conform to the conventions— the narrative biographies of agency, intent, and closure—that it developed (Dube 2002:127). Indeed, much has been made of the haphazard methods deployed by the commission for recovering truth, assessing testimony, and evaluating authenticity (Posel and Simpson 2002:vii; Simpson 2002).

It may well be that ambiguities of this sort are inherent in processes of truth and reconciliation, being an essential element of the poetics that give ritual everywhere the power to infuse social norms with ineffable fervor (Turner 1967). But it is precisely here that the authority of the law came into its own. Perhaps because its patchwork of procedures were so fraught with uncertainty, so inchoate and contingent, so lacking in clear forensic standards of practice that the TRC relied so heavily on the language of jural facticity to give it an imprimatur of disciplinary rigor, a means of arriving at grounded truth, and a yardstick by which to measure contrition amidst conflicting understandings and unsettling emotions. Despite its judicial trappings, as we have said, the legal status of the commission and of its findings were to prove questionable in the longer run. The standing of its evidence in subsequent court proceedings—against those denied amnesty, for example—has been contested (Wilson 2001:11; du Toit 1999). There has also been the vexed matter of how its findings should relate to reparations. The belated payment of a paltry sum to the 19,000 "victims of apartheid"[19] selected to give testimony—much less than the TRC itself recommended—led to complaints of a miscarriage of justice. Meanwhile, efforts to find alternative means to redress the enduring effects of structural violence and suffering, to make good on the "restitutionary equality" at the core of the new national constitution (Ackerman 2004:679), have faltered. Talk of more general compensation for the systemic ravages of apartheid has sparked a furor among many of its former beneficiaries. But then, as has often been noted, the TRC was from the start a product of political compromises, above all in respect of amnesty, deemed necessary to secure a relatively peaceful transition of power from the old regime to the new.

As an organ of state, the TRC sought to found a new democracy on the public acknowledgment of past abuse. It endorsed a view of history as the stuff of individual intention, action, and accountability, of justice as a calculus of human rights, of citizenship as vested in the recognition of injury, entitlement, and indemnity. It also validated a sense of a political subjectivity rooted in suppressed histories of suffering. This has expressed itself in other judicial forums as well, particularly those in which the civil law has been deployed in class actions to establish identity, exact reparations, and prove liability for past harms. In this, the South African story is one instance of the global movement for indigenous rights and the rights of victims, a movement that has been greatly abetted by the expanding reach of international tort law. More than ever before, corporations are being held responsible for past wrongdoing, as were the Swiss banks that, in 2000, were ordered by a New York judge to pay $1.25b to survivors of the holocaust.[20] That precedent was cited in the suit, mentioned in Chapter 1, filed in the US[21] on behalf of victims of apartheid against businesses that allegedly colluded with the old nationalist regime—a regime that knowingly perpetrated murder, torture, and forced labor—by breaching sanctions intended to bring it down.

Among the plaintiffs was Lulu Peterson, whose twelve-year-old brother, Hector, died in the 1976 Soweto uprising. The two were immortalized by one of the most famous photographs of the struggle years. A museum exists today in Hector Peterson's name near the place where he fell, mortally wounded by a police bullet. The siblings became iconic of anti-apartheid resistance in the "new" South Africa: "We want reparations from those international companies ... that profited from the blood and misery of our fathers and mothers, brothers and sisters," Lulu Peterson declared, echoing the rationale of the movement for reparations among descendants of slaves in the US.[22] Like the North American case, this one has proven controversial. The US State Department opposed it at first, asserting that it jeopardized the commercial interests of both countries; Thabo Mbeki, then president of South Africa, was equally antagonistic, claiming, as we noted earlier, that it undermined the sovereignty of the state. The suit, initially filed in the US District Court in Manhattan, was duly dismissed. But in 2007 it was reinstated by the 2nd US Circuit Court of Appeals on the ground that the corporations named *had* wittingly colluded with the notorious apartheid regime. The latest court papers do not specify the level of damages sought, laying more stress on a desire to set straight the historical record and deter future multinational collaboration with repressive regimes.[23] In the meantime, in an about-face, the South African justice minister has offered support to all the litigants in the search for a settlement.[24] The campaign to have the case heard has been spearheaded by the Khulumani Support Group,[25] founded in 1995 to empower survivors of apartheid. On its website, the words *Memory, Truth, Reconciliation,* and *Reparations* flash in large white letters. Not perhaps Walter Benjamin's (2005:255) unsettling "flash of memory" in a time of danger. Instead, this chain of association seems to signal the resolve to transform traumatic experience into a more solid currency, the stuff of identity-as-recognition and reparation.

Which returns us to where we began. Modern history may have served the nation-state well by writing and authorizing its hegemonic narrative, projecting from it a progressive, collective future; this by contrast to memory, which is situated in subjective, locally grounded experiences of the past (Anderson 1991:205; see above). But the modernist telos of nationhood, and the kind of historiography it mandated, has been seriously undermined. Nowadays *both* the future and past—even the oppressive colonial past, the struggles to which it gave rise, and the revolutionary possibilities toward which liberation pointed (Dlamini 2009)—radiate an aura of lost certainty, lost momentum. In the grip of what Charles Piot (2010) calls a *Nostalgia for the Future,* it is not merely born-again traditionalists who invoke the dead in the hope of reanimating life's forward thrust. As we have seen, genealogies of pain and sacrifice are very widely mobilized in efforts to revitalize identity, to conjure new sources of value, to galvanize a purchase on the here and now. This is a "remembered" past that, despite its assertions of authenticity, is explicitly tailored to underwrite indictments, to secure recognition, to claim entitlements, to elicit reparations. It makes memory the alibi of class actions that, in neoliberal times, tend to supplant class struggle as a mode of political action—and displace history as a national charter.

How well this sort of lawfare from below serves the cause of "little people"—or, indeed, of social justice—is yet to be seen. The record is distinctly mixed (Comaroff and Comaroff 2006b:26f). So, too, are its effects on the history-making of those who seek to redeem their pasts in court. Take a suit brought in the US under the Alien Tort Claims Act in 2004 by victims of military violence perpetrated in El Salvador in 1979. Jonah Rubin (2008) tells of the plaintiffs' dismay when their lawyers, eager to secure a victory and establish precedent, expurgated what they understood to be the broader historical significance of their stories in order to impress the jury with incontrovertible evidence of atrocities committed against them personally by the defendants. Legal procedures operate with narrow conventions of culpability, facticity, and proof. They have little tolerance for ambiguity or excess. Judgment insists on an authoritative, slimmed-down reading of the past, a past explained with reference to specifiable human intentions and actions. Just as history-on-trial cannot handle narrative overload, so it cannot brook indeterminacy, nothing of what Schama refers to as its "subversion," its attachment to the "bud of awkward alternative outcomes."[26] Litigation, in other words, demands a tactical reduction of the past if it is to be made to work for those who claim it as a means to an end: it has to demonstrate individual or collective guilt and take the measure of suffering as a debt to be repaid. No more, no less. Very different, this, from approaching abuse and injury as a problem of political action or social analysis. Different, also, from the idea of history as the interrogation of a past that, to invoke Nietzsche (1957:7) again, cannot simply be "subdued," a past that requires constantly to be revisited because it bears down upon the present in unforeseen ways.

## Conclusion: Memories, Plastic and Otherwise

Well, *are* we in danger of being rendered "unhistorical" by dint of an excess of partisan recollection? Are we being seduced by the romance of memory that, at once authenticated and purified by pain, is invested with a capacity to speak truth to power, to make claims for recognition, rights, and recompense? And what of the fate of modernist history, discredited for its putative inability to posit a plausible past, present, or future?

The production of an archive—or its reduction—in the service of victims' rights poses a problem for historians and political activists everywhere; above all, for those who have long dreamed that decolonization would bring with it a collective reclamation of the past, emancipating it in the service of a new nationhood. On one hand, we have witnessed a welcome repossession of that past by some postcolonial populations. Who would not be deeply moved, as was Shula Marks (1997) in South Africa, by efforts to retrieve the bones of ancestors abducted by former colonial rulers or their scientific sidekicks; this in a context in which the restoration of the violated black body has become a powerful ritual for recovering national dignity?[27] Yet, as Marks implies, the poignant pursuit of relics in post-apartheid South Africa—a practice replicated in many parts of the post-totalitarian world (cf. Verdery 1999)—has its darker sides. Some are made uneasy by the fact that the repatriation of bodily remains of genocide victims—as though this might redress the destruction of a *people*—ironically reproduces the efforts of their former oppressors to reduce them to their biophysical essence. Others observe that processes of repossession frequently lead to strife among ethnic groups[28] and, within them, to a hardening of the lines between inside and out, thus conducing to the exclusion of many. Yet others find it unnerving that memory, deployed in the service of identity-based struggles, tends to silence the flux and indeterminacy of social and cultural life in times past (Lalu 2009).

This conundrum presents itself as a theoretical problem as well. Modernist critics, from William Wordsworth to Walter Benjamin, have long believed memory to have unique powers to subvert the authority of reigning narratives. Set against history-as-hegemony, that view celebrates it as a vestige of innate, unruly, incorruptible humanity. Never truly separable from imagination and the life of images, from dreaming, affect, and the embodied mind, memory promises escape from a politics of brute interest, coming and going unbidden, re-presenting us with traces of what we have been made to forget. For the likes of Benjamin (2005:255), it was the spark, the flash that enabled a fleeting recognition of the truth, of social contradictions suppressed by "historicism's picture of history." Appealing though this is, we should be wary of seeing memory as a form of "weak messianic power" (p.254), a sublime force from elsewhere uniquely capable of breaking the conventions of its time and place, of cutting the present to the quick, of laying bare its animating conflicts. As those threatened by AmaZulu World have learned, even at its most fleeting, memory is time-bound, "plastic," interest-bearing; as much so, indeed, as any other socio-historical phenomenon. Human beings can be as readily dispossessed as redeemed by the sudden return of the past, especially when it comes back with the imprimatur of the law, or in the guise of Memory, Inc. On the other hand, if it is to live up to its subversive promise—if memory *is* to give creative voice to the unruly imagination without giving play to the darker side immanent in its politics—it has to be reunited, as subjective consciousness, with history as an account of the *collective* production of the present. Not with history as a reified, always-already authoritative chronicle, but as itself subversive, itself capable of immanent critique of the present from within; this by re-membering what has been divided, by questioning what is certain, by vexing the taken-for-granted. Including, of course, the authenticating power of memory itself. Recuperating the positive, perennially open dialectic of history and memory ought not merely to put populist and identitarian politics in proper perspective. It ought to interrogate just how things came to be as they are. And how they could be otherwise.

# CHAPTER 7

# Alien-Nation

*Zombies, Immigrants, and Millennial Capitalism*

... productive labor—or even production in general—no longer appears as the pillar that defines and sustains capitalist social organization. Production is given an objective quality, as if the capitalist system were a machine that marched forward of its own accord, without labor, a capitalist automaton.

*Michael Hardt (1995:39)*

*Automaton,* n. Thing imbued with spontaneous motion; living being viewed materially; piece of machinery with concealed motive power; living being whose actions are involuntary or without active intelligence.

*Oxford English Dictionary*

WHAT MIGHT ZOMBIES HAVE TO DO WITH THE EXPLOSION OF neoliberal capitalism at the end of the 20th century? What might they have to do with postcolonial, postrevolutionary nationalism? With labor history? With the metamorphosis of the modernist nation-state? Why have these spectral, floating signifiers made an appearance in epic, epidemic proportions in several parts of Africa recently? And what might they have to do with immigrants, those wanderers in pursuit of work, whose proper place is always elsewhere;

those the pariah citizens of a global order in which, paradoxically, old borders are said everywhere to be dissolving (see Chapter 4)? What, indeed, do any of these things, which bear the distinct taint of exoticism, tell us about the hard-edged material, cultural, epistemic realities of our times? Indeed, why pose such apparently perverse questions at all when our social world abounds with practical problems of immediate, unremitting *gravitas?*

So much for the questions. We shall cycle slowly back toward their answers. Let us move, first, from the interrogative to the indicative, from the conundrums with which we shall be concerned to the circumstances whence they arose.

## SPECTRAL CAPITAL, CAPITALIST SPECULATION: FROM *PRODUCTION* TO *CONSUMPTION*

Consumption.

In the 18th and 19th centuries it was the hallmark illness of the First Coming of Industrial Capitalism. Of the age in which the ecological conditions of production, its consuming passions (Sontag 1989; cf. J. Comaroff 1997), ate up the bodies of producers. Now, more than a hundred years later, semantically transposed into another key, it has become, in the words of van Binsbergen and Geschiere (1999), the "hallmark of modernity." Of its wealth, health, and vitality. Too vast a generalization? Maybe. But the claim captures popular imaginings, and their mass-mediated representation, from across the planet. It also resonates with the near-universal truism that the (post)modern person is a subject made by means of objects. Nor is this surprising. Consumption, in its ideological guise—as consumer*ism*—refers to a material sensibility actively cultivated, ostensibly for the common good, by Euro-American states and commercial interests, particularly since World War II.[1] In social theory, as well, it has become a prime mover, the force that determines definitions of value, the construction of identities, even the shape of the global ecumene.[2] As such, it is the invisible hand that animates the political and material imperative of the Second Coming of Capitalism, of capitalism in its neoliberal, global manifestation. Note the image: the *invisible hand.* It recalls a moving spirit of older vintage, one that dates back to the Time of Adam. To Adam Smith, that is, and the first debut of liberalism. Gone is the trope of the *deus ex machina,* a figure all too mechanistic for the post-industrial era.

As consumption has become the prime medium for producing selves and identities since the late 20th century, so there has been a concomitant eclipse of production; an eclipse, at least, of its *perceived* salience for the wealth of nations. This has been accompanied by a shift, across the world, in ordinary understandings of the nature of capitalism. The workplace and labor, especially work-and-place, securely sited in local configurations of class and community, are no longer the anchors of social existence. *Per contra,* especially in the global north, the factory and the workshop are increasingly experienced by virtue of their vanishing; this either because they are no longer competitive with enterprise elsewhere—where labor is cheaper, less assertive, unprotected by states and unions, where corporations are less taxed, less hemmed in by law—or by dint of their replacement by nonhuman means of manufacture. Which, in turn, has left behind a legacy of part-time piece work and menial make work, relatively insecure occupations that are tellingly dubbed "non-productive" labor. For many populations, industrial production has been replaced, as the *fons et origo* of wealth, by an altogether more precarious service economy and by finance capital, the inscrutable realm of speculation and transaction in which money appears to give birth to money.

Symptomatic, in respect of the latter, are the changing historical fortunes of gambling. Until quite recently, living off its proceeds was, normatively speaking, the epitome of immoral accumulation: the wager stood to the wage, the bet to personal betterment, as did depravity to virtue. But, in the era of finance capital, gambling has been routinized in a widespread infatuation with, and popular participation in, high-risk ventures that involve ever more abstract, abstruse instruments whose value accrues from, among other things, betting quixotically on the fortunes of diverse assets, be they pork bellies, life insurance policies, real estate, stocks and bonds, toxic debt, or derivatives of these "products." It also expresses itself in a fascination with futures and with their down-market counterpart, the lottery; banal, if symbolically saturated fantasies these of abundance without effort, of beating capitalism on its own terms by drawing a winning number at the behest of unseen forces.[3] Once again, that invisible hand. We have written about this at greater length elsewhere (Comaroff and Comaroff 2000a): at a time when, in most places, taxes have become anathema to the majoritarian political center, gambling is a favored means of raising revenues—of generating cultural and social assets—in what were once welfare states.

It has become commonplace to see in the turn to an economics of speculation the triumph of so-called casino capitalism. Argues Susan Strange (1986:1–3; cf. Harvey 1989:332; Tomasic 1991), who likens the global financial order to an immense game of luck, undignified even by probability theory:

> Something rather radical has happened to the international financial system to make it so much like a gambling hall. What that change has been, and how it has come about, are not clear. What is certain is that it has affected everyone ... [It] has made inveterate, and largely involuntary, gamblers of us all.

A literal manifestation of just this is evident in Native American reservation gambling, where tribes have staked their futures on the capacity of casinos to finance their social regeneration and their sovereignty (Cattelino 2008).

But we seek to make a slightly different point here: that the gaming room has become iconic of the central impulse of capital, namely, its capacity to make its own vitality and growth appear to be the natural yield of speculation and consumption, independent of all human labor (Hardt 1995:39). This is in spite of the fact that crisis after crisis in the global economy—not to mention growing income disparities, hunger, and poverty on a planetary scale—make it painfully plain that there is no such thing as capitalism *sans* production, that the neoliberal faith in finance and consumption as the *ur*-sources of value is palpably problematic. At once in perception, in theory, and in practice. In the late 1990s we noted that, while scholars had been somewhat slow to reflect on all this, people all over the world have not, especially those in places where there have been sudden infusions of commodities, of exploding money markets, of wealth without work. Many have been quick to give voice, albeit in different registers, to their perplexity at the enigma of this wealth. Of its origin and the capriciousness of its distribution, of the opaque, even occult, relation between means and ends embodied in it (Comaroff and Comaroff 1999a). Our concern in this chapter emerges directly out of these perplexities, these imaginings: out of worldwide speculation, in both senses of the term, at the specters conjured up by real or imagined changes in the conditions of material existence at the end of the 20th century and the beginning of the 21st.

We seek here, in a nutshell, to interrogate the *experiential* contradiction at the core of neoliberal capitalism in its global manifestation: the fact that it appears to offer up vast, almost instantaneous riches to those who control its technologies—and, simultaneously, to threaten the very survival of those who do not. More specifically, our objective is to explore the ways in which this conundrum is resolved, the ways in which the enchantments of capital are addressed, through efforts to plumb the mysterious relation of consumption to production as mediated by speculation; efforts that take a wide variety of local, culturally modulated forms; efforts that reveal much about the nature of economy, society, culture, and politics in the postcolonial, postrevolutionary present. As anthropologists are wont to do, we ground our excursion in a set of preoccupations and practices both concrete and historically particular: the obsession, in rural post-apartheid South Africa, with a rush of new commodities, currencies, and cash; with things whose acquisition is tantalizingly close, yet always just out of reach to all but those who understand their perverse secrets; with the disquieting figure of the zombie, an embodied, dispirited phantasm widely associated with the production, the possibility and impossibility, of these new forms of wealth. Although they are creatures of the moment, zombies have ghostly forebears who have arisen in prior periods of social disruption, periods characterized by sharp shifts in control over the fabrication and circulation of value, periods that also serve to illuminate the here and now.

We shall argue that the half-life of zombies in South Africa, past and present, is linked to that of compromised workers of another kind: immigrants from elsewhere on the continent, whose demonization is an equally prominent feature of the postcolonial scene. Together, these proletarian pariahs make visible a phantom history, a local chapter in a global story of changing relations of labor to capital, of production to consumption—indeed, of the very *pro* and *con* of capitalism. Their manifestation here also allows us to ponder a paradox in the scholarly literature: given that the factory model of capitalist manufacture has been said—confidently, and quite recently—to infuse *all* forms of social production (e.g., Deleuze 1986), why does labor appear less and less to undergird the social order of the present epoch?

Thus we bring you the case of the Zombie and the (Im)Migrant, this being the sequel to an earlier inquiry into work, labor, and historical consciousness in a South Africa then still palpably proletarian (Comaroff and Comaroff 1987). But first a brief excursion into the problematic status of production in the age of global capital.

## Labor's Lost

The emergence of consumption as a privileged site for the fashioning of society and identity, it may be argued, is integrally connected to the changing status of work under contemporary conditions. For some, the economic order of our times represents a completion of the intrinsic "project" of capital: namely, the evolution of a social formation that, as Tronti (1980:32) puts it, "does not look to labor as its dynamic foundation." Others see the present moment in very different terms. Lash and Urry (1987:232f), for instance, declare that we are witnessing not the *denouement* but the demise of organized capitalism, of a system in which corporate institutions could secure compromises between employers and employees by making appeal to the national interest. The internationalization of market forces, they claim, has not merely dislocated national economies and state sovereignties. It has led to a decline in the importance of domestic production in many once-industrialized countries. All of which, along with the worldwide rise of the service sector, the discounting of wage work, and the casualization of labor, has eroded the bases of proletarian identity and its politics—dispersing class relations, alliances and antinomies, across the four corners of the earth. The globalization of the division of labor reduces workers everywhere to the lowest common denominator, to a disposable cost, compelling them to compete with sweatshop and family manufacture.[4] It has also put such a distance between sites of production and consumption that their relationship becomes all but unfathomable, save in fantasy.

Not that Fordist fabrication has disappeared. Neither is the mutation of the labor market altogether unprecedented. For one thing, as Marx (1967:635) observed, the development of capitalism has always conduced to the cumulative replacement of "skilled laborers by less skilled, mature laborers by immature, male by female ..." For another, David Harvey (1989:192f) reminds us, the devaluation of labor power has been a traditional response to falling profits and periodic crises of commodity production. What is more, the growth of a global free market in commodities and services has not been accompanied by a correspondingly free flow of workers; most nation-states still regulate their movement to a greater or lesser extent. Nonetheless, the likes of Harvey insist, the current moment *is* different in that it evinces significant features that set it apart, rupturing the continuing history of capital—a history that "remain[s] the same and yet [is] constantly changing."[5] Above all else, the explosion of new monetary instruments and markets, aided by ever more sophisticated means of planetary coordination and space-time compression, have allowed the financial order to achieve a degree of autonomy from "real production" unmatched in the annals of modern political economy. Indeed, the ever more virtual qualities of fiscal circulation enable the speculative side of capitalism to appear independent of manufacture—and relatively unconstrained either by the exigencies or the moral values of virtuous labor.

How might any of this be connected to conditions in contemporary South Africa or to the preoccupation there with reserve armies of spectral workers? What might we learn about the historical implications of the global age by eavesdropping on popular anxieties at this coordinate on the postcolonial map? How do we interpret mounting local fears about the preternatural production of wealth, about its fitful flow and occult accumulation, about the destruction of the labor market by technicians of the arcane?

The end of apartheid might have fired utopian imaginations around the world with a uniquely telegenic vision of rights restored and history redeemed. But South Africa has also been remarkable for the speed with which it has run up against problems common to societies—especially to postrevolutionary societies[6]—abruptly confronted with the prospect of liberation under neoliberal conditions. Not only was its miraculously peaceful passage to democracy marred by a disconcerting upsurge of violence and crime, both organized and everyday. It continues to evince an uneasy fusion of enfranchisement and exclusion, hope and hopelessness, as the chasm between rich and poor widens, as efforts are made to realize a modern utopia by decidedly postmodern means. Gone is any prospect of an egalitarian, socialist future, of work for all, of the welfare state envisioned in the Freedom Charter that, famously, mandated the struggle against the *ancien regime*.[7] Gone for the most part, too, are the critiques of the free market and of bourgeois ideology once voiced by the anti-apartheid movements, their idealism reframed by the perceived reality of global economic forces (cf. Sharp 1998:245f).[8] Elsewhere (2000a) we have suggested that these conditions, and similar ones in other places, have conduced to a form of millennial capitalism. By this we mean not just capitalism at the millennium, but capitalism invested with salvific force, with an intense faith in its capacity, if rightly harnessed, wholly to transform the universe, including the lot of the most marginalized, immiserated, and disempowered. At its most extreme, this faith is epitomized by forms of money magic, ranging from pyramid schemes to prosperity gospels, that pledge to deliver immense, immediate wealth by largely inscrutable means; in its more mundane manifestation, it accords the market itself an almost mystical capacity to produce and deliver ever more wealth.

Of course, as we intimated in speaking of consumption and speculation, market redemption is now a worldwide creed; although stirred by the crisis of 2008, it seems not to have been badly shaken. But its millennial character is decidedly more prominent in some places than in others, especially those in which there has been a relatively abrupt conversion to *laissez-faire* from tightly regulated material and moral economies; where evocative calls for entrepreneurialism confront the realities of marginalization in the distribution of resources; where totalizing ideologies have suddenly given way to a spirit of deregulation, with its taunting mix of desire and disappointment, liberation and limitation. Individual citizens, many of them marooned by a rudderless ship of state, attempt to clamber aboard the good ship *Enterprise.* In so doing, however, they find themselves battling the eccentric currents of the "new" world order, which forge expansive connections between the local and the translocal, short-circuit established ways and means, disarticulate conventional relations of wealth and power, and render received borders within and between nation-states at once more and less porous (see Chapter 4). In the space left by attenuated national ideologies—or, more accurately, by ideologies increasingly contested in the name of identity politics—people in these societies are washed over by a flood of mass media from across the earth, media depicting a cargo of objects and lifestyles that affirm the neoliberal message of freedom and self-realization through consumption.

Under these conditions, where images of desire are as pervasive as they are inaccessible, it is only to be expected that there would be an intensification of efforts to grasp the hidden logic of supply and demand, to restore a measure of transparency to the connection between production and value, work and wealth, and to experiment with modes of accumulation, both fair and foul. The occult economies of many postcolonies, and the spectacular rise within them of organized crime, are alike features of millennial capitalism. They are disturbing caricatures of market enterprise in motion, of the impetus to acquire vast fortunes *sans* labor or its costs. Yet, distinctive as they are, the conditions of which we speak here are not unprecedented. In Africa, they recall a prior moment of global expansion, of dramatic articulations of the local and the translocal, of the circulation of new goods and images, of the displacement of indigenous orders of production and power. We refer to the onset of colonialism. It, too, occasioned world-transforming, millennial aspirations (cf. Fields 1985).

With this parallel in mind, we turn to contemporary South Africa.

## ALIEN-NATION

*The Nightshift: Workers in the Alternative Economy*

> ... no job; no sense
> Tell him, Joe, go kill
> Attention, quick march ...
> Open your hat, fall in, fall out, fall down ...
> Order: dismiss!
>
> *Zombie, Fela Anikulapo Kuti & Africa 70*[9]

There can be no denying the latter-day preoccupation with zombies in rural South Africa.[10] Their existence, far from being the subject of elusive tales from the backwoods, of fantastic fables from the veld, is widely taken for granted. It is treated as a simple matter of fact. In the 1990s, respectable local newspapers began to carry banner headlines like "'Zombie' Back from the Dead," illustrating their stories with conventional, high-realist photographs.[11] Similarly, defense lawyers in provincial courts have sought, by forensic means, to have clients acquitted of murder on grounds of having been driven to their deadly deeds by the zombification of their kin; illicit zombie workers have also become an issue in large-scale labor disputes.[12] Public culture is replete with invocations of the living dead, from popular songs and prime-time documentaries to national theatrical productions.[13] Not even the state has remained aloof. A *Commission of Inquiry into Witchcraft Violence and Ritual Murders* (Ralushai *et al.* 1996), appointed in 1995 by the Northern Province (now Limpopo) administration to investigate an "epidemic" of occult violence, reported widespread fear of the figure of the zombie. The latter, it notes in a tone of ethnographic neutrality (p.5),[14]

> is a person who is believed to have died, but because of the power of a witch, he is resurrected ... [and] works for the person who has turned him into a zombie. To make it impossible for him to communicate with other

people, the front part of his tongue is cut off so that he cannot speak. It is believed that he works at night only … [and] that he can leave his rural area and work in an urban area, often far from his home. Whenever he meets people he knows, he vanishes.

Speechless and unspeakable, this apparition fades away as soon as it becomes visible and knowable. It is a mutation of humanity made mute.

The observations of the commission are amply confirmed by our own experience in the Northwest Province since the early 1990s; although our informants added that zombies (*dithotsela;* also *diphoko*)[15] were not merely the dead-brought-back-to-life, that they could also be killed specifically for the purpose. Here, too, reference to them permeates everyday talk on the street, in private backyards, on the pages of the local press, in courts of law. Long-standing notions of witchcraft, *boloi,* have come to embrace zombie-making, the brutal reduction of others—in South Africa, largely unrelated neighbors—to instruments of production: insensible beings stored, like tools, in sheds, cupboards, or oil drums, at the homes of their creators (cf. Ralushai *et al.* 1996:50). In a world of flex-time employment, it is even said that some people are made into "part-time zombies" (cf. Ralushai *et al.* 1996:224–25), whose exhaustion in the morning speaks of an unwitting nocturnal mission, of involuntary toil on the night shift.

Thus do some build fortunes with the lifeblood of others. And, as they do, they are held to destroy the job market—even more, the very essence of self-possessed labor—in the process. Those typically said to conjure up the living dead tend, unsurprisingly, to be persons of conspicuous wealth, especially new wealth, whose source is neither visible nor readily explicable. Such things, of course, are highly relative. In very poor rural communities, where (almost) all things are relatives, it does not take a great deal to be seen to be affluent. In point of fact, those actually accused of the mystical manufacture of night workers, and assaulted or killed as a result, are not always the same as those suspected. Much like peoples assailed elsewhere as witches and sorcerers, they are often elderly, relict individuals, mostly female. Note: not all, although there is a penchant in northerly South Africa to refer to anyone alleged to engage in this kind of magical evil as "old women."[16] Conversely, their primary accusers and attackers, more often than not, are young, unemployed men.

Zombie-makers, moreover, are semiotically saturated, visually charged figures. In contrast to their victims, who are rendered sexless by being reduced to pure labor power, they are stereotypically described as perverts whose deformed passions and poisonous secretions make them unable to reproduce. Worse yet, they spoil the fertility of others, whether it be individuals, families, clans, or communities. This is why they have become iconic of a perceived crisis of household and collective futures in rural South Africa.[17] To be sure, they fuse, in a single grotesque, the very essence of negative value (cf. Munn 1986), the simultaneous destruction of *both* production and reproduction. On one hand, by manufacturing spectral workers, they annihilate the very possibility of productive employment, imaginatively if not manifestly; on the other, by taking work away from young people, they prevent them from securing the wherewithal to establish families, thereby making it impossible for communities to ensure their futures. No wonder that, in one of the most poignant witch-killings of the 1990s, an old woman set alight by morally outraged youths—determined to save their village by removing all evil-doers— was to hear, in her final agony, the words: "Die, die you witch. We can't get work because of you!" (Ralushai *et al.* 1996:193f).

Discourse in a range of overlapping public spheres—from customary tribunals and provincial courts, through local religious and political assemblies, to the print and broadcast media—makes it clear that, for many, the threat of a spectral workforce is all too concrete. And urgent. On more than one occasion, large crowds have gathered in the Northwest to watch the epic effort of healers to "liberate" zombies from their captors; in vernacular parlance, to "return them home." Here the spectral becomes spectacle. The fantasy of forcing underground evil into public visibility, of reversing the arcane alienation that creates phantom workers, is a palpable feature of the domestic cultural scene. Local newspapers, widely Africanized since the fall of apartheid, have been crucial in all this. They have taken the conventions of investigative reporting far beyond their orthodox rationalist frame in order to plumb the enigma of new social realities (Fordred 1998); harsh realities whose magicality, in the prevailing historical circumstances, does not permit the literary conceit of magical realism, demanding instead a deadly serious engagement with the actuality of enchantment.

Thus the long-running saga in 1993 on the pages of *The Mail*—formerly the *Mafeking Mail,* a small town newspaper, now a Northwest provincial weekly with large circulation—in which a pair of journalists sought to verify the claims of a healer, one Mokalaka Kwinda. Kwinda claimed that he had revived a man who had been living for four years as the "slave" of witches in the nearby Swartruggens district; this before the "eyes of his," the zombie's, "weeping mother."[18] Likewise a quest that same year to cover the efforts of four diviners to "retrieve" a "zombie woman" from the clutches of a malevolent in the nearby Luhurutshe District.[19] These stories marry the surreal to the banal, the mystical to the mundane. In the former case, the healer told the reporters that his elusive patient was undergoing "preliminary" treatment, a debriefing as it were, so that he might be "able to speak and return to normal life."[20] Nor are such events confined to the outback. In Mabopane, in the eastern part of the province, "hundreds of students and workers" reportedly filled the streets one weekday in May 1994, eager to witness a "zombie hunt."[21]

The fear of being reduced to ghost labor, of being abducted to feed the fortunes of a depraved stranger, occurs alongside another kind of specter: a growing mass, a shadowy alien-nation, of immigrant workers from elsewhere on the continent. As we saw in Chapter 4, these workers are held to disrupt local relations of production and reproduction—to "steal" scarce jobs and resources, foster prostitution, and spread AIDS—and have been openly harassed, or worse, on South African streets. Like zombies, they are nightmare citizens, their rootlessness threatening to siphon off the diminishing prosperity of the indigenous population. Interestingly, like zombies, too, they suffer from impaired speech; recall that the common term for immigrant, *makwerekwere,* is a Sesotho word that implies limited competence in the vernacular and, concomitantly, an incapacity to enter fully into South African society.[22] And like zombies, they are prone to provoking public violence.

In September 1998, for example, a crowd returning by train from a march in Pretoria—held, significantly, to protest mass unemployment—threw three *makwerekwere* to their deaths, purportedly for taking scarce jobs. Two were Senegalese, one from Mozambique.[23] Three months later, in December, there came alarming reports of a band of hoodlums in Johannesburg who seemed bent on the "systematic elimination" of foreign nationals.[24] Since then, there have been intermittent attacks, some of them fatal, a few notoriously brutal. Immigrants from neighboring countries, and from farther abroad, have worked in industry, on farms, and across the service sector in South Africa for over a century. But, in the 1990s, the tight regulation of these labor flows gave way to less controlled, often subcontracted sources of supply.[25] Employers are attracted by the potential of this cheap labor. It is said that as many as 80 percent of them use casual, "non-standard" workers (Horwitz, cited in Adam *et al.* 1998:209). An investigation just before the millennium showed that, while the preponderance of immigrants in the past decade have actually been male entrepreneurs plying their trade in large cities, a large number do find their way into other areas of the economy, often in provincial towns.[26] Some, especially those lacking legal documentation, many of them women and children, land up in the highly exploitable reaches of rural agriculture—in places like the Northwest Province.

Wherever they land up in South Africa, immigrants take their place on a fraught historical terrain. Anxieties about unemployment have reached unprecedented levels: by common agreement, the rate is much higher than the unofficial 38 percent to which the state admits. According to one estimate, 500,000 jobs, virtually all of them held by blacks, evaporated in the five years after 1994.[27] And this is probably a conservative reckoning, based primarily on shrinkage in the formal sector. "No jobs means our youth are destroyed," a resident of Soweto told a reporter from the *Chicago Tribune* in February 1999.[28] Even that eternal optimist Nelson Mandela, just before his retirement, quipped, "In a few months, I'll be standing by the road with a sign: Please Help. Unemployed with a new wife and a big family."[29]

In the northerly provinces, among the poorest in the country, there has been little evidence of the prosperity and redistribution that was expected to follow the fall of apartheid. True, the newly deregulated economy has granted some blacks a larger share of the spoils. Postcolonial South Africa has seen an elevated standard of living for sections of the African middle class. It has also given rise to a "liberation aristocracy," some of whose cadres have become very wealthy and serve as living personifications of the triumph of nonracial, neoliberal capitalism (Adam *et al.* 1998:203). In spite of all this, or perhaps because of it, the so-called transition, as we noted earlier, has kindled a millennial faith in the opportunities of free-market enterprise, now ostensibly open to all. "I want every black person to feel that he or she has the opportunity to become rich and only has himself to blame if he fails," declared Dan Mkhwanazi, launching the National Economic Trust (Adam *et al.* 1998:217).[30]

For the vast majority, however, millennial hope runs up against material impossibility. The much vaunted post-apartheid Reconstruction and Development Plan (RDP), designed to root out endemic poverty, had minimal impact. Indeed, its reformist objectives, which harked back to the age of the welfare state, quickly hardened into GEAR, the government's Growth, Employment, And Reconstruction strategy, which privileged development though privatization, wage flexibility, enterprise, and public service cuts. Little of the positive effects of these policies, or of the post-Fordist expansion of "industries" like tourism, find their way into the rural landscapes of Limpopo or the Northwest. Here a living has to be eked out from pitifully small-scale subsistence farming and (very) petty commerce: from such things as brewing, sex work, and the refashioning of used commodities, classically the pursuits of women. Such assets as pensions and social grants, paltry though they may be, have become the subject of fierce contention. Their beneficiaries, mainly widows and old men, are prime targets of jealousy, allegations of avarice, even bodily violence. Meanwhile, the migrant labor wages that long subsidized agrarian endeavors, and gave young men a degree of autonomy, have diminished dramatically. This, in turn, has exacerbated their sense of threatened masculinity, adding fuel to the gendered, generational conflicts of the countryside. Which is why the overwhelming proportion of those accused of witchcraft and zombie-making are older and female. And why their accusers are overwhelmingly out-of-work young adult males.

At the same time, provincial towns in these northerly provinces are home to small, bustling black elites, many of them spawned originally by the "ethnic homelands" into which the apartheid regime pumped endless resources over several decades. Well positioned to soak up novel business opportunities and to engage in behind-the-scenes dealings, they quickly took charge of a sizeable proportion of retail marketing and the provision of services in the countryside. For them, the conspicuous consumption of prized commodities—houses, cars, TVs, cell phones—does more than just signal accomplishment. It also serves to assuage the inequities of the colonial past. But, as it does, it also marks the growing inequalities of the postcolonial present. These distinctions, to those who gaze upon them from below, also seem to be a product of enchantment: given that they appeared with indecent speed and with little visible exertion, their material provenance remains mysterious. So, even more, does the cause of joblessness amidst such obvious prosperity. In the upshot, the two sides of millennial capitalism, post-apartheid style, come together: on one is the ever more distressing awareness of the absence of work, itself measured by the looming presence of the figure of the immigrant; on the other is the constantly reiterated suspicion, embodied in the zombie, that it is only by magical means, by consuming others, that people may enrich themselves in these perplexing times.

The symbolic apotheosis of this syllogism is to be found in a commercial advertisement run by a self-styled traditional healer in the Northwest. It appears in, of all places, the *Mafikeng Business Advertiser,* a local trade weekly. Top among the occult skills on offer is a treatment that promises clients "to get a job early if unemployed." The healer in question, Dr. S.M. Banda, should know. He is an immigrant.[31]

*Precursors: The Ghosts of Workers Past*

> … phantasmagoria comes into being when, under the constraints of its
> own limitations, modernity's latest products come close to the archaic.
> *Theodor Adorno (1981:95)*

On the face of it, much of this is new. When we did research in the Northwest in the late 1960s and mid-1970s—it was still then the Tswana ethnic "homeland"—most males were, or had been, away as migrants to the industrial centers. There was barely a black middle class to speak of and no manifest anxieties about immigrants. Laborers had long come from elsewhere to seek employment in local towns and on the farms of the neighboring Western Transvaal. "Foreigners"—Zimbabweans, for instance, and descendants of Xhosa who had built the railroad at the turn of the century—lived amicably with Tswana-speaking populations. There was also no mention of zombies. True, many people spoke of their concern about witchcraft, understood as an unnatural means of garnering wealth by "eating" others and absorbing their capacity to create value. On occasion, moreover, malevolents would cause young migrants to lose their moorings, to forsake their kin at home, and to eschew the demands of domestic reproduction.[32] But there was nothing like the current preoccupation with the danger of humans being made into toiling automatons. Nor was there the sense that a spectral economy, founded on the labor of these and other aliens, might be draining the productive and reproductive potential of the community at large.

At the same time, these late 20th-century anxieties are not entirely unprecedented either. In disinterring vernacular conceptions of work, labor, and consciousness during the high apartheid years in Chapter 2, we noted that Tswana regarded certain modes of migrant toil (*mmèrèkò*) as alienating, that they spoke of the way in which its disciplined routines reduced humans to draft animals, even to "tinned fish."[33] These tropes implied a contrasting notion of self-possessed work (*tiro*), typically work-at-home, which created social value. This form of exertion constructed personhood in a positive key through the simultaneous building up of others; it also added to the commonweal of a collective world. But the historical record indicates that Tswana ideas of estranged labor were not limited to the experience of proletarianization alone. Recall, again from Chapter 2, J. Tom Brown's (1926) account of *sehihi* or *sefifi,* a condition linked to the eclipse of self-possession—and, with it, the capacity to accumulate wealth and social power. Typically associated with witchcraft, it was a condition that "alienated [the afflicted individual] from fellowship with his kith and kin" (p.137–38). As Brown went on to note, and we repeat most of the passage here:

> ... [*sefifi*] signifies that though the body lives and moves it is only a grave, a place where something has died or been killed. The essential manhood is dead. It is no uncommon thing to hear a person spoken of as being dead when he stands before you visibly alive. When this takes place it always means that there has been an overshadowing of the true relationships of life ...

Here, patently, we have a precursor of the zombie. But, whereas the latter is conjured from a corpse, either killed for the purpose or already deceased, *sefifi* is a state of eclipse effected by the appropriation of the essential selfhood of a living person, leaving behind a sentient shell as mute witness to the erasure of the social being it once housed. Moreover, where *sefifi* entailed the loss of *all* human creativity—often said to have been eaten whole by witches to enhance their own physical, political, and material potency—the zombie is transformed purely into alienated labor power, abducted from home or workplace, and made to serve as someone else's instrument of production.[34] He or she was stored, like tools, remember, in the cupboards or shed of their owners.

Evidence from elsewhere in southern Africa fills out this phantasmagoric history of labor, enabling us to track its fitful figurings, its continuities and breaks. Thus Harries's (1994:221) study of the world of Mozambican migrants to South Africa between 1860 and 1910 shows that witches (*baloyi*), held to be prevalent on the mines, were said to seize the "life essence" of others, forcing them to toil for days as zombies (*dlukula*) in closed-off subterranean galleries, where they lived on a diet of mud. The poetic particularity of phantom workers, here as elsewhere, is a sensitive register of shifting experiences of labor and its value. The introduction of compensation pay for miner's phthisis, for example, quickly led to a notion that zombies returned from below ground with numbers—potential payouts, blood money—chalked on their backs. Junod (1927:298–99,513; cf. Harries 1994:221), classic ethnographer of southeastern Africa, remarked on similar fears in rural southern Mozambique around 1910. "Modernized" witches there, anticipating their latter-day South African counterparts, were thought capable of reducing their fellows to a nocturnal agrarian workforce, masquerading by day as innocent children.[35] Some could even induce young men to wander off to the Witwatersrand mines, never to return. Once more we see the zombie as a "walking specter," an object of collective terror and desire, to invoke Clery's (1995:174) description of the "terrorist genre" of haunted Gothic fiction in late 18th-century England, where industrialization was similarly restructuring the nature of work-and-place. Like those "Horrid Mysteries," zombie tales dramatize the strangeness of what had become real; in this instance, who or what it is that controls the relation of work to the production of social being, secured in time and space.

Other instances of ghost workers in Africa underline the point. Take Ardener's (1970) piquant narrative of zombie beliefs among the Bakweri of West Cameroon. These beliefs—an intensification, it appears, of older ideas about witchcraft—arose at the time of the Great War, with the relatively sudden penetration of German colonizers into the region. Their fecund agricultural land expropriated for plantations manned largely by foreigners, the Bakweri found themselves crowded into inhospitable reserves. As a result, they fell into a period of impoverishment and reduced fertility. It was then that the zombie labor force (*vekongi*) first made itself felt, sheltering in tin houses built by those locals who had somehow managed to profit from the unpromising circumstances.[36] The living dead, many of them children, were said to be victims of the murderous greed of their own kin. They were sent away to work in distant plantations, where witchmasters had built a town overflowing with modern consumer goods.

Here, as in newly colonized Mozambique, we see the sudden conjuncture of a local world—in which production is closely tied to kin groups—with forces that arrogate the capacity to create value and redirect its flow. Above all, these forces fracture the meaning of work and its received relation to place; place, that is, in both its social and ethical aspects. Under such conditions, zombies become the stuff of "estranged recognition" (Clery 1995:114):

recognition not merely of the commodification of labor, or its subjection to deadly competition, but of the invisible predations that seem to congeal beneath the banal surfaces of new forms of wealth. In their iconography of forced migration and wandering exile, of children abused and relatives violated, the living dead comment on the disruption of an economy in which productive energies were once visibly invested in the reproduction of a situated order of domestic and communal relations, an order through which the present was, literally, kept in place. And the future was secured.

Ardener (1970:148) notes the complex continuities and innovations at play in these constructions, which have, as their imaginative precondition, ideas of the occult widely distributed across Africa and the New World; in particular, the idea that witches, by their very nature, consume the generative force of others. Zombies themselves seem to be born, at least in the first instance, of colonial encounters: of the precipitous engagement of local worlds with imperial economies that seek to exert control over the essential means of producing value, means like land and labor, space and time. It is in this abstract, metaphorical sense that René Depestre (1971:20) declares colonialism to be "a process of man's general zombification."[37] In purely historical terms, the affinity between colonization and zombification is less direct. Colonialism does not always call forth zombies, and zombies are not always associated with colonialism. What they *do* tend to be associated with, however, are rapidly changing conditions of work under capitalism in its various guises; conditions that rupture not just established relations of production and reproduction, but also received connections of laborer to species-being, persons to place, the material to the moral, the individual to the communal, past to future. In this respect, the living dead join a host of other spectral figures—vampires, monsters, creatures of Gothic "supernaturalism"—who alike have been vectors of an affective engagement with the visceral implications of the factory, the plantation, the market, the mine (cf. Ardener 1970:156; Clery 1995:9).

As this suggests, however abstract a set of ideas may be embodied in the living dead *sui generis,* any particular zombie congeals the predicament of human labor at its most concrete, its most historically specific. How, then, might those we have encountered in rural South Africa be linked, in more precise terms, to the late 20th-century transformations with which we began? Or to the impact of millennial capitalism in this postcolony?

## Toward a Conclusion

These questions have been anticipated, their answers foreshadowed, elsewhere. Thus Harries (1994:221) has argued that, among early 20th century Mozambican miners in the Transvaal, zombie-making magic was a practical response to the unfamiliar—specifically, to the physical depredations of underground work and to the explosion of new forms of wealth amidst abject poverty. Witchcraft, in a virulently mutated strain, he says, became a proxy for capitalist exploitation, witch-hunting, a displacement of class struggle. Niehaus (1993, 1995, 2001:197f), writing of the rural Mpumalanga Province at the other end of the century, arrives at a similar conclusion: mystical evil is a "cultural fantasy" manipulated by the dominant to defend their positions of privilege. Explanations of this sort belong to a species of interpretation that brings a critical understanding of ideology to bear on Evans-Pritchard's (1937) classic conception of witchcraft as a "socially relevant" theory of cause (Ferguson 1993; Comaroff and Comaroff 1993; Geschiere 1997). Many would agree with their underlying premise: that witches and zombies are to be read as etiological principles that translate structural contradictions, experiential anomalies, and aporias—force-fields of greater complexity than is normally implied by "class struggle"—into the argot of human agency, of interpersonal kinship, of morality and passion.

But here lies the rub. How does this very general truism, as valid for early colonial witchcraft as it is for latter-day zombies, relate to the implosive, shifting histories of which we have spoken? If the living dead are merely walking specters of class struggle, why have they not been a permanent fixture of the modern South African scene? What accounts for their comings and goings— and, to return to our opening conundrums, for the dramatic intensification of their appeal in the postcolony? How, furthermore, do we make sense of the particular poetics of these fantasies, whose symbolic excess and expressive exuberance gesture toward an imaginative play infinitely more elaborate than is allowed by a purely pragmatic, functionalist explication?

We have tried, in the course of this narrative, to show that the mounting preoccupation with zombies and immigrants here is owed to a specific, if large-scale clutch of historical conditions—conditions that have congealed in a postcolonial moment experienced, by all but the most affluent, as an unprecedented mix of hope and hopelessness, promise and impossibility, the new and the continuing. They have their source in social and material transformations sparked by the rapid rise of neoliberal capitalism on a global scale, a process that, among other things, has intensified market competition; translocalized the division of labor; rendered national polities and economies increasingly porous, less sovereign; set many people in motion and disrupted their sense of place; dispersed class relations across international borders; and widened the gulf between flows of fiscal circulation and sites of concrete production, thus permitting speculative capital to appear to determine the fate of postrevolutionary societies. What is more, because corporate enterprise chases cheap, tractable labor all over the earth, searching out optimally (de)regulated environments, it often erodes the social infrastructure of working communities, adding yet further to the stream of immigrants in pursuit of employment—and to the likelihood that they will be despised, demonized, even done to death.

The backwash of this process, as we have seen, is readily evident in contemporary South Africa, where rapid deregulation, labile employment arrangements, and the gross shrinkage of the job market have altered the generic meaning of work, the specific relationship of production to reproduction, and the connection of both to place. What is more, labor migration, which had become a rite of passage to social manhood, has all but vanished. In the void left behind, especially in the countryside, there have risen new, unaccountable manifestations of wealth, wealth not derived from any discernible or conventional source. In this void, too, jobs seem available only for "non-standard" workers—those, like immigrants, who will take anything they can get. Zombies, the ultimate non-standard devalued workers, take shape in the collective imaginary as figurations of these conditions. In their silence they give voice to a sense of dread about the human costs of intensified capitalist production, about the loss of control over the terms in which people alienate their labor power, about the demise of a moral economy in which wage employment, however distant and exploitative, had "always" been there to support the founding of families and the well-being of communities. This bears its own measure of historical irony. In the colonial epoch, the migrant contract system was regarded as a social, moral, and political travesty, breaking up black households and forcing men to toil under exacting conditions for pitiable earnings. Then a frequent object of protest, it is seen, in retrospect, as having been one of the secure foundations of the social landscape. Shades, here, of earlier revolutions, earlier metamorphoses in the articulation of capital and labor.

Here, then, is what is unique about the moment in the South African postcolony, what it is that has called forth an alien-nation of pariah proletarians, dead and alive. It is an historical moment that, in bringing together force-fields at once global and local, has conduced to a seismic mutation in the ontological *experience* of work, selfhood, gender, community, and place. Because the terms of reference for this experience are those of modernist capitalism—indeed, these are the *only* terms in which the present may be reduced to semiotic sense-and-sensibility—it is framed in the language of labor lost, factories foreclosed, communities crumbling. Which is why the concern with zombies in the northerly reaches of the country, while in many ways a novel confection, replays enduring images of alienated production. In Adorno's (1981:96) phrase, "it sounded so old, and yet was so new." Much like the story of labor itself, which, in an abstract sense, is still subject to the familiar "laws" of capitalism—yet, as concrete reality, has been substantially altered by the reorganization of the world economy as we know it. To reiterate: it all "remain[s] the same and yet [is] constantly changing."

One final point. Although we have tried to subdue the fantasy of spectral labor by recourse to historical reason, its key animus still eludes us. What, finally, are we to make of its symbolic excess? What does the intricate discourse about alien workers tell us of the subterranean workings of terror, of the life of standardized nightmares in a world of "daylight reason" (Duncan 1992:143)?[38] There is little question that this discourse gives motive and moral valence to disturbing events: that, in the classic manner of ideologies everywhere, it links etiology to existing orders of power and value. But zombie-speak seems to do much more. Its productive figurations feed a process of fervent speculation, poetic elaboration, forensic quest. The menacing dangers of zombification— the disoriented wanderings, the loss of speech, sense, and will, the perverted practices that erase all ties to kith and kin—serve to conjure with inchoate fears, allowing free play to anger and anguish and desire. Also to the effort to make some sense of them. Like Gothic horror, the elaboration of these images "encourage[s] an experience of estranged recognition" (Clery 1995:114). Nor only at the immiserated edges of polite society. The hardboiled social analyst might insist that the obsession with the living dead misrecognizes the systemic roots of deprivation and distress. But its eruption onto the fertile planes of post-apartheid public culture—via sober press reports, TV documentaries, and agitprop theater—has had a tangible impact. It has forced a recognition of the crisis in the countryside, of the plight of displaced youth, of the devaluation of work and workers, of an alien-nation within the postcolony itself. As the very conditions that called forth zombies erode the basis of a conventional politics of labor and public interest, we would do well to pay careful attention to the lessons of history embodied in these dread creatures.

# CHAPTER 8

# Beyond Bare Life

*AIDS, (Bio)Politics, and the Neo World Order*

IT IS IMPOSSIBLE TO CONTEMPLATE THE SHAPE OF LATE MODERN history, in Africa or elsewhere, without the polymorphous presence of HIV/ AIDS, the signal pandemic of the global here and now. In retrospect, the timing of its onset was uncanny. The disease appeared like a *memento mori* in a world high on the hype of Reaganomics, deregulation, and the end of the Cold War. In its wake, even careful observers made medieval associations. "AIDS," wrote Susan Sontag (1989:122), "reinstates something like a premodern experience of illness," a throwback to an era in which sickness was, by its nature, immutable, mysterious, and fatal. Such reactions make plain how the genesis of the pandemic affected our very sense of history, imposing a chronotope of its own, a distinctly *un*modern sense of fate unfolding, of implacable destiny. By unsettling scientific certainties, AIDS also prefigured an ironic, postmodern future. As Sontag intuited, it marked an epochal shift, not merely in the almost omnipotent status of medical knowledge and its sanitized language of suffering; nor even in the relationship with death, so long banished from the concerns of those preoccupied with life and the capacity to control it. AIDS also cast a premodern pall over the emancipated pleasures, the amoral, free-wheeling desires that animated advanced consumer societies. Epidemics everywhere tend to be seen as coming from outside, especially when they well up within the antiseptic heartlands of reason. When Western order is polluted from within, the contagion is frequently identified with Africa—as primal other, as object of dangerous desire, as projection of a self never fully tamed or tameable.

In more ways than one, then, AIDS represented the return of the repressed, the suppressed, the oppressed. Quickly overwhelming the received limits of virology and immunology—indeed, of the restricted lexicon of bioscience *tout court*—it set off an avalanche of myth-making. There have been those, in the tradition of Nietzsche (1910:77), who insist that modernity has banished this sort of myth-making, that it has condemned us to pain without meaning. In our day and age, suggests Jean-Luc Nancy (1997:149), suffering is "no longer sacrificial." Our bodies are broken and repaired, leaving "nothing to say." But there certainly has *not* been a shortage of things to say about AIDS. On the contrary, it has sparked a veritable plague of images; what Treichler (1988), memorably, refers to as an "epidemic of signification." Striking the unstable landscape of the late 20th century like a "lightning bolt" (cf. Nancy 1997:146), it cut a swathe at once awesome and absolute, marking out the path of economic and environmental change that sped the evolution and transmission of unfamiliar viruses both within and among species (Davis 2005:55). In the process, it signaled emerging biopolitical insecurities: unrecognizable aliens threatening existing immunities, penetrating once-secure boundaries at a time of deregulated flows and exchanges. In the north, the disease prefigured a new order of post–Cold War terrors, of protean, deterritorialized invaders capable of hijacking our defenses and coexisting with us in a deadly symbiosis, setting off rapidly mutating, mimetic forms of violence and counter-violence—a process that W.J.T. Mitchell (n.d.) has called the "cloning of terror."

As all this suggests, AIDS has been rewriting the global geopolitical coordinates within which we think and act. We may lack the nerve or imagination to theorize it adequately, but it has certainly been theorizing us for quite a while. "It doesn't matter if you are HIV-positive or negative," insists South Africa activist Adam Levin (2005:226; see Chapter 1), "the world has AIDS. And if you give a shit about the world, you have it too." The ready mutability of the disease challenges efforts to impose stable categories of recognition and exclusion on an already disrupted late-modern topography. The pandemic is savagely cosmopolitan, having made blatant the existence of dynamic, translocal intimacies and connections across received lines of segregation, difference, and propriety. It has also revived old specters, marking out pathologized publics and crystallizing latent contradictions and anxieties. And, in so doing, it has exacerbated economic and moral divides on an ever more planetary scale. Coming as it did at the time of a radical restructuring of the axes of a bipolar world, of the liberal-democratic nation-state, and of the workings of capitalism itself, the disease served as both a sign and a vector of a global order-in-formation. And with it, a new sense of the nature and possibilities of the political.

Here again, the timing has not been coincidental. It scarcely needs saying anymore that, as governments have outsourced many of their operations, retreating from a politics of redistribution, the grand disciplinary institutions of the modernist state have shrunk. Or that the task of social reproduction—of schooling, healing, law enforcement, elder care—has been ceded to public-private institutions, to corporations, to volunteer workers, and to more or less viable "communities" under the sway of regimes of "expert" knowledge. If family values are the all-purpose glue meant to ensure social reproduction under these conditions, AIDS has been read as social pathology incarnate, a quintessential sign of all that imperils a civilized future-in-the-world. In its primal association with non-normative sexuality, it also lends itself to a language of revelation and retribution, evoking strong emotions that, in the north, point to barely repressed anxieties about sexual selfhood and desire; this at a time of profound upheaval in gendered relations of power and production (Butler 1997:27).

At play, in all this, is also the uncertain issue of citizenship. Here, too, AIDS has figured as standardized nightmare (Wilson 1951). As states have become less invested in sustaining national economies of production, the political subject is defined less as a patriotic producer, *homo faber,* than as a consumer of services. Government, reciprocally, is expected to superintend service delivery, security, and the conditions of "healthy," untrammeled enterprise. With the erosion, if not the erasure, of social categories rooted in nation, territory, and class, being-in-the-world inheres ever more in individual, identity-bearing bodies: bodies defined as objects of biological nature, subjects of commodified desire. Statesmen represent the predicament of contemporary governance as a battle to reduce its bureaucratic footprint and its costs while maximizing personal safety and self-realization, their rhetoric focusing on "quality of life," understood in simultaneously moral and material terms. AIDS embodies, all too literally, core contradictions at issue in all this. For some, its onset made plain the dangers of *laissez-faire* and a drastic reduction of the reach of the polis—the erosion of institutions of public health, for example, in the name of corporate science (Brazier 1989). But such critical, *social* reflection, at least in the global north, has been overpowered by another process already noted: a tendency to project the dystopic implications of neoliberalism onto the victims themselves. Thus it is that the archetype of the homosexual AIDS sufferer became the specter of a world driven by desire *sans* moral commitment. The hysteria that erupted in the US with the first awareness of the epidemic made plain how central is the register of sexual "perversion" to the neoconservative imagination (Berlant 1997). It is an imagination that strives to reduce expansive, supple vocabularies of politics, social debate, and intimacy to a straitjacket of absolute oppositions, of nature and abomination, truth and deception, good and evil.

In the upshot, sex is seen, for good and ill, to hold the key to life. It is a fetish, attributed with the decisive capacity to move people and motivate action. Productively channeled, it builds moral communities. Left to its own hedonistic designs, it destroys them. Much has been written about this, of course. What we wish to emphasize here is how non-normative sexuality has come to instantiate the dark underside of the commodity form and the world it makes possible. It stands in for transaction cut free from moral regulation and social constraint, transactions that "pervert" responsible reproduction and the "wholesome" family-oriented appetites that ought to animate market-driven sociality. Indeed, an older politics of class and ideological struggle has given way to what Simon Watney (1990:100) has dubbed a "politics of intense moral purity" (see Chapter 1); the sort of politics made evident in the disproportionate part played by gay marriage in partisan electioneering and public discourse in the US and beyond in the early 21st century.

Just how pervasive is this politics of moral purity? A liturgy of seamy evidence springs readily to mind. Recall a report that, in the 1990s, the US Air Force's Wright Laboratory proposed to develop an "aphrodisiac" chemical weapon to deliver a "non-lethal blow to the morale of enemy troops by provoking homosexual behavior among them."[1] In a reflection on "'Brokeback' and Abu Ghraib," Jesse Kornbluth asks why it is that "gay sex [is] unacceptable within our borders, but ideal to export to foreign torture chambers."[2] Pictures from Abu Ghraib, he notes, confirmed a systematic effort to attack Islamic values—in terms that often mimic what he dubs S&M gay porn. "Our interrogators strip the Iraqis of their heterosexual masculinity, then force them to reenact somebody's idea of gay scenarios." As in Abu Ghraib, so also in Guantanamo:[3] the attempt to assert Euro-American dominance over what appears to be a decidedly post-Euro-American world involves the projection of depraved sexuality onto others at the same time as US forces engage in a depraved sexualization of warfare. In doing this, the enterprise revisits technologies of an earlier colonial era, invoking a history whose consequences are writ large in the contemporary politics of HIV/AIDS in Africa.

But we are running ahead of ourselves. Our broad concern here is how, and with what consequences, HIV/AIDS is implicated in the world-altering processes that have reshaped the late 20th- and early 21st-century global order: how it has played a role in the redefinition of our moral geography and sense of biosecurity, in the rise of new kinds of political subjectivity and sociality, in the emergence of new patterns of integration, exclusion, prosperity, and immiseration on an ever more planetary scale.

## EXPORTING THE EPIDEMIC: AIDS GOES SOUTH

In the decades since HIV/AIDS was first identified, therapeutic advances have rendered it more manageable. As South African "actorvist" Pieter-Dirk Uys has put it, it is now a "life sentence ... not a death sentence."[4] Or rather, it should be. In point of fact, the most devastating burden of suffering has shifted to parts of the world where, from the vantage of the privileged, misery is endemic, life is cheap, and people are disposable. As has often been noted, mass-mediated images of the disease have had a signal impact on contemporary constructions of "Third World Peoples" as abject, intractable, doomed (cf. Treichler 1999:210). Mbembe and Nuttall (2004:348) suggest, in respect of Africa, that these archetypes exceed even the otherness implied in Edward Said's Orientalist paradigm. They are correct. Global geopolitics have produced new zones of exclusion in which alterity becomes highly relative. The Muslim terrorist might have emerged as the acme of frenzied opposition to American dominance in the post–Cold War world, but disease-ridden Africa epitomizes another otherness, the product less of an axis of evil than, in northern eyes, an axis of irrelevance. Bereft of its former strategic significance, and until recently unpromising to those in search of profitable commodity markets, the continent disappears once more behind colonial images of nature red in tooth-and-claw. Once more it becomes a site for philanthropy, adventurism, extraction. Once more it is depicted as a horrific exemplar of all that threatens the "natural" reproduction of life: mothers whose wombs gestate death, chauvinist leaders who court dissident science, men who rape virgins and even babies to rid themselves of infection, children bereft of innocence who are driven to preternatural sex, drugs, and violence for a pittance.

These circulating discourses intersect in complex ways with HIV/AIDS as a lived reality in the postcolony. There, the condition is deeply contested. It is at once a sign and a source of sociality, of altered states of collective consciousness, and of new forms of politics in pursuit of rights, recognition, and entitlement. For AIDS makes scandalously plain the human costs of economic and political marginalization, of insufficient humanitarian intervention where it is most needed, and of an ever more monopolistic control over the means of life itself. In many African countries, HIV revivifies scarcely suppressed memories of the violence and medical neglect of times past, jibing with enduring legacies of scientific racism, material extraction, and technological dependency. Small wonder the disease animates traumas that invert the phobias of Euro-America: suspicions that it was inflicted on black populations by genocidal racists, by careless experimentation, by the CIA, or by pharmaceutical firms and their craven local sidekicks.

At the same time, across Africa, Euro-American nightmares interbreed with a host of local anxieties and etiologies. Discourses of perversion and shame have been common, for instance. Despite all the evidence that its transmission on the continent is predominantly heterosexual, the spread of AIDS has spurred the vilification of homosexuality—and its depiction as an import from the decadent, double-dealing countries of the north. It has also licensed the policing of other forms of sexuality not securely under the control of normative authority; hence the demonization of independent women, immigrants, and youth. As Neville Hoad (2005) observes of South Africa, the sexualized tropes of colonial racism have continued to stalk the politics of HIV/AIDS, provoking official denial at the behest of the "silencing phantasm of sexual respectability." Studied refusal to acknowledge the pandemic by government perpetuated the association of race, sex, and pathology. For their part, AIDS activists and educators have struggled to break these associations and the conspiracies of suppression and displacement that solidify them. They have sought to open up public forums in which sufferers can assert their status in unambiguous terms. It is in light of this struggle that a small gesture by Nelson Mandela in 2005 took on enormous significance. In announcing that his sole surviving son had succumbed to the disease, he declared, "The only way of making [HIV/AIDS] appear a normal illness like TB or cancer is to come out and say that someone has died of [it]."[5] Local commentators referred to this as their "'Rock Hudson' moment."[6]

But the inaudibility of talk about AIDS is often less a matter of brute repression or secrecy than of complicated communicative practices under conditions of dread and uncertainty. Nuanced registers and indirect forms of speech flourish in a field haunted by the ubiquitous presence of the disease, a field in which death is the silent referent around which much everyday signification has been reoriented. In South Africa, the national prevalence rate in 2010 hovered around 11 percent; one in three women aged twenty-five to twenty-nine, and over a quarter of men between thirty and thirty-four, were living with HIV.[7] In this context, maintaining the ambiguity of one's "status," or the presence or absence of *the* disease, can be an act of self-preservation, defiance, or resignation. Adjectives like fat or thin, sharp or sluggish, sallow or pumped, prime the delicate labor of framing identities and futures in the shadow of the pandemic. The work of sustaining the self in the face of it also takes on a discernible spatio-temporal aspect. Frédéric Le Marcis (2004:454) speaks of the distinctive map of Johannesburg drawn by sufferers as they traverse the city in search of care. Their journeys chart a metropolis partly visible, partly hidden from sight. In their tenacious quest for treatment, their ailing bodies chart the intersections of the public and the private, the official and the unofficial, the said and the unsaid.

All this suggests that AIDS, as fetish and taboo, disputed truth and irreducible reality, has been prolifically productive in Africa. We use this last term, in the manner of Marx and Foucault, to imply that it has given birth to unfamiliar forms of sociality and signification, enterprise and activism—both negative and positive. The pandemic has redrawn the parameters of human existence as intimate pleasures turn into mortal risks, as trust and fidelity are freighted with deadly salience, as patterns of physical and cultural continuity are eroded in unexpected ways, as entire generations are "stolen," as children become mothers and schools become orphanages.[8] Where adult workforces are depleted and domestic incomes dry up, new orders of dependency, debt, care, and custody take shape. So, too, do new etiologies, utopian vocabularies, and visions of apocalypse, all intensified by fears of human malevolence and witchcraft (Ashforth 2002). Such circumstances breed desperate sorts of inventiveness, representation, and enterprise. Vibrant expressive genres have sprung up around the pandemic; notable among them is the Body Maps Project, in which South African artists and activists commemorate those who, in the words of Ingrid de Kock (2004–05:58), "die of love's lesions." But the impact of AIDS is also evident in the less elevated business of everyday exchange. The banal accoutrements of death jostle other domestic commodities on sidewalks and in markets: coffins, wreaths, all manner of medicaments, sacrificial beasts. Communities struggle to find the time and place, the ritual and financial means, to process the weight of mortality, thus to avoid the ultimate abjection of "bare death."[9] For the prospect of being unable to dispatch the dead with due ceremony, to consign them properly to the ancestral world, marks the null point of social continuity. It is as threatening to an imagined future as is bare life in the present.

While AIDS often unfixes received signs and practices, it can also authorize assertive associations and visions of the common good. Those who embrace a "positive" politics defy silence and invisibility by becoming emphatic embodiments of the disease. Members of the South African Treatment Action Campaign (TAC) wear its brightly colored T-shirts like a uniform, using diagnostic indices as terms of personal identification. They introduce themselves at support group meetings, for example, by announcing their CD4 T-cell counts and viral loads (Robins 2005:11). Here, claiming a positive identity is tantamount to a conversion experience, literally a path to salvation, since it may bring access to medication and material support. A neophyte in an anti-retroviral (ARV) program put it thus: "I am like a born again … It's like committing yourself to life because the drugs are a life-time thing. ARV's are now my life" (Robins 2005:10). These testimonies redeploy the register of regeneration common in the Pentecostal churches that have burgeoned across the global south in recent times, churches that have had ambivalent relations with AIDS movements; they frequently claim, for instance, that Jesus alone can effect a cure. But religious and secular NGOs alike find the language rebirth appropriate to their mission, laying stress on the role of personal witnessing in making manifest new-found certainties and commitments—and in countering pressures toward deception and secrecy among their following. Like Susan Sontag (1989) in her vain attempt to banish metaphor from the representations of illness, AIDS activists often fetishize the "value-free" argot of science in the effort to curb the semantic resonance of the disease;[10] although, as we shall see, they also strive to reconnect popular science to a vocabulary of critical politics.

The various forms of advocacy and enterprise, anger and argument, cooperation and conflict that have emerged in response to AIDS belie images of African abjection. Not only have several countries—like Uganda, Senegal, Burkina Faso—made notable inroads into rates of infection. The pandemic has also triggered energetic forms of mobilization that, often in stark contrast to their counterparts in the north, extend to a more embracing politics of life couched in the idiom of rights, citizenship, and the scandal of deepening social inequality. To this end, AIDS activists have forged broad, heterogeneous alliances with international movements, NGOs, and private philanthropists, as well as with various corporations acting in the name of conscience, public relations, or opposition to biotech monopolies. They have pressed a range of questions, from the entitlement to life-saving drugs to treatment for HIV-positive migrants, from the ethics of medical experimentation to the implications of intellectual property law for access to technology and treatment. In an era in which Euro-American intellectuals lament the "lasting eclipse" of politics (Agamben 1998:4), and anti-globalization cadres find it hard to confront their rapidly mutating, elusively deterritorialized opponents, AIDS campaigners in Brazil, South Africa, and India have developed innovative repertoires of popular insurgency. Recuperating anticolonial idioms of mass struggle, they infuse them with a fresh understanding of the uses of the courts, media, and the agitprop arts, the better to come to grips with complex configurations of power within and beyond the state (cf. Farmer 2003; Robins 2008). Joao Biehl (2004:111) claims that, in Brazil, medical professionals and activists have been adept at fashioning strategies aimed at maximizing equity within a liberalizing nation-state. Their initiative, he argues, has become one of the most viable sites for recrafting a vision of democratic politics and ethics. As we shall see, there are grounds on which to question some of the claims made for a politics of health citizenship: to ask whether the terms in which it frames its biopolitical goals buy into "magic bullet" treatments and perpetuate "neoliberal governmentality" (see Biehl 2007:84; Kistner n.d.). But it is also undeniable that medical advocacy in the south has proven vexing to states seeking to reconcile the privatization of public services with constitutional empowerment, particularly where governments are battling to assert sovereignty against the force of global markets, corporations, and organizations.

This has been very obvious in the heated battle in South Africa between AIDS activists and the African National Congress regime. The movement in support of a constitutional right to anti-retrovirals (ARVs)—centered on an alliance between the Treatment Action Campaign and *Médicins Sans Frontières*[11]—has been uniquely capable of exploiting the kind of public-private, local-translocal collaborations that characterize government in the neoliberal age. In its attempt to link its biopolitical demands to the more capacious terms of enfranchisement written into the Freedom Charter of 1955 (see Chapter 7, n.7), TAC has adopted the songs and commemorative calendar of the anti-apartheid struggle (Robins 2004:667).[12] Yet it also has a thoroughly 21st-century appreciation of the sites and vehicles of extra-institutional, transnational politics: of the fact that corporate interest, no less than humanitarian empathy and guilt, can be mobilized to its cause—in large part, by playing on the productivity of media images.[13] In addition, AIDS activists evince a shrewd understanding of the degree to which politics itself has migrated to the domain of the law (see Chapter 7); thus their defiant "smuggling" of cheap generic drugs into a country that refused to provide them and their boldness in suing the government over its legal obligation to make ARVs available to all. As this suggests, the movement fully embraces a politics of shame and passion. *Pace* Nancy, it deploys the rhetoric of sacrifice, even martyrdom, epitomized in the compelling figure of its "positive" leader, Zackie Achmat. In an unfolding drama broadcast across the nation, an ailing Achmat refused to take ARVs—entreaties by the likes of Nelson Mandela notwithstanding—until the government, in 2003, undertook to provide them for all in need.

These techniques of mobilization have their own limitations, of course. As a result, AIDS activists in South Africa and elsewhere have suffered many reverses. Still, their tactical creativity underlines the ever greater salience of health in the reciprocal engagement of rulers and subjects across the world. But why has the biomedical definition of life become so central a site of contestation where other kinds of populist politics—the politics of labor movements, for instance—appear to be eroding? Why is it that citizenship, equity, and justice have come to be epitomized in so many places by access to medicine rather than by, say, the right to a job, clean air, personal safety, or freedom from war (cf. Petryna 2002; Biehl 2004)?[14] How might this fact shed light on contemporary theory about the shape of late modern politics, be it focused on the impact of liberalization, the state of exception, or the labile intersection of governmentality with sovereignty?

## LIFE AND NOTHING BUT?: *HOMO SACER*
## AND THE POLITICS OF SALVATION

It has become commonplace to reflect on the rising centrality of biopolitics. Hannah Arendt (1958:320–21) long ago identified a preoccupation, in the modern world, with what she termed the "immortality" of "life itself." This fixation, she argued, was the consequence of a growing sense of individual mortality, which had led to a compensatory concern with the "everlasting process of the species mankind." Foucault (1978), famously, linked the preoccupation with life to the birth of modernist politics. Almost as famously, Agamben (1998:6) takes this a critical step further. The *"production of a biopolitical body,"* he argues, *"is the original activity of sovereign power"* (original emphasis). Nor is this unique to our age: the secret of modern and archaic power alike is its capacity to control "bare life" by excluding it from a meaningful social existence. Bare life is thus paradoxically made part of "the political" by the very fact of its exclusion.

But what is distinctive about modern politics, for Agamben, is that it "knows no value ... *other* than life" (p.10; emphasis added). Bare life is simultaneously its object *and* its subject: the object of state enforcement, the subject of struggles for democratic emancipation. As exception becomes the rule, a contradictory process manifests itself. A predisposition to human liberation and a tendency toward state fascism collapse into each other, rooting themselves in the same ground: in the "new biopolitical body of humanity" (p.9). This con/fusion drives the political history of Euro-America, culminating in a polis in which an unprecedented capacity and concern to enhance life is rivaled only by the capacity to destroy it. As is well known, Agamben personifies this predicament in the enigmatic figure of *homo sacer,* one who can be "killed, but not sacrificed." We are returned here to Nancy's view that, in these times, mortality is no longer sacramental—although Agamben is less concerned with the existential meaninglessness of modern existence than with the fact that it is at once sacred, and scandalously dispensable.

More than one contemporary observer has seen the apotheosis of *homo sacer* in the HIV/AIDS sufferer of the global south: a scarcely human being who is excluded in an age of humanitarian empathy, untreated in an era of pharmacological salvation, left to die without significance or sacrificial value (Biehl 2001; Kistner 2003). If, in Agamben's (1998:84) words, "all men are potentially *homines sacri*" in relation to sovereign power, the immiserated AIDS sufferer would indeed appear to be the everyman of our time. There, but for the accident of geography, go we all ... And yet, as we have seen, the moral politics of AIDS belies these observations. It insists on making death sacrificial once more.

In the world after 9/11—in which crisis and exception have become routine, in which the classical Weberian view of state sovereignty seems less and less credible—Agamben's passionate provocations have proven compelling. He has been credited, among other things, with "repoliticizing" Foucault (Kistner 2003:152) and with moving political philosophy beyond "mere" metaphysics (Hansen and Stepputat 2005:16). It is largely for these reasons that his perspective has appealed to many who grapple with the political valence of HIV/AIDS. For Joao Biehl (2001:140), the destitute communities of undocumented, infected persons that have arisen in Brazil with the so-called Africanization of AIDS there are zones of abandonment, zones populated by *homines sacri* who belong to neither the living nor the dead. Even as activists, NGOs, and the state collaborate to provide medication on a national scale, new lines of exclusion spring up to separate those worthy of salvation from those condemned to death camps. Biotechnology, in that context, thrives alongside structural violence. Jeffrey Kahn's (n.d.) account of the detention of HIV-positive Haitian refugees at Guantanamo Bay in the 1990s makes a similar claim. Held by the US Immigration and Nationalization Service without access to legal counsel, this population offers unnerving evidence of the ways in which early AIDS policy foreshadowed the politics of terror. For Kahn, this is a prime example of Agamben's model of sovereignty: the power to banish and to disregard the law. Ulrike Kistner (2003:135f) argues that this same conception of sovereignty makes sense of the notorious South African "AIDS war," enabling scholars to move beyond moral condemnation to more reasoned historical-critical analysis. The Mbeki government stance on the disease was less "eccentric," she suggests, than evidence of a shift in the generic nature of power. At issue was a "new role [for] the State in the arena of health and medicine," one that returned to a classic notion of sovereignty as control over life and death (p.3).

In each of these three instances, Agamben's allegory—the act of sovereign exception, the purgatory of *homo sacer*—is used to show how modern government stages itself by dealing directly in the power over life: the power to exclude, to suspend the law, to strip human existence of civic rights and social value. Agamben's historico-philosophical argument is propelled by a number of forceful images. Chief among these is the camp, understood less as historical fact than as a paradigm, the "hidden matrix" against which normal, healthy political subjects everywhere have come to be defined (Agamben 1998:166).

But the very appeal of this mode of argumentation raises theoretical issues. For one thing, it moves by way of a very limited set of archetypes and metaphors—the ban as originary political act, the production of bare life as the threshold from nature to culture, the camp as hidden matrix—to which all modern politics is reduced. For another, it hovers ambiguously between metaphysics and history. While this species of ambiguity can be highly suggestive, it can also, when applied literally to circumstances in the world, lead to oversimplification and category confusion. In respect of contemporary Africa, for example, it blurs precisely what demands to be specified in the quest to plumb the shifting political salience of AIDS. What is more, it is unclear what kind of historical justification Agamben might offer for his contention that naked life, life shorn of civic and political rights, has become the *sole* preoccupation of modern sovereignty; unclear, especially, in comparison with the views of Arendt (1958), who links the mounting obsession with "life itself" to the decline of *homo faber*, the civic-minded worker, turned inward by the privatizing thrust of capitalism. If, for Agamben, a fixation on biopolitics is the defining feature of modernity *sui generis*, how are we to account for the *late* modern struggles currently under way over the definition of life itself, over the ways that it is mediated, interpreted, abstracted, patented? These struggles are critical to an understanding of the power-play that surrounds AIDS in Africa and elsewhere, power linked to the rise of the life sciences, among other things, whose engagement with biotechnology and capital have had a significant impact on the characterization of human existence and the control of its value—and hence, on the shape of biopolitics. Just how useful, in confronting these issues, is the concept of bare life, spoken of in terms of pure subjection and gross biological being, meaningful only as a sign of sovereignty? These questions are critical if we are to take seriously Agamben's own exhortation to engage in a politics that recuperates civic being.

More immediately, they are consequential if we are to make sense of the various ways in which HIV itself has been politicized—and politics biologized. For the stigmatizing rhetoric of the disease, above all that pertaining to so-called African AIDS (Patton 1988), has all too often fed off the slippage between metaphysics and history, archetype and instance. All too often, complicated local histories and sociologies of the disease are obscured by grand, Conradian allegories of exclusion, crisis, apocalypse. While the will to power, or the effect of structural violence, might significantly sever life from civic protection and social value, no act of sovereignty, except perhaps in fantasy, can actually alienate human beings entirely from entailment in webs of relations, meanings, and affect. Darrell Roodt's film *Yesterday*[15] cogently underscores this insight. In it, an HIV-positive woman in rural KwaZulu-Natal, ostracized by her neighbors, builds a scrap-metal hospice in the bush for her husband, who is dying of AIDS. Here, in a zone of exclusion and erasure, bare life asserts a stubborn connection to human existence. In the face of the social death endured by many AIDS sufferers, the will to assert visibility, dignity, kinship, and attachment fuels the task of everyday survival. The insistence on "positive" life—imbued with ordinary, future-oriented expectations—is palpable in the forms of mobilization that press for recognition of the disease. So, too, once again, is the rejection of bare death, of disposability without salience. Exclusion here is less a total exile from the law or from social order than a dis/location between different moments and sites of their inhabitation (cf. Bull 2004:6).[16]

This takes us back, briefly, to the three examples we introduced a moment ago, those that use Agamben's insights to explore historically specific instances of the contemporary politics of HIV/AIDS.

## From Bare Life to Biocapital

While the stories of AIDS sufferers abandoned in Brazil or detained at Guantanamo show how readily late-modern authority may root itself in a sovereign politics of exclusion, focus on this alone yields only a partial account of the dialectics at play here. This on three counts. *First,* sovereignty in the older sense of the term is *also* very much at issue in these cases. As Bull (2004:3) notes, states have hardly ceased trying to maintain a monopoly over the means of coercion. Whatever the degree to which they deal with immiserated subjects by means of exclusion, their use of direct violence in the management of their citizens, *within* the ordinary workings of the law-as-usual, can be at once awesome and all-embracing. This is a point cogently made by Walter Benjamin (1978) and others, a point to which treatment of the poor, the indigent, the ill, the alien, and the outlaw readily attests. *Second,* those stories speak volubly to the impact upon nation-states of neoliberal forces that have undermined their capacity to manage their economies, to control their borders, and to meet the needs of their citizens. As a result, and the Brazilian example makes this plain, social abandonment nowadays may have less to do with the willful exercise by governments of sovereign exclusion or direct violence than with their *in*ability to subject the workings of transnational corporations to their own interests and to those of their populations—thus to secure access to, among other things, the pharmaceutical products that have become the elixir of life itself. In short, exclusion from the means of survival may be due more to the operations of global capital than to the will of sovereign authority. It is noteworthy, in this respect, that, in Latin America, left-leaning regimes have sought to tame the excesses of corporate *laissez-faire* by an "old fashioned" return to state regulation (Lomnitz 2006). And *third,* evidence from around the world suggests that prolonged periods of emergency in the exercise of sovereign control often spawn political and legal counter-practices that work the aporias between exception and the norms made palpable by their very suspension (see Agrama 2005 on Egypt, for instance); *vide,* for example, the forms of insurgent lawfare that we encountered in Chapter 7. The conclusion? That neither in Brazil nor in Haiti are the politics that emerged in the wake of abandonment and exclusion adequately captured by Agamben's conception of sovereignty. Save at the level of metaphor.

However we wish to explain the abandonment of impoverished AIDS populations, especially in the global south, their exclusion, as we have seen, is producing new political subjects and sources of mobilization: a fight for access to the means of survival that arises out of opportunities to forge identities around a "politicized biology" (Biehl 2004:122). While it is arguable that the latter, a politicized biology, emerges from *within* the field of biopower, it *does* nonetheless seek to give voice to tensions within that field—and to contest many of its truth effects. If life itself has become the prime medium for the exercise of governmentality, it is also the stuff of political striving; hence the various kinds of activism that have sprung up around the world to deal with HIV/AIDS, activism that aims to make intelligible and reversible the impact of exclusion on afflicted bodies, blighted lives.

This species of counter-politics, then, may indeed be a product of govern-mentality: of the process, that is, by which the means and ends of organized power diffuse, without any apparent unity or telos, throughout a body politic. And it may also be a corollary of the forms of rogue sovereignty, of lawless, "prerogatory" power that, according to Judith Butler (2004:56), are increas-ingly part of the contemporary world. But it also makes clear that the structural dynamics at play in north-south relations demand a more nuanced analytic apparatus than is afforded by terms like "sovereignty" and "governmentality" alone. The rhetoric of grassroots activism, for instance, presumes that forces of large scale, of extraction and ideology and value accumulation, shape local worlds, often in ambiguous, obscure ways. Identifying and disambiguating those forces—translating them into the language of exploitation, accountabil-ity, human rights, democratic process, and the like—is the primary work of counter-politics. Claims to entitlement based on suffering are central here; they speak of injury, abjection, and disposability. But AIDS organizers also aspire to build a more capacious politics, an ethics of social justice based on critical analyses of material inequality, of the social mechanisms that configure their world, of the means by which capital exerts control over life and death—and of the constellation of actors who personify those means, mechanisms, and materialities. Just how this politics of personification occurs was brilliantly exemplified in a drama staged outside the high court in Pretoria in April 2001, during the hearing of a case brought by thirty-nine drug companies against the South African government for breaching international trade rules against importing generic drugs. Crystallizing a campaign that fired international opinion and a global web of support, activists donned large, life-like card-board masks of the CEOs of several of the pharmas involved, each identified by name and corporate logo.[17] As these eerie, grinning visages were broadcast across world, the companies, belatedly realizing the damage being done to their image, halted the case (Figure 2).

Social justice pursued by these means is not easily achieved, of course. A political practice that might connect an older conception of social movements to the romance of a defiant "multitude" seems as inchoate to would-be activists as it is to those who seek to study them. What has recently been termed a "politics of citizenship" remains tethered to some degree to a liberal model of subject and social contract (Robins 2008). And, while movements like the Treatment Action Campaign have been able to use it to win significant collective rights, their victories have not been unequivocal. TAC, for one, has been accused—despite its affinities with a legacy of mass action—of individualizing AIDS and of failing to deal adequately with its "socio-politico-economic" roots and implications (Decoteau n.d.:15). But, like others striving to define a commons amidst the "debris of empire" (Chari n.d.), AIDS organizers build with what comes to hand, seeking to forge alliances and to experiment with cocktails of techniques, the better

*The Guardian* (London), 19 April 2001. Photo by Juda Ngwenya/Reuters.

to engage the shifting assemblage of national and transnational forces that control access to the means of life.

As this suggests, a crucial feature of AIDS activism in the global south is that it focuses overtly on biocapital (Rajan 2005:21): on the knowledge, patents, commodities, and systems of transaction that make the difference between life and death. For healing is increasingly vested not merely in corporate bioscience, but in the drug as *ur*-commodity, liberated from regulation, even on the part of the medical and caring professions. This returns us to the issues with which we began: the manner in which subjectivity, sexuality, pathology, and citizenship are inflected more and more tightly by the logic of the commodity in both its productive and dystopic forms. Drugs have come to embody the means of life itself: the means to control body and mind and subject them to the terms of the market. Pharmaceutical companies now aim to sell their products directly to the consumer ("Ask your doctor about Lipitor ..."). We are *all* interpolated incessantly as proto-patients. No wonder that access to medicaments is the most contentious issue surrounding the World Trade Organization. Or that ARVs have become the sacrament through which born-again AIDS sufferers enter into cults of salvation. The hold of biotechnology, and the pharma-industrial-complex, over life itself makes it a consequential force in the operation of sovereignty in our day and age. This is very clear in the plain-speak of African AIDS politics. The UN special envoy for HIV/AIDS to the continent reported in 2005, for example, that, while the use of triple-dose therapy in the north had cut the numbers of children with HIV practically to zero, in Africa, only 10 percent of pregnant, infected women had access to the drugs needed to prevent mother-to-child transmission. Furthermore, there were still no adequate, dedicated pediatric ARVs on the market. The prevention of infant pain and death, he added, seemed insufficient incentive to pharmaceutical companies in a world in which some "children are ... consigned to the coffins of history."[18]

It would appear that no account of biopolitics in the modern world, no notion of bare life, can neglect this imploding history of biocapital. It is integral to the ways in which the substance of human existence—blood, organs, drugs, patents, and the distribution of essential resources—are objectified, regulated, struggled over. AIDS activists know well that, if there *is* to be a redemptive politics of life, one that reconnects *homo sacer* to civic entitlement and ethical being, it must find innovative ways of contesting the monopolies that determine access to the essence of survival; hence the targeting of patents, intellectual property rights, and the bald rhetoric that equates life with profit. As conventional politics falters in the face of elusive collaborations of wealth, power, and the law, AIDS activism has sought to exploit the incoherence inherent in the neoliberal order, finding productive footholds within the aporias of the market system. While this has hardly forced a capitulation on the part of governments or corporations, it *has* won some significant concessions.

This returns us to our third example, Kistner's account of the politics of life at stake in the South African "AIDS war." The notorious conflict over the disease that was waged between government—above all, former President Thabo Mbeki—and the national AIDS movement would seem to exemplify biopolitics at its most literal. Here, Kistner (2003:153) suggests, the effort to assert sovereignty entered directly into the dispensation of life and death. Biomedical discourse became a critical affair of state. Nor just of the state, also the nation. President Mbeki refused to accept definitions of HIV/AIDS that portrayed it as a sexually transmitted disease: he argued that they perpetuated both Western racist stereotypes and the Euro-American propensity to use African bodies for experimentation and profit (Hoad 2005:104). AIDS, for him, marked the impact on African immune systems of an enduring legacy of imperialism. From this perspective, remedies ought to lie less in costly or haz-ardous drugs, which prolong neocolonial dependency, than in the reversal of inequality; although it should be noted that, during the Mbeki administration, the ANC did support experimentation with anti-AIDS drugs—the notorious Virodene being an example—and has subsequently fostered a pharmaceuti-cal industry to follow India and Thailand in manufacturing cheap generics.

How useful is it, then, to see in this fractious history, as Kistner (2003:152) does, "a new regime of biopolitics" that draws directly on the control of bare life, a regime whose sovereignty relies more on medical defi-nitions than on the racial classification of governments past? Here again, we would caution against too monolithic a conception of politics, too reified a conception of bare life, too shortsighted a view of the present. Colonial regimes also ruled by putting the lives of their subjects on the line: by sepa-rating them from political being and the means of survival—from economic viability, health care, civic rights—thereby striving to reduce them to a naked biological existence under the sign of physical difference. But there, too, life could never be fully severed from social and civic entailment at the behest of sovereign power. What is more, the colonized suffered as much from the exquisite exercise of the law as by its suspension.

We would argue that, while his regime was admirably postcolonial in many respects, Thabo Mbeki's stance on AIDS spoke less to a new mode of sovereignty than to the continuing impact of colonial ideologies that have tied life, even at its most bioscientific, to racialized sexuality. AIDS dissidents rejected the coital transmission of the disease because they saw it as an ac-cusation of black promiscuity. They remained doubtful that Euro-American biological definitions could *ever* free themselves from stigmatizing deter-minations, that hegemonic science could *ever* escape imperial associations of perversion with race. This is why their rhetoric sounded uncomfortably similar to the writings of some colonial discourse theorists—on whom they drew. Those who opposed their views argued cogently for the possibilities of relatively independent scientific knowledge; as we have noted, the Treatment Action Campaign has sought to purify AIDS talk from the ravages of metaphor. But, while activist politics advocate the uses of a non-sexist, non-racist science, it also struggles against entrapment in a reductionist biology. Above all, it seeks to reconnect bioscience to a critical, redemptive sociology, dedicating itself to mass education about the social etiology of the disease, about drugs and the political economy of their global distribution, about the constitutional entitlement of ordinary citizens to health. In short, to a politics that links a not-so-bare conception of life to a more robust practice of citizenship (Robins 2005).

## Conclusion

The singular productivity of AIDS, then, flows from its status as both a sign and a consequence of late modernity: of the promise and risks of bold new freedoms, of the unruly conflation of love and death, of life and capital, of longevity and species annihilation. In other words, of the ever more intense, intensive interplay of creation and destruction. To return to Agamben, AIDS epitomizes the paradoxical coexistence of inclusion and exclusion, human emancipation and inhuman neglect. But what it also makes jarringly visible is that these conundrums are caught up in an ongoing dialectic of history and power, capital and geopolitics. Thus the disease, like Hurricane Katrina or the burning *banlieues* of Paris (see Chapter 1), also lays bare colonial frontiers etched across the ostensibly integrated landscape of our Brave Neo World. In the north, as among the more-than-equal everywhere, AIDS may have been brought to heel. It has slipped behind what John Pilger calls the "one-way moral mirror" separating the secure from the indigent.[19] The AIDS activism we have described seeks to shatter that mirror, to break into our self-insulating, self-referential circuits of concern and communication. In the process, it reminds us of something that, in Euro-America, has been all but forgotten: a disarmingly unalienated sense of politics as a positive calling.

# Editorial Note

With the exception of Chapters 1 and 6, the essays in this volume have all been published elsewhere—in part, in whole, or in different versions. Chapter 2 was written in 1997 for a conference at the University of Heidelberg on "The Autonomous Person—A European Invention?" It appeared in *Social Identities* 7:267–83 (2001) and, in German translation, in *Die autonome Person—Eine europäische Erfindung,* edited by K. Koepping, M. Welker, and R. Wiehl (Heidelberg: Wilhem Fink Verlag, 2002). Chapter 3 began its life as one of our Jensen Lectures at the Johann Wolfgang Goethe University, Frankfurt, in 2001; it first came out, under the title "Reflections on Liberalism, Policulturalism, and ID-ology: Citizenship and Difference in South Africa," in *Social Identities* 9:445–74 (2003). Chapter 4 reworks substantially material originally included in "Naturing the Nation: Aliens, Apocalypse and the Postcolonial State" in *Hagar: International Social Science Review* 1:7–40 (2000).

Chapters 5 through 8 were first presented as lectures. Chapter 5 was given by John Comaroff as the 1996 *Journal of Anthropological Research* Distinguished Lecture; it came out in that journal the following year (53:123–46) under the title "Postcolonial Politics and Discourses of Democracy: An Anthropological Perspective on African Political Modernities." Chapter 6 was delivered as a keynote address by Jean Comaroff to the International Conference on History and Memory, held at the Indian Institute of Advanced Study in Shimla in May 2010. Both of these essays have been heavily revised for present purposes. Less so the final chapters, which are published here with relatively minor alteration. An earlier rendering of Chapter 7, prepared for a meeting in Senegal in 1998, is to be found in the *Codesria Bulletin* 3–4:17–28 (1999). Chapter 8, first presented by Jean Comaroff to a symposium on AIDS and the Moral Order at the Freie Universität Berlin in 2005, appeared in *Public Culture* 19:197–219 (2007).

# Notes

## CHAPTER I

1. For just one effort to bring together "social theory from the world periphery"—albeit with a rather different emphasis from our own—see Raewyn Connell's *Southern Theory* (2007); we are indebted to Lauren Coyle, a doctoral student at the University of Chicago, for drawing our attention to this volume. In recent years there has also been intermittent discussion of what Krotz (2005:147) refers to as "new 'anthropologies of the South.'"

2. Similar arguments were to be made later by Afrocentric scholars in the US, most notably, perhaps, by Bernal in *Black Athena* (1987–2006), a study that evoked a storm of criticism; see, e.g., Lefkowitz and Rogers (1996).

3. As Fernando Coronil (2004:223) notes, a tradition of leftist writings in the 1960s, later subsumed into dependency theory, produced a "formidable body of work ... designed to understand Latin America's distinct historical trajectory ... auguring ... the postcolonial critique of contemporary imperialism."

4. The term—"constitutive outside"—has been deployed in broadly similar ways by others, among them Laclau (1990:84, 17 after Derrida). However, Butler's use of it to describe "exclusions that are nevertheless internal to [a] system as its own nonthematized necessity" is closest to what we intend here.

5. We learned of DeLay's statement from Darian-Smith (2010). She quotes it from "The Real Scandal of Tom DeLay," Mark Shields, CNN.com, 9 May 2005; www.cnn.com/2005/POLITICS/05/09/real.delay. The original article in the *Washington Post,* "A 'Petri Dish' in the Pacific: Conservative Network Aligned with DeLay Makes Marianas a Profitable Cause," Juliet Eilperin, 26 July 2000, has been reprinted many times; we read it at www.freedomworks.org/news/a-petri-dish-in-the-pacific-conservative-network-a-0, accessed 6 July 2010. The article details how conservative activists and lobbyists went about making the fourteen islands, formally the Commonwealth of the Northern Mariana Islands (CNMI), into a living experiment in free-market economics.

6. Note, in this respect, the existence of an Institute of Comparative Modernities at Cornell University (www.icm.arts.cornell.edu), one of whose objectives is to study "conflicts and complexities within the West."

7. R.V. Selope Thema, "The Test of Bantu Leadership," *Umteteli wa Bantu,* 26 November 1926.

8. We, among many others, have used "alternative" in the past to describe African modernities, although we have usually intended it as a synonym for "vernacular." In retrospect, it would have been better to use the latter term rather than the former—even though, in some contexts, "alternative" *does* describe the intention behind self-conscious African efforts to carve out an indigenous modernity in explicit contrast to its European counterparts.

9. As Duara (2007:293–4) points out in an insightful review, it is as if Cooper "has had it with theorists discouraging historians from getting on with the job of discovering facts." He also criticizes Cooper for setting up straw men: few historians, says Duara, actually write about modernity in the generalized manner he suggests.

10. And to deconstruct the opposition between the universal and the particular. *Pace* Taylor (2010:280–81)—who rather caricatures the literature on the subject—the idea of "multiple or plural modernities" emerged specifically to implode that opposition; this by provincializing, and relativizing, the Western conceit of universalism *tout court*. Taylor seems also to miss another crucial point: the analytic appeal to "alternative modernities," whatever its shortcomings, does *not*, as he claims, tacitly support the idea that Western modernity is "the generic form against which all other versions become weighed as lesser approximations" (p.281). Quite the contrary.

11. Stoler and Cooper (1997:32), in discussing the impact of colonialism, say explicitly that colonized men and women "could be 'modern' in a variety of ways."

12. There are ironic echoes here of Evans-Pritchard's (1956:63) classic argument with Western scholars of religion who would not credit that, for the Nuer of the Southern Sudan, God (*Kwoth*) could be simultaneously one thing and many, that this did not imply conceptual incoherence or an instance of "primitive mentality."

13. There is a large, fast-growing critical literature on these aspects of the "new" age of capital, beginning, perhaps, with Mandel (1978) and Harvey (1982, cf. also 1989); since that literature is not directly salient to our present concerns, we make no effort here to address it.

14. These accounts do not come from marginal scholars: Wilkinson and Pickett are, respectively, a professor emeritus at the University of Nottingham (and an honorary professor at University College London) and a professor at the University of York; Jackson's volume is based on a report he wrote as Economics Commissioner of the Sustainable Development Commission, the UK government's independent watchdog. For commentary on the two accounts from an African perspective, see "A Bridge Across the Wealth Gap," Richard Calland, *Mail & Guardian,* 21–27 May 2010, p.32.

15. The rise of populist political leaders in Latin America and Africa, leaders who cast themselves against global neoliberalism, is an expression of this. In South Africa, critiques of market fundamentalism have been the stuff of everyday mass media discourse since the 1990s; see, e.g., Bond (1997).

16. This is documented in a recent report by the McKinsey Global Institute; see Roxburgh *et al.* (2010).

17. The World Bank reported that FDI in Africa yielded the highest returns in the world in 2002; see "Africa 'Best for Investment,'" www.globalpolicy.org/socecon/develop/africa/2003/0408fdi.htm, accessed 1 May 2005. This raises unnerving parallels with earlier moments of colonial extraction. The pattern has continued. Guo (2010:42), citing the IMF, notes that "in 2007 and 2008, southern Africa, the Great Lakes region of Kenya, Tanzania, and Uganda, and even the drought-stricken Horn of Africa had GDP growth rates on par with Asia's two powerhouses. Last year, in the depths of global recession, the continent clocked almost 2 percent growth, roughly equal to the rates in the Middle East, and outperforming everywhere else but India and China." In the same vein, Tostevin (2010:8) points out that $1,000 invested in the Nigerian or Kenyan stock markets at the start of 2010 would have yielded approximately $150 by mid-year; the same investment in US shares from the S&P 500 index would have lost money.

18. Seabrook here cites James Dyson, who—in an influential report written in 2010 for the British Conservative Party on the revival of the UK economy—not only uses the term "re-balancing" (Dyson 2010:70), but makes it the basis of his plan for a healthier economic future, one much less reliant on finance capital.

19. On Sweden, see Henning Mankell, one of that country's most celebrated crime novelists, quoted in "Brightening Thrillers with a Gloomy Swedish Detective," Sarah Lyall, *New York Times,* 13 November 2003, pp.B1, 5; on Scotland, see Ian Rankin's *The Complaints* (2009), which ends with one of the older characters lamenting " … Scotland's in meltdown, and for all I know the rest of the world's about to follow …" (p.381).

20. Cf. Simon Watney (1990) in his powerful analysis of AIDS, race, and Africa; see also Chapter 8.

21. A historical precursor of this form of "production" is described by Luise White (1990) for colonial Kenya.

22. For a thoughtful analysis of new forms of counter-politics in Latin America, see Lomnitz (2006).

23. This aphorism is cited in any number of collections of quotable phrases. We were struck by its relevance to our discussion here when we came across it in an insightful essay by Adam Gopnik (2008:52) on the "troubling genius of G.K. Chesterton."

24. Nancy Banks-Smith, on the anthropological series "Face Values," *Guardian,* 21 July 1988.

25. "The Pivotal Presidency," Andrew Sullivan, Daily Dish, *The Atlantic,* 30 December 2009; http://andrewsullivan.theatlantic.com/the_daily_dish/2009/12/the-pivotal-presidency.html, accessed 20 January 2010.

26. "Leviathan Inc.," Leader, *Economist,* 7 August 2010, pp.9–10.

27. See "Father and Sons: For Ralph Miliband Government Could Never Tame Capitalism," John Gray, Review, *Saturday Guardian,* 4 September 2010, p.20. Gray echoes the point, made earlier in the paragraph, that the crisis of 2008 has had a major negative effect on growth in the "developed" economies of the north.

28. At the time of writing, the US Congress was engaged in a battle over a reform bill whose objective was to limit—under the so-called Volcker Rule—the extent to which commercial banks might indulge in high-risk speculation, thus to distinguish their operations from those of investment houses. However, this legislation, a political minefield despite being a relatively minor form of regulation, had run into difficulties. Even if it does eventually pass, it would not curb the more aggressive gambling practices of the finance industry at large; see, e.g., Cassidy (2010).

29. Already in 2008, a survey by the FAO reported that a billion people would go seriously hungry in 2009 despite "bumper harvests," primarily because of rising food costs caused largely by profiteering. See "1 000 000 000 People: That Is How Many Will Go Hungry in 2009," Geoffrey Lean, *Sunday Independent* (South Africa), 4 January 2009, p.15. This account, first printed in the *Independent* (UK), was widely syndicated. For FAO publications on the world food situation, see www.fao.org/worldfoodsituation/en. The latest warning of an impending global crisis came at an FAO meeting in August 2010; see, e.g., "New Food Crisis Looming," John Vidal and Agencies, *Guardian Weekly,* 1 October 2010, p.6.

30. Contrary to Michael Hardt, who envisions a new "commons" rising with the death of neoliberalism—which he takes to be a "walking zombie"—we find little evidence to support this proposition. Moreover, in the spirit of Mark Twain, we regard pronouncements of this particular death somewhat premature. See "The Commons in Communism," Michael Hardt, Lecture to the European Graduate School, 2 September 2009; www.youtube.com/watch?v=FqtW_elBbLo, accessed 5 March 2010.

31. *Vide* the much heralded Khulumani Support Group suit on behalf of victims of apartheid against corporations that allegedly conspired in violence perpetrated by the nationalist party government in South Africa prior to 1994. We discuss the case, heard in the New York courts, in Chapter 6, specifically with respect to the claim on the part of then President Thabo Mbeki that it constituted a violation of national sovereignty.

32. For Przeworski (1991), the minimalist conception of democracy had, as its essential criterion, the requirement that elections be held in which ruling parties might lose, thus permitting the transfer of power. Practically speaking, however, the version of democracy exported to the south from the late 1980s onward seems to have been less concerned with the transfer of power than with producing congenial regimes; its dominant demand was "free and fair elections," although the standards by which these things were judged tended also to be tempered by outcomes, acceptable ends sometimes justifying highly dubious means.

33. This number comes from *World Fact Book,* 14 July 2005; www.odci.gov/cia/publications/factbook/fields/2063.html, last accessed 27 July 2005.

34. Shechtel's (2010) study, which summarizes findings from the widely respected *Afrobarometer,* is both confused and confusing; apart from all else, its empirical data contradict narrative statements made in the body of the article. Nonetheless, those data show clearly that elections rank low in the democratic desiderata of the Africans surveyed; government performance, embodied especially in that of national leaders, comes first (p.53). They also suggest that delivery is taken here to be integral to democracy, especially the delivery of economic goods—*pace* those political scientists

who argue that what Africans want, above all else, is "political goods" (e.g., Bratton, Mattes, and Gyimah-Boadi 2005).

35. "Poetry Gets Political Again," Gordon James, *Guardian* (UK), *Society Guardian,* 1 September 2010, p.2.

36. In some places, victims have gone so far as to sue the state for failing to protect them against violence, another way in which the criminal is folded into the civil law. We are grateful to Dennis Davis, Judge President of the Competition Court in South Africa, for pointing this out to us (personal communication, 11 February 2010).

37. "Truth Commissions," Eric Brahm, *Beyond Intractability,* June 2004; www .beyondintractibility.org/essay/truth_commissions, accessed 3 September 2010.

38. "Previous Pope Apologies," *News24.com,* 18 September 2006; www.news24 .com/world/News/Previous-pope-apologies-20060917, accessed 7 September 2010.

39. "Television and the Trouble With History," Simon Schama, Inside Story, *Guardian,* 18 June 2002, pp.6–7.

40. "History Is Everywhere—But Whose History Is It?" Yasmin Alibhai-Brown, Editorial and Opinion, *Independent,* 22 July 2002, p.13.

41. "Teachers Drop the Holocaust to Avoid Offending Muslims," Laura Clark, 2 April 2007, *Mail Online;* www.dailymail.co.uk/news/article-445979/Teachers-drop -Holocaust-avoid-offending-Muslims.html#ixzz0hUwG0FFM, accessed 6 March 2010.

42. See Organization of American Historians (2004) and "The 'Loss of History' in Schools is a 21st Century Crisis," Nancy McTygue, *Dateline UC Davis,* 2 March 2007; http://dateline.ucdavis.edu/dl_detail.lasso?id=9334, accessed 2 February 2008.

43. This was written not by a critic of neoliberalism—or by George Stiglitz, whom we quoted earlier to similar effect—but by a reporter syndicated on FoxNews. See "Special Report," Charles Krauthammer, Panel on the Economy and McCain's Foreign Policy Speech, FoxNews, 27 March 2008; www.foxnews.com/story/0,2933 ,342137,00.html, accessed 10 March 2009.

44. We discuss Miracle 2000 in Comaroff and Comaroff (2003). There and elsewhere (e.g., 1999a, 2000a) we give further examples of similar schemes. On the rise and fall of Bernard Madoff, see, e.g., Kirtzman (2009).

45. "Zombie Bank" was among the words of the year listed by the Oxford English Dictionary in 2009. See "'Tweetups,' 'Unfriend' New Words in Oxford Dictionary," *Newsx on Facebook;* http://newsx.com/story/69529, accessed 20 January 2010.

46. "Zombie Banks Feed Off Bailout Money," Chris Arnold, National Public Radio, 11 March 2009; www.npr.org/templates/ story/story.php?storyId=100762999# commentBlock, accessed 11 March 2009; "How Zombie Debt Works," Sarah Siddons, WelcomeBackVeterans.org; http://money.howstuffworks.com/personal -finance/debt-management/zombie-debt3.htm, accessed 12 March 2009; "With-Profits Ravaged by Zombie Funds," Sylvia Morris, *Money Mail,* 28 May 2008; www .thisismoney.co.uk/mortgages/endowments/article.html?in_article_id=442203&in_ page_id=55, accessed 12 March 2009.

47. "In the Shadow of the Zombie Hotels," Henry McDonald and Julia Kollewe, *Guardian,* 6 September 2010, p.23.

48. "Human Face Masks Same Old Barbarism," Slavoj Žižek, *Guardian Weekly,* 8 October 2010, p.19.

49. See "Financing Equity: The Campaign for a Basic Income Grant," *Policy Innovations for a Fairer Globalization,* Carnegie Council, 8 July 2005; www .policyinnovations.org/ideas/briefings/data/000015, accessed 7 October 2010.

50. See *Media Statement on the Development of a Humanities and Social Sciences Charter,* Ministry of Higher Education and Training, Republic of South Africa, 6 October 2010; www.education.gov.za/dynamic/dynamic.aspx?pageid=310&id=10648, accessed 7 October 2010. The words from the statement quoted here are those of the Minister of Higher Education and Training, Blade Nzimande.

51. It is ironic that "bloc" should have been used for the international alliances composed of the major powers and their satellites during the Cold War, alliances that cast their differences in deeply ideological terms. Bloc, or "historical bloc," was the concept deployed by Gramsci (1988, Part 2, VI, 4), after Sorel, to describe the union of social forces that underpins general consent—across vertical lines of difference—to a social order, thus to assure the hegemony of its ruling classes and their ideology. The two usages have an interestingly orthogonal overlap, while being obviously quite distinct.

52. This phrase—among other things, the title of a well-known book (Bell 1960)—itself has a long genealogy. It continues to be invoked, although not always to denote precisely the same phenomena, or for the same reasons.

53. We have been struck by the frequency with which we have heard this phrase in Europe and the USA since early 2010. For a particularly acute reflection on the "grim New Normal" in the European media—it is where our addition of the adjective "grim" comes from—see "If It's a Recovery, Why Does It Feel So Bad?" Michael Powell and Motoko Rich, *International Herald Tribune,* 13 October 2010, pp.1, 15.

54. It will be clear from this formulation that we intend something quite different from the pure inductivism essayed—famously and controversially—as "grounded theory" by Glaser and Strauss (1967).

## CHAPTER 2

1. We are hardly the first to ask this question. See, for just one example, Burridge (1979:4). The individual, he says, lies "at the center of our civilization ... [Is] the development of [this figure] a universal in human experience, or is it in some sense culturally specific?"

2. Also one with a complex history, as Mauss ([1938] 1985) classically pointed out (cf. also MacFarlane 1978). Mauss, whose own characterization of the development of personhood was distinctly evolutionary, took pains to point out that "other societies have held very different notions of the self, and [that] each society's notion is intimately connected with its form of social organization" (Carrithers, Collins, and Lukes 1985:vii); echoes here, too, of Durkheim, for whom the modern person is a "product of specific social factors" (Collins 1985:63).

3. Similarly, for example, Melanesian notions of personhood, as Konrad (1998:645) has recently reminded us, citing the seminal work of Strathern (1998)

and Wagner (1991) among others. For a rather different, older account, however, see Read (1955)—and, on the contrast between Melanesia and India, Busby (1997).

4. On the ethnogenesis of the Southern Tswana peoples during the early colonial period, see Comaroff and Comaroff (1997:387–95; 1991:306–08); also, more generally, on the concept of ethnogenesis, see J.L. Comaroff (1987).

5. The person, in short, was irreducible to an autonomous *individual*. A point of definitional clarification is in order here. As La Fontaine (1985:124–26) notes, orthodox anthropological usage has long distinguished the person from both the individual and the self. The individual refers to a biologically distinct, socially discrete, indivisible being, a unity of body and mind; the person, to an ensemble of social roles and relations; the self, to a uniquely subjective identity. In analytic practice, however, this distinction is often blurred; to be sure, it is difficult to sustain—especially in the West, where, given the ideological predominance of individualism (cf. MacFarlane 1978; Dumont 1970), there has long been a tendency to collapse the person into the individual, and both into the self. In late colonial Africa, there is the opposite tendency: to see the individual purely in terms of personhood.

6. The received opposition between ascription and achievement, like many of the great antimonies of modernist social theory, has played a major part in stereotypic (mis)perceptions of African personhood; note, again, the spurious singular. We would argue that nowhere in Africa does a purely ascriptive society exist outside of the imagination of social theorists (cf. J.L. Comaroff 1978).

7. See, classically, Murphy and Kasdan (1959, 1967); also, Barth (1973) and Comaroff and Roberts (1981:31–33). For here, it is enough to note that unions among close kin have the effect of generating relations that are overlapping and inherently ambiguous, relations at once agnatic, matrilateral, and affinal. Among Tswana these forms of connection carried quite different, even inimical, social expectations; they had, therefore, to be reduced to one thing or another in the pragmatic course of everyday life—which, *of necessity,* made them an ongoing object of negotiation (see Comaroff and Comaroff 1981).

8. They form the predominant population of neighboring Botswana as well, but we are concerned here with those Southern Tswana who live in the Northwest Province of South Africa. Due to the unreliability of census data published by the apartheid regime, and to the fact that ethnic identities have long been somewhat malleable in this part of the world, it is impossible to establish the precise number of Tswana in the country. Somewhere in excess of 1.5 million is probably a fair estimate, however.

9. Cf., in this respect, Marks (1978) on Zululand.

10. For an account of the ways in which rules of rank and status were negotiated, see J.L. Comaroff (1978); also, see again n.7 for the effect of endogamous marriage practices on the ambiguity and negotiability of social ties.

11. It is striking how—at least until recently in the history of anthropological thought—marriage featured as *the* atom of society and social formation in all major theoretical traditions. Thus, for example, notwithstanding their differences, structural functionalist and structuralist approaches, in the guise of descent and alliance theory, agreed that marriage rules (especially prohibitions) were fundamental in the construction of non-Western societies; for foundational works, see, e.g., Fortes (1953,

1969) and Lévi-Strauss (1969). Even revisionist Marxist approaches emphasized the significance of marriage and its prestations for structuring relations of production and exploitation in "precapitalist formations" (see, e.g., Meillassoux 1972).

12. Elsewhere (1987) we deal at length with the opposition between *tiro*, self-possessed labor, and *mmèrèkò* (from *bereka* [Afrikaans]), wage work for others, usually whites. The contrast between these two terms—each had a broad fan of referents—was of enormous salience to Southern Tswana in the late colonial years. It underlay the way in which they imagined, and navigated, South African economy and society under apartheid.

13. See Comaroff and Comaroff (1997:153–54) for details. The anthropologist was Z.K. Matthews, one of South Africa's great black scholars and political figures, whose field notes are housed in the Botswana National Archives.

14. Welker outlined his concept of *autoplexy* to us in a letter (Heidelberg, 16 September 1998): "a person's playing and shifting with a multiplicity of ascribed and assumed roles and identity patterns to secure individual freedom and importance, in short: to use this sort of complexity in analogous ways to the use of modern autonomy." Clearly, the concept is intended to elide *autonomy* with *complexity*. We have paraphrased Welker's words here to fit more closely the terms of our own analysis.

## CHAPTER 3

1. The statement, first made in an article written for the African-American Institute, is published in Tutu (1984:121). It has been much quoted. For just two recent examples, see Lijphart (1995:281) and Oomen (2002:3).

2. "Revisit Cultural Values," Zandile Nkutha, Sowetan, 17 November 1999, p.2. Maduna made the statement in an address to a conference on constitutionalism. His audience included leaders of the South African Development Community (SADC).

3. Elsewhere (see, e.g., 1987, 1992, 1993) we have sought to problematize the concept of tradition and, by extension, of "traditional" leadership. We deploy the term here strictly to refer to vernacular usage. "Traditional leadership" has become a generic label in South Africa for all forms of indigenous African rule.

4. See "Ideology Is Dead, Long Live ID-ology," Rapule Tabane and Ferial Haffajee, *Mail & Guardian*, 27 June–3 July 2003, p.6. To our knowledge, this is the first time that the term "ID-ology" appeared in public discourse. Tabane and Haffajee use it in a manner slightly different from the way we do here and elsewhere.

5. Most notably but not only by Pagad, "People Against Guns and Drugs," a Muslim organization that arose in Cape Town in the 1990s; see, e.g., Jensen (2005:218f).

6. The best known case is that of Mapogo a Mathamaga, a large organization led by Monhle Magolego, about whom much has been written (see Comaroff and Comaroff 2007). In an interview with us at Acornhoek on 11 March 2000, Magolego, who has been indicted several times, insisted that the justice carried out by his cadres was "the African way of stopping crime" and was inflicted "with the cooperation of local chiefs."

7. *Prince v The President of the Law Society of the Cape of Good Hope and Others,* CCT 36/00.

8. "Top Politicians for Witchcraft Summit," *Cape Argus,* 7 September 1999, p.9.

9. It is easier, of course, for the state to ignore the "minority" cultural claims of Khoe-San, Coloreds, and Afrikaners.

10. But not all. Nelson Mandela, for one, has—famously—always shown great respect for traditional leadership and for the political processes associated with it; see his autobiography (Mandela 1994).

11. Govan Mbeki (1964) once said that "when a people have developed to a stage which discards chieftainship ... then to force it on them is ... enslavement." This statement has been widely quoted; see, e.g., "The Chieftancy System Is Rooted in Apartheid," Lungisile Ntsebeza and Fred Hendricks, Crossfire, *Mail & Guardian,* 18–24 February 2000, p.33.

12. This is a virtual paraphrase of the Local Government: Municipal Structures Amendment Bill, 2000; see www.pmg.org.za/bills/municipalstructures2ndamd .htm, accessed 5 June 2002.

13. "The Chieftancy System Is Rooted in Apartheid," Lungisile Ntsebeza and Fred Hendricks, Crossfire, *Mail & Guardian,* 18–24 February 2000, p.33.

14. *A National Conference on Traditional Leadership,* Eskom Conference Centre, Midrand, 17–18 August 2000, Department of Provincial and Local Government. We attended the conference on the formal invitation of the Minister for Provincial and Local Government, the Hon. F.S. Mufamadi, and wish to thank him and the staff of his ministry for making our presence possible.

15. The conference was preceded by, and organized around, a *Draft Discussion Document Towards a White Paper on Traditional Leadership and Institutions* issued by the Department of Provincial and Local Government on 11 April 2000.

16. These were the words of Mangosuthu Buthelezi, leader of the Inkatha Freedom Party, in a speech made to rally Zulu support in the "fight for autonomy of the[ir] kingdom"; see "Unite Against ANC Treachery—Buthelezi," Mawande Jubasi and Thabo Mkhize, *Sunday Times,* 4 August 2002, p.4.

17. "The Chieftancy System Is Rooted in Apartheid," Lungisile Ntsebeza and Fred Hendricks, Crossfire, *Mail & Guardian,* 18–24 February 2000, p.33.

18. Act 108 of 1996 as adopted on 8 May and amended on 11 October by the Constitutional Assembly.

19. "Constitutional Tower of Babel," Goloa Moiloa, *Sunday World,* 31 October 1999, p.16.

20. Supreme Court of Appeal, *Mthembu v Letsela,* 30 May 2000 (Case No: 71/98), www.law.wits.ac.za/sca/scadate.html, p.31–32; see also Chapter 8.

21. See "Customary Law Undermines Constitutional Rights," Khadija Magardie, *Mail & Guardian,* 15–22 June 2000, p.33.

22. "Customary Law in the Dock," Fatima Schroeder, *Cape Times,* 19 June 2003, p.5.

23. *Bhe and Others v Magistrate, Khayelitsha and Others,* 15 October 2004, CC149/03; see Chapter 8 for further discussion of this case.

24. Justice Mokgoro has written on the topic as well; see Mokgoro (1994) for her early views.

25. Since we first drafted this essay, a great deal more has been written on the topic. We ask the reader to forgive the anachronism; in point of fact, it does not affect the substance of what is to follow.

26. Much the same point was made just before the UK parliamentary elections of 2001: "[W]ith a basically pre-set macroeconomic framework, government becomes a matter ... ultimately of microeconomic management. [Labour] is set to be elected as managers of Her Majesty's Public Sector, plc." See "Whatever Happened to Big Economics," Faisal Islam, *The Observer* (London), 3 June 2001, Business Section, p.3.

27. *Vide,* in this respect, McMichael's (1998:113) suggestion that the "citizen state" has been replaced by the "consumer state." Cf. Hegeman (1991:72), who argues that identity, at all levels, has come to be defined by consumption (see also Vanderbilt 1997:141); not merely by the consumption of objects, but also by the consumption of the past.

28. The argument summarized in this paragraph was first developed, and is more extensively stated, in J.L. Comaroff (1998).

29. See *World Fact Book,* 14 July 2005; www.odci.gov/cia/publications/factbook/fields/2063.html, accessed 27 July 2005. The number includes only countries that had either enacted entirely new constitutions (92) or had heavily revised existing ones (13).

30. The train was operated by *Legal i,* a Section 21 (i.e., non-profit) company with a board of directors representative of the local law societies—among them, the Black Lawyers Association and the National Association of Democratic Lawyers—and consumer agencies. It was supported by the European Union.

31. Such critics span the political spectrum from radical (e.g., Dirlik 1990) to conservative. One British "View from the Right," Minette Marrin, *The Guardian* (UK), 29 May 2001, p.7, puts it thus: "[W]hat we must have to live together in harmony is a tolerant, over-arching common culture." But the very idea of such a culture is "denounced by multiculturalists as supremacist and racist."

32. "Clash of Custom, Constitution," *The Mail,* 31 July 1998, p.17.

33. Tribal authorities are officially recognized administrative bodies made up of chiefs and chiefly advisors. Instituted by the apartheid regime as part of the system of "homeland" governance, they were explicitly modeled on an African political institution that endures in many rural areas.

34. The HRC is an independent commission set up under the Constitution to investigate alleged violations of its terms.

35. Case No. 618/98, in the High Court of South Africa (Bophuthatswana Provincial Division), p.3.

36. "Women Present Memo to the Chief," *The Mail,* 30 June 1995, p.3.

37. Case No. 618/98, in the High Court of South Africa (Bophuthatswana Provincial Division), Founding Affidavit, p.3.

38. Interviews with Advocate Pansy Tlakula (Human Rights Commission), 19 July 2000; Simon Ruthwane (Department of Traditional Affairs, Northwest Province), 20 July 2000; Reginald Mpame (Registrar, High Court, Mmabatho), 10 July 2000; and Elizabeth Tlhoaele (House of Traditional Leaders, Northwest Province), 24 July 2000.

39. Case No. 618/98, in the High Court of South Africa (Bophuthatswana Provincial Division), Answering Affidavit, Nyalala Molefe John Pilane, 13 November 1998, p.28.

40. Case No. 618/98, in the High Court of South Africa (Bophuthatswana Provincial Division), Founding Affidavit, pp.5–6.

41. The speaker was introduced as Paramount Chief of the Kgatla; this despite the fact that, while Tswana chiefdoms recognize an order of ritual seniority among their rulers, they have never had paramount chiefs *per se.* Paramountcy has been claimed from time to time, however, for political purposes.

42. Advocate Pansy Tlakula (personal communication).

43. Case No. 618/98, in the High Court of South Africa (Bophuthatswana Provincial Division), Founding Affidavit, p.6.

44. Pilane's communication here is multiply resonant. At this point in his reply he invoked a hallowed aphorism: *kgosi ke kgosi ka morafe,* a chief is chief by [with] the people.

45. Letter from Kgosi Nyalala M.J. Pilane to M.C. Moodliar, Human Rights Commission, 29 June 1998; item B4 attached to the case record of the Bophuthatswana High Court.

46. "Clash of Custom, Constitution," *The Mail,* 31 July 1998, p.17. Other resonances are at work here. House arrest was a mechanism commonly used by the apartheid government to silence its opponents; its invocation by Mrs. Tumane associates the actions of the tribal authority with the tactics of the *ancien régime.*

47. Member of the Executive Council of the House of Representatives of the Northwest Province. MECs are the heads of provincial government departments.

48. "Clash of Custom, Constitution," *The Mail,* 31 July 1998, p.17.

49. Case No. 618/98, in the High Court of South Africa (Bophuthatswana Provincial Division), Answering Affidavit, Nyalala Molefe John Pilane, 13 November 1998; all our citations in this paragraph are from p.7–10.

50. Constitutionalism has been a feature of independent African churches from their inception (J. Comaroff 1974; Sundkler 1961). But its centrality in the "new" South Africa to popular notions of organizational legitimacy has given church constitutions new salience.

51. See the statement made to this effect by Advocate Tlakula during the debate on the case in the Northwest House of Traditional Leaders; "Clash of Custom, Constitution," *The Mail,* 31 July 1998, p.17. According to Tlakula (personal communication), she told the chiefs that the matter rested with them: either they would reform their traditions or the matter would be taken out of their hands.

52. Case No. 618/98, in the High Court of South Africa (Bophuthatswana Provincial Division), Answering Affidavit, Nyalala Molefe John Pilane, 13 November 1998, p.19.

53. "Clash of Custom, Constitution," *The Mail,* 31 July 1998, p.17.

54. While they have increasingly been drawn into such litigation, traditional rulers feel relatively disadvantaged by its terms. Pilane and other royals publicly expressed the view that the *mogaga* case should have been conducted elsewhere than in the High Court. In their view, African authority, enshrined in the chiefship and chiefly courts, ought to be constitutionally recognized. Hence the insistence, at the Midrand Conference on Traditional Leadership and Institutions (see above) that the Constitution be amended to recognize their sovereignty.

55. Contrary to some formulations (cf. Modood 2000:177), we use "hybridization" not as an analytic concept but as a descriptive term for one among many self-conscious strategies deployed to address the paradox of difference here. We do not see the concept, conventionally understood, as providing an adequately theorized account of processes of this nature.

56. There are, of course, "traditional" practices that chiefs have themselves banished, on grounds of one or another principle, in order to address social and political transformations. Nor is this a purely postcolonial phenomenon. Schapera (1943, 1970) has documented the history of vernacular legislation and legal innovation among various Tswana groupings.

## CHAPTER 4

1. See, e.g., "Ash City: Why the Fires Were So Bad," B. Jordan, *Sunday Times,* 23 January 2000, p.7.

2. See "Force Landowners to Clear Invading Alien Plants," J. Yeld, *Sunday Argus,* 22–23 January 2000, p.7; also "Take Decisive Steps to Avoid Future Fire Disaster," L. de Villiers, Chair of Peninsula Mountain Forum, Letter to the *Cape Times,* 28 January 2000, p.11.

3. See "*Ukuvuka* the Biggest Ever," Editorial, *Cape Times,* 7 February 2000, p.10.

4. For early technical accounts of *fynbos* and its ecology, see, e.g., Kruger (1978) and Day *et al.* (1979).

5. "They Seem to Have a Problem With Aliens," Chip Snaddon, *Cape Argus,* 27 January 2000, p.23.

6. For a thoughtful, Africa-centric reflection on this tendency, see Geschiere and Nyamnjoh (2000).

7. See, e.g., "Official Figures for Brain Drain Released," *The Star,* 14 March 2000, p.2.

8. This was confirmed by botanists working on the Fynbos Biome, although *fynbos* seems first to have appeared in a publication in 1916 (Dave Richardson, personal communication). Regular academic usage begins in the early 1970s. The term appears on a list of summer school lectures at the University of Cape Town in 1972, for example, and in Kruger (1977). We certainly do not recall it being in circulation while we were growing up in the Cape.

9. Simon Pooley (2010) argues, in a suggestive new essay, that botanists in early 20th-century South Africa also sought urgently to popularize and protect the region's unique indigenous flora, and that invasive alien imports became a focus for their advocacy—resonating with efforts to forge a common white identity in the country at the time. The politically integrative potential of this discourse, he insists, has a history that predates the current, postcolonial moment. Pooley's essay, which dwells on the unfortunate consequences for local flora of foreign theories of ecology and its management, usefully enriches our sense of the enduring significance of imported species here. It does not alter our point, however, that the meaning and political connotations associated with what became known, in the late 20th century, as *fynbos,* were a distinctive product of their time. This is evident in the manner in which the issue became a popular obsession, and an affair of state, despite attempts

of local botanists to stem anxieties. Clearly, plant imports have become infused with a decidedly late-modern connotation of the term "alien" and the threat it poses to national belonging.

10. See "Row over 'Mother of the Nation' Winnie Mandela," David Beresford, *Guardian Century,* 27 January 1989; http://century.guardian.co.uk/1980-1989/Story/0,,110268,00.html, accessed 17 August 2010.

11. It was replaced by the Aliens Control Act No.96 (1991) and subsequent amendments.

12. "Take Decisive Steps to Avoid Future Fire Disaster," L. de Villiers, Chair of Peninsula Mountain Forum, Letter to the *Cape Times,* 28 January 2000, p.11.

13. For further detail on official discourse concerning invasive alien plants during the 1990s, see the original, rather longer version of this essay (Comaroff and Comaroff 2000b).

14. Message from President Mbeki, read by Valli Moosa, Minister for Environmental Affairs and Tourism, at the international symposium on *Best Management Practices for Preventing and Controlling Invasive Alien Species,* Kirstenbosch, 22–24 February 2000; see also "Only the Truly Patriotic Can Be Trusted to Smell the Roses, and Weed Them Out," Karen Bliksem, *Sunday Independent,* 22 February 2000, p.8.

15. "Only the Truly Patriotic Can Be Trusted to Smell the Roses, and Weed Them Out," Karen Bliksem, *Sunday Independent,* 22 February 2000, p.8.

16. A controversial investigation into racism in the mainstream press, both overt and "subliminal," was being conducted by the South African Human Rights Commission at the time; see, e.g., "Journalists Must Do Their Jobs Without Interference," E. Rapiti, Letter to the *Mail & Guardian,* 10–16 March 2000, p.28.

17. "Forget Alien Plants, What About Guns?" Carol Lazar, *The Star,* 7 March 2000, p.8.

18. "Loving the Alien," M. Aken'Ova, *Mail & Guardian,* 18–24 February 2000, p.29.

19. "Racists and Hypocrites," Jeremy Seabrook, *Mail & Guardian,* 18–24 February 2000, p.22.

20. "Time We Became a Bit More Neighbourly," Hopewell Radebe, *The Star,* 16 March 2001, p.13.

21. "My Four Hours as an Illegal Immigrant," Lungile Madywabe, *Mail & Guardian,* 3–9 March 2000, p.16.

22. See also the findings of the South African Migration Project, summarized in "Immigrants Are Creating Work—Not Taking Your Jobs," Chiara Carter and Ferial Haffajee, *Mail & Guardian,* 11–17 September 1998, p.3.

23. "Troops Called in as SA Burns," Sapa, 21 May 2008, *Independent Online;* www.iol.co.za/index.php?set_id=1&click_id=79&art_id=nw20080521184209735C690777&newslett=1&em=177481a1a20080522ah, accessed 6 April 2009.

24. "In a Populist Vice-Grip," Steven Robins, *Mail & Guardian Online,* 12 August 2008; www.mg.co.za/article/2008-08-13-in-a-populist-vicegrip, accessed 6 April 2009.

25. "In a Populist Vice-Grip," Steven Robins, *Mail & Guardian Online,* 12 August 2008; www.mg.co.za/article/2008-08-13-in-a-populist-vicegrip, accessed 6 April 2009.

26. "US-Style Bid to Rid SA of Illegal Aliens," R. Brand, *The Star,* 14 February 2000, p.1.

27. There have been many reports in the mass media of violence at the center. In one case, the Cameroonian embassy lodged a formal protest to the South African government; see "Cameroon to Lodge Protest Over Repatriation Centre Beating," C. Banda and G. Clifford, *The Star,* 17 March 2000, p.1.

28. "The US Is Clamping Down on Illegal Migrants, But It Relies on Their Labor," Gary Younge, *The Guardian,* 11 June 2007, p.29. All quoted phrases in this paragraph and the next are from the same source.

29. "How War Was Turned into a Brand," Naomi Klein, *The Guardian,* 16 June 2007, p.34.

30. "How War Was Turned into a Brand," Naomi Klein, *The Guardian,* 16 June 2007, p.34.

## CHAPTER 5

1. The opening of this essay is taken from notes written in Cape Town by John Comaroff at the time of the first free South African elections, April–May 1994. Some of these notes appeared in J.L. Comaroff (1994).

2. "Political Cowards Fear One-Party State," Argus Africa News Service, *The Argus* (South Africa), 17 July 1990, p.8.

3. See "Democracy in Africa: More Than Votes and Free-Market Economics," *Africa: Africa World Press Guide,* World Views; http://worldviews.igc.org/awpguide/democ.html, accessed 1 August 2009.

4. This point is made with particular acuity by Basil Davidson (1992).

5. The first phrase refers, of course, to Bayart (1993), the second to Mbembe (1992b).

6. See, e.g., Colclough and McCarthy (1980:41), Shepherd (1984), and, more recently, Bratton (2002:13). Perhaps the most comprehensive discussion of democracy in Botswana as it is conventionally seen from within is to be found in Holm and Molutsi (1989). Van Binsbergen (1995:22f), however, argues that, *pace* prevailing stereotypes, this nation-state "is far from a totally convincing democracy" (cf. also Picard 1987; Crowder 1988a; Good 1992; Charlton 1993). We shall return to some of these more skeptical views below.

7. At the first election, held in 1965, the BDP had won 90 percent of the thirty-one seats in the national assembly; in 1969, it won 78 percent. By 1974, the parliament had been enlarged to thirty-two seats, of which it won twenty-seven (see Republic of Botswana 1970, 1974).

8. See, e.g., *Botswana Daily News,* 14 October 1974, 31 October 1974, 4 November 1974, and 13 November 1974. In all cases, the articles and reports appear on p.1.

9. See "President Won't Decree One-Party," *Botswana Daily News,* 31 October 1974, p.1.

10. See "President's Stand on One-Party Rule Lauded," *Botswana Daily News,* 4 November 1974, p.1. This article cites an editorial in *The World,* a black South

African newspaper, that congratulated Khama on the fact that "Botswana ha[d] evolved a truly non-racial democracy."

11. We were doing research in southern Botswana at the time (July 1974–August 1975). The primary data for this essay derive from our ethnographic study of the 1974 elections.

12. See "Voters Are Told: President at Oodi," Paul Rankao, *Botswana Daily News,* 14 October 1974, p.1.

13. Botswana is both sociologically and ethnically more diverse than is often allowed in older scholarly and popular writings. Official state discourses, both colonial and postcolonial, have long tended to portray the nation as highly homogenous, a representation that is increasingly contested these days.

14. For summary histories of Bechuanaland/Botswana, and especially the incorporation into it of the indigenous chiefdoms and other communities, see, e.g., Sillery (1952), Maylam (1980), and Picard (1985).

15. See, e.g., Gillett (1973) and Schapera and Comaroff (1991:76–79).

16. See, for just a few examples, Schapera (1938, 1940), Tlou (1974), Vengroff (1975), and J.L. Comaroff (1974, 1975, 1978).

17. Received wisdom, usually attributed to Schapera (e.g., 1938), has it that Tswana political systems, especially in the past, were "ascriptive," with access to all offices determined by primogeniture; indeed Crowder (1988b:105) once referred to this as the "iron law of succession" (but see 1988a:466 n.17). We have offered the counterview that these systems were much more dynamic, complex, fluid, indeed *political,* than orthodox accounts allow; also that, while all succession to office had to be legitimized in terms of primogeniture—there was no choice in the matter, which is what made them *appear* ascriptive—it was not the rules of rank but the *realpolitik* of the public sphere that determined status and position, since multiple claims could almost always be made (J.L. Comaroff 1974, 1978). Crowder, Parson, and Parsons (1990:12f) take issue with us, asserting that our "case" is aberrant and our evidence flawed. We have answered them (J.L. Comaroff 1990:561 n.14; Comaroff and Comaroff 1992:47 n.22), demonstrating that their critique, and their own reading of the historical record, confuses the *determination* of political processes with their culturally prescribed *representation.*

18. The "*kgotla* system" is often portrayed, especially by political scientists, as an African analogue of the Greek *polis* of classical times. Here, says Crowder (1988a:465–66), "free adult males under the presidency of the chief debated political, administrative and judicial matters" (cf. Shepherd 1984), the ruler having to take into account the views of the majority in arriving at his decisions—this being essayed as proof of the existence of a healthy local tradition of participatory democracy. Others, however, see the *kgotla* in a less flattering light, a point to which we shall return. Neither side in this unjoined debate, however, goes into any real depth in analyzing the substance, style, and political culture of the public sphere, the workings of which turn out to be very complex indeed (see J.L. Comaroff 1975:*passim*).

19. Because of space constraints, we do not annotate our historical sources here. For those sources, and for collateral evidence, see Comaroff and Comaroff (1991: Chapter 4).

20. See, e.g., Campbell (1822,2:156–57) and, for further discussion and additional sources, Comaroff and Comaroff (1991:148f, 329 n.29); also, n.22 below.

21. Tswana chiefs and ruling cadres in Botswana and South Africa varied a great deal in their willingness to open public assemblies and courts to females and members of those ethnic minorities regarded as serfs and clients.

22. See J.L. Comaroff (1975:146f). It is no surprise, therefore, that early accounts differ in their characterization of the authority of Tswana sovereigns. (Indeed, the variance among these accounts itself provides *prima facie* evidence for our analysis of the dynamics of Tswana chiefship.) For example, at one extreme, Lichtenstein (1930,2:414) described their power as "nearly uncircumscribed"; likewise Burchell (1824,2:376), although he noted the moderating effect of "men of property" on the will of rulers. Others stressed that the latter had always to respect "the sentiments of the people" (Barrow 1806:399; Mackenzie 1871:371). At the other extreme, Moffat (1842:389) tells of a Rolong ruler who lost all legitimacy and was deposed because of a "want of energy."

23. It will be self-evident that we refer here to governance *within* the chiefdoms. The ultimate limits of chiefly authority were increasingly delimited and defined, though not always closely regulated, by the colonial state—and then, yet more restrictively, by its postcolonial successor.

24. Until the middle of the 19th century, a powerful chief could also monopolize external trade and levy tariffs on scarce commodities; see Comaroff and Comaroff (1991:Chapter 4).

25. Turnouts in 1994 and 2004 were much higher again, over 76 percent. Although we did not conduct election studies in those years, we would suggest that the elevated figure for 1994 was owed in major part to the fact that, at the time, President Quett Masire's regime was under fire for its lackluster performance in office. The 2004 ballot seems to have sparked public interest largely because of internal politics within the ruling party, due in some measure to the entry of Seretse Ian Khama, son of Seretse Khama, into its leadership cadres—and the longer run prospect of a succession struggle that this heralded. Both explanations would, if correct, be consistent with our analysis. Note, here, Swatuk's (1999:17) comment, made between those two elections: "In power for 33 years, complacency on the part of government and apathy on the part of the electorate characterize the general political mood." To combat these things, he goes on, the BDP "commissioned a well-known South African professor, Lawrence Schlemmer, to undertake a study exploring ways to reinvigorate the ruling party and make it more relevant for the post-Masire era."

26. See "Democracy in Africa: More Than Votes and Free-Market Economics," *Africa: Africa World Press Guide,* World Views; http://worldviews.igc.org/awpguide/democ.html, accessed 1 August 2009.

27. We owe the point to Steven Friedman, a leading South African political scientist and public intellectual. In his own book in progress on African democracy, Friedman includes an insightful critique of the original version of this essay, which he was kind enough to permit us to read in manuscript—thus allowing us to sharpen our own argument (see also Friedman 2007). It is also due to him that we address the electoral turnouts of 1994 and 2004 (see n.25 above).

28. "One-Party Democracy," Thomas L. Friedman, *International Herald Tribune,* 10 September 2009, p.7.

29. See "Our 'Second Liberation' Will Need Ethics and Ubuntu," Archbishop Njongonkulu Ndungane, *Sunday Times* (South Africa), Review, 9 August 2009, p.12.

## CHAPTER 6

1. See J. Comaroff (2005:126). This chapter develops ideas first explored in that essay.

2. Hartog (2003) makes a similar point about the move away from the modernist "regime of historicity" in favor of a preoccupation with the past. Because the future is no longer fully predictable, he says, we have become locked in a pessimistic "presentism," reading that past purely in relation to current political demands. Our own understanding of this move away from the modernist "regime of historicity" has less to do with the loss of predictive power than with a fundamental erosion of the vision of progress, and of the shared teleology, on which modernist imaginings of history were based. What is more, the material we discuss here does not evince a pessimism, or an unusually "political" use of the past—which has always been mediated by the concerns of the here and now. Our interest, rather, is in the precise *nature* of that mediation in the contemporary moment: in explaining why it takes increasingly forensic, privatized forms—and how this affects efforts to produce a future. We thank Paulo Israel for his valuable input on this point.

3. "AmaZulu World Plans Unveiled," Suren Naidoo, *The Mercury,* 8 October 2008, p.1. See also "Re: Forced Eviction of 10 000 Families from eMacambini for AmaZulu World," Letter from the Centre on Housing Rights and Evictions (COHRE) to KwaZulu-Natal Premier, Mr. Sibusiso Ndebele, 16 January 2009; www.abahlali.org/node/4752, accessed 10 January 2009.

4. "The End of History, Revisited: The Ex-Communist States of Eastern Europe Are Leaving Their Pasts Behind," Europe.view, *The Economist* online, 25 February 2010; www.economist.com/world/europe/displaystory.cfm?story_id=15577511, accessed 1 March 2010.

5. See Readers' Comments on Europe.view; www.economist.com.hk/node/15577511/comments?page=1, accessed 5 July 2010.

6. "Historical Memory Law"; http://en.wikipedia.org/wiki/Historical_Memory_Law, accessed 8 May 2010. See Rubin (n.d.:1).

7. The team includes scholars from a variety of disciplines and is directed by Gonzalo Sánchez, a leading historian of violence in Colombia (Castaño n.d.). On the Truth and Reconciliation Commission established by the Canadian government to gather testimony from survivors of the Indian Residential School System, see Weiss (n.d.).

8. "British Lawyer Prepares for Mau Mau Suit," Gakuu Mathenge, *Daily Nation on the Web* (East Africa), 25 November 2002; www.nationaudio.com/News/Daily/Nation/Today/News/News; "Mau Mau Rebels Threaten Court Action,"

Mike Thompson, *BBC News—World: Africa;* http://news.bbc.co.uk/1/hi/world/africa/2429227.stm, accessed 6 June 2003.

9. "New Lease for History," Nawaal Deane, *Weekly Mail & Guardian,* 31 August 2002; www.sn.apc.org./wmail/issues/010831/OTHER84.html, accessed 20 December 2002.

10. See "The 'Loss of History' in Schools is a 21st Century Crisis," Nancy McTygue, *Dateline UC Davis,* 2 March 2007; http://dateline.ucdavis.edu/dl_detail.lasso?id=9334, accessed 2 February 2008. See also Osborne (2003) on the Canadian case.

11. "Reviving South African History: Academics Debate How to Represent and Teach the Nation's Past," Sasha Polakow-Suransky, *Chronicle of Higher Education,* International, 14 June 2002; http://chronicle.com/weekly/v48/i40.40a03601.htm, accessed 20 December 2002.

12. Terence Ranger (n.d.:4) argues that history has remained more vital in Zimbabwe than in South Africa, mainly due to the greater dependence of the Zimbabwean regime on historical validation. In fact, the protracted political crisis in that country probably mediates many of the influences considered here. At the same time, Ranger does provide evidence that, in both school and university, Zimbabwean history might well be "dying a natural death" (p.8).

13. "Television and the Trouble With History," Simon Schama, *The Guardian,* 18 June 2002, Inside Story, pp.6–7.

14. Recall, in this regard, the announcement made by the Ministry of Higher Education and Training in South Africa of its initiative to strengthen the social sciences and humanities. We cite excerpts from it in our epigraph at the beginning of the book and, again, in Chapter 1. The piece of the statement relevant here: "The work of South African social scientists, historians and writers was of great assistance in helping our leaders and people to guide our struggle ... [I]n the last two decades, the social sciences and humanities have taken a back seat." Media Statement on the Development of a Humanities and Social Sciences Charter, Ministry of Higher Education and Training, Republic of South Africa, 6 October 2010; www.education.gov.za/dynamic/dynamic.aspx?pageid=310&id=10648, accessed 8 October 2010.

15. Wilson (2001:60–61) notes, for instance, that the two truth commissions held in Guatemala have been able to develop a richer social and political history of local patterns of violence, in large part by drawing on the unifying perspective of liberation theology.

16. *Truth and Reconciliation Commission of South Africa Report,* Volume 5, Chapter 1 lays out the methods used in gathering statements and selecting witnesses. It notes that the TRC "devised a form, referred to as a protocol or 'statement form,' for recording the statements made to the Commission by people who believed they had suffered gross violations of human rights." Trained "statement takers" recorded these accounts "in a manner which would facilitate their entry into the Commission's database." They "listen[ed] to the stories told by people in their chosen language, ... distil[led] the essential facts, and ... record[ed] them in English." The report stresses that "statement takers ... carried a heavy burden of responsibility and were the front rank of those who gathered the memories of the pain and suffering of the

past"; www.justice.gov.za/trc/report/finalreport/Volume%201.pdf, accessed 30 June 2010.

17. *Truth and Reconciliation Commission of South Africa Report,* Volume 1; www .justice.gov.za/trc/report/finalreport/Volume%201.pdf, accessed 30 June 2010. See also Ross (2003:12).

18. *Truth and Reconciliation Commission of South Africa Report,* Volume 1; www .justice.gov.za/trc/report/finalreport/Volume%201.pdf, accessed 30 June 2010.

19. "Reparations and the South African Truth and Reconciliation Commission," Speech by Brandon Hamber to the "Implementation of the TRC's Recommendations Workshop," 16 February 2000; brandonhamber.com/issues_reparations.htm, accessed 26 January 2005.

20. "Holocaust Victims Win $1.25bn," Julian Borger, *The Guardian,* 27 July 2000; www.guardian.co.uk/world/2000/jul/27/julianborger, accessed 6 July 2010.

21. There is a growing tendency for non-Americans to turn to the US Alien Tort Claims Act in the effort to press for reparations against international bodies, corporate or political (e.g., Shamir 2004). This act is a section of the United States Code that reads: "The district courts shall have original jurisdiction of any civil action by an alien for a tort only, committed in violation of the law of nations or a treaty of the United States" (Henner 2009:13). The statute is notable for allowing US courts to hear human rights cases brought by foreign citizens for conduct committed outside the United States. Its rising popularity underscores the hegemony of American legal procedures across the world. This seems ironic in light of the fact that the US itself is not a member of the International Criminal Court.

22. "Seeking Justice for 'Sins' of Apartheid ... ," Fred Bridgland, *Daily Herald,* 23 June 2002; www.commondreams.org/headlines02/0623-03.htm, accessed 5 August 2002.

23. "Landmark Ruling Allows Apartheid Victims to Sue Multinationals," Khadija Sharife, *African Business,* 1 June 2009; www.allbusiness.com/legal/trial-procedure -suits-claims/12368326-1.html, accessed 18 February 2010.

24. "State Backs Apartheid Victims' Case," Mmanaledi Mataboge, *Mail & Guardian Online,* 9 September 2009; www.mg.co.za/article/2009-0-09-state-backs -apartheid-victims-case, accessed 18 February 2010.

25. See www.khulumani.net, accessed 18 February 2010. The suit remains controversial in South Africa. In December 2009, a group of international law professors there, including former education minister Kader Asmal, filed papers as friends of the court, contesting the existence of corporate liability in international law. They maintained that it was a "gross impertinence" for the case to be heard in the US and that, as a sovereign state, South Africa should deal with the issue at home. See "Asmal's Loyalty to Comrades Questioned," *Cape Argus,* 12 January 2010; http:// allafrica.com/stories/201001120626.html, accessed 20 February 2010.

26. "Television and the Trouble with History," Simon Schama, *The Guardian,* Inside Story, 18 June 2002, pp.6–7.

27. Marks (1997) was most directly concerned with the search in the Scottish highlands for the head of Hintsa, the Xhosa king killed and dismembered in 1835 during the colonial expansion of the British into the eastern Cape Province. Other South African instances include the successful campaign of the Khoi people for

the repatriation of the remains of Saartje (Sara) Baartman, the so-called Hottentot Venus who was abducted to Europe in the early 19th century and whose genitalia were, until recently, on show in the Musée de l'Homme in Paris; also, the bones of Griqua leader Cornelius Kok II, lately returned to his descendants by Dr. Phillip Tobias of the University of the Witwatersrand Medical School. See "African Woman Going Home After 200 Years," David Hearst, *The Guardian,* 30 April 2002; "Griqua Chief Fumes as Tobias Hands Over Bones," Adam Cooke, *The Star,* 21 August 1996, p.1. A further case, as yet unresolved, involves the missing skeleton of the man held to have been the first king of the rapidly "re-traditionalizing" Mamone Bapedi of Sekhukhune, who was hanged by the Boers a century ago (Oomen 2005:194).

28. The repatriation of the remains of Saartje Baartman (see above, n.27) set off one such dispute. The Griqua group of Khoe people in the Northern Cape Province had claimed her as "family," although she was known to have been born among Khoe in the coastal area where the Eastern and Western Cape Provinces meet. After months of debate among groups vying for the right to bury her, Baartman was finally laid to rest in Hankey, near the Gamtoos River and her birthplace. See "'Hottentot Venus' Burial Wrangle Laid to Rest," Judy Damon, *The Star,* 25 July 2002; www.iol .co.za/?click_id=13&art_id=ct20020725001729761S610452&set_id=1, accessed 2 March 2010.

## Chapter 7

1. Not only by them. By the early 1990s, Dirlik (1996:194) notes, even Deng Xiaoping was calling for "consumption as a motor force of production."

2. "Ecumene" refers to a region of "persistent cultural interaction and exchange" (Kopytoff 1987:10; cf. Hannerz 1989:66).

3. The millennial allure of lotteries across the globe in the late 20th century made itself felt in many media, from Euro-American cinema to press reports in Asia. Note, in respect of the former, the film *Waking Ned Divine* (1998), which replayed the ideology of the national lottery in Britain, fantasizing about the way in which a large win might enable communal regeneration in a peripheral, impoverished village. In India, newspapers claimed that "lottery mania" lay behind a number of suicides and mobilized the state to take action; see "Lottery Mania Grips Madhya Pradesh, Many Commit Suicide," *India Tribune* (Chicago), 2 January 1999, 23(1), p.8.

4. Terence Turner (2003) has argued, in this respect, that the globalization of the division of labor has elevated class conflicts to the level of international relations.

5. Friedrich Engels, as cited by Andre Gunder Frank (1971:36).

6. By "postrevolutionary" societies we mean societies—such as those of the former Soviet Union—that have witnessed a metamorphosis of their political, material, social, and cultural structures, largely under the impact of the growth of the global, neoliberal market economy.

7. The Freedom Charter was, for all practical purposes, the founding document in the fight against the apartheid state. Signed in 1955 by all the protest organizations of the Congress Alliance, it made a commitment, among other things, to national-

ize major industries and to mandate a heavily state-run, welfare-freighted political economy (see, e.g., Walshe 1971; Lodge 1983).

8. Robins (1998:13) makes the point cogently in noting how quick the African National Congress government was to disparage John Pilger's film *Apartheid Did Not Die,* which provides harsh evidence of the continuing contrast between white opulence and black poverty: "Whereas critiques of racial capitalism were once accepted as truth within the liberation movements, they are now dismissed by the new ruling class as pure polemic and/or naive utopian socialist rhetoric."

9. We are grateful to Nathan Sayre for alerting us to this song; also to Joshua Comaroff for transcribing it and, more generally, for availing us of his creative imagination.

10. In our discussion of rural South Africa, we focus primarily on two provinces, Limpopo and the Northwest. These, along with Mpumalanga, have been the sites of the most concentrated occult activity in the country over the past two decades or so. The Northwest is also the region in which we have done most of our research since 1969.

11. "'Zombie' Back from the Dead," Sonnyboy Mokgadi and Moopelwa Letanke, *The Mail* (Mafikeng), 11 June 1993, pp.1, 7. See also "Zombie Missing," Sonnyboy Mokgadi and Moopelwa Letanke, *The Mail* (Mafikeng), 17 December 1993, pp.1, 4; "Apartheid Is Over, But Other Old Evils Haunt South Africa: Witch-Burning Is on the Rise as Superstitious Villagers Sweep House of Spirits," Joe Davidson, *Wall Street Journal,* 20 June 1994, pp.A1, A10. Sonnyboy Mokgadi, co-author of the first two stories and many others on the topic, was killed some two years later, in mysterious circumstances involving a "township fight." Rumors had it that his violent death was due to his investigation of zombies.

12. See, e.g., "Petrol Murder Denial," *The Mail* (Mafikeng), 2 June 1995, p.2; "Bizarre Zombie Claim in Court," Nat Molomo, *The Mail* (Mafikeng), 31 March 1995, p.2.

13. See "Disturbing Insight into Kokstad Zombie Killings," Ntokozo Gwamanda, *Sowetan,* 15 July 1998, p.17; also the SABC2 documentary series, *Issues of Faith,* whose program on 12 July 1998 dealt with the topic. The program made reference to a much acclaimed play entitled *Ipizombi,* by Brett Bailey, which was featured at the Standard Bank National Arts Festival in July 1996 and was later televised by the SABC. The appearance of this play on a prominent national stage points to the fact that the phenomenon was entering into the mainstream of public consciousness at the time. We are grateful to Loren Kruger, of the Department of English at the University of Chicago, for sharing with us a review of the production.

14. The report of this commission, chaired by a retired professor of anthropology, Professor V.N. Ralushai, speaks in two different registers. On one hand, it gives an orthodox ethnographic account, couched in cultural relativist terms, of African beliefs; on the other, it offers a stark condemnation, phrased in Euro-American legal language, of the evils of occult violence. What is more, it speaks explicitly of the contradiction between European law, which criminalizes witchcraft, and its African counterpart, which accepts it as a pervasive, mundane reality (Ralushai

*et al.* 1996:61). For their own part, the commissioners do not call the actuality of witchcraft itself into doubt.

15. The use of *diphoko* for zombie—*diphoko* being from the Afrikaans, *spook* (earlier, from the Dutch; see n.35 below)—points to the existence here of a cultural interplay, across lines of race and language, of ideas of haunting and enchantment.

16. Our own collection of narratives about zombies and ritual murder in the Northwest, where we elicited both descriptive accounts of the phenomena and specific case histories, evinced a sharp gender distinction. Ritual murder—i.e., the killing of people to harvest their body parts for medicine—could be perpetrated by either men or women, with or without the help of a "traditional" healer. But zombie conjurers were, more often than not, said to be female.

17. For an unusually fine analysis of the crisis of domestic reproduction in South Africa, centered in northern KwaZulu-Natal, see White (2001). Of course, the connection between a shrinking labor market and the threat to community is not purely a South African phenomenon. Several films from Britain, a few of them popular successes like *Brassed Off* and *The Full Monty,* make it clear that the north of England has suffered precisely the same unhappy conjuncture, ushered in by the Thatcherite campaign to force a neoliberal revolution.

18. "'Zombie' Back from the Dead," Sonnyboy Mokgadi and Moopelwa Le-tanke, *The Mail* (Mafikeng), 11 June 1993, pp.1, 7; "Healer Vows to Expose Those Behind Zombie Man," Sonnyboy Mokgadi, *The Mail* (Mafikeng), 18 June 1993, p.7; "Death and Revival of 'Zombie' Man Still a Mystery," Sonnyboy Mokgadi, *The Mail* (Mafikeng), 25 June 1993, p.2; "Zombie Missing," Sonnyboy Mokgadi and Moopelwa Letanke, *The Mail* (Mafikeng), 17 December 1993, pp.1, 4.

19. "New 'Zombie' Claims, But Now About a Woman," Sonnyboy Mokgadi and Moopelwa Letanke, *The Mail* (Mafikeng), 13 August 1993, p.1, 5.

20. "Healer Vows to Expose Those Behind 'Zombie' Man," Sonnyboy Mokgadi, *The Mail* (Mafikeng), 18 June 1993, p.7.

21. "Witch-hunt Sets Town Ablaze," Mthake Nakedi, *The Mail* (Mafikeng), 27 May 1994, p.2; also "Petrol Murder Denial," *The Mail* (Mafikeng), 2 June 1995, p.2, which describes a similar exorcism in a village in the Molopo District.

22. See, e.g., "Meet SA's Strange New 'Racists,'" Chris Barron, *Sunday Times,* 13 September 1998, p.19. The connection between immigrants and zombies is visible elsewhere as well. In rural Zimbabwe, for instance, stories abound about figures termed *ntogelochi* (from *thokolosbe,* the Nguni term now universally used for witch familiars in South Africa). Said to be brought from South Africa, they are purchased as general factotums to do all manner of work. But they come to haunt their pos-sessors, following them everywhere—onto planes, into church—like unruly shadows. Or like the alienated essence of their own labor (Dana Bilsky and Thomas Asher, personal communication).

23. "Jobless Mob Goes on Death Rampage," *Cape Argus,* 4 September 1998, p.9.

24. "African Foreigners Terrorized," Tangenu Amupadhi, *Mail & Guardian,* 18–23 December 1998, p.3.

25. A refugee bill was promulgated by the South African parliament in 1998, aim-ing to bring the country into line with international and constitutional obligations in respect of migrants and refugees (previously regulated under the provisions of

the Aliens Control Act). The move was also seen to be related to growing national concerns about immigration and other cross-border traffic, in particular those involving gun-running, drugs, money laundering, and organized crime. See "New Bill for Asylum Applications," Chiara Carter, *Mail & Guardian,* 11–17 September, p.6.

26. See the findings of the South African Migration Project, reported in "Immigrants Are Creating Work—Not Taking Our Jobs," Chiara Carter and Ferial Haffajee, *Mail & Guardian,* 11–17 September 1998, pp.6, 7.

27. "Mandela Stresses Success, Struggle," Paul Salopek, *Chicago Tribune,* 6 February 1999, p.3.

28. "South Africa's Uncertain Future," Paul Salopek, *Chicago Tribune,* 31 January 1999, pp.1, 14.

29. "Mandela Stresses Success, Struggle," Paul Salopek, *Chicago Tribune,* 6 February 1999, p.3.

30. In a telling irony that speaks volumes about the Midas touch of neoliberalism, Adam *et al.* (1998:207) note that, at the time, even the South African Communist Party was considering establishing an investment arm in order to "trade its way out of the red."

31. Dr. S.M. Banda claims to be "[o]ne of the best traditional healers from Malawi." His special expertise, he says, includes a knowledge of the means "to get promoted" and "to help your business be successful"; *Mafikeng Business Advertiser,* December 1998, 2(1):11.

32. This point is made in a divination sequence in the film *Heal the Whole Man* (Chigfield Films, London, 1973), based on our research in the Mafikeng District.

33. See also Alverson (1978:225f). The reference to tinned fish captures the spatial congestion of the notorious mine hostels in which workers' bunks were stacked above each other in tight rows.

34. Geschiere (1999:232), writing of similar beliefs about zombies in Cameroon, observes that "witches see their fellow men no longer as meat to be eaten ... as life to feed upon in order to strengthen one's own life force—but rather as laborers that have to be exploited."

35. These unfortunates were termed *sipoko* (from the Dutch *spook;* "ghost"), a word borrowed, Junod (1927:488) notes, from European animism; see also n.15 above.

36. Ardener's (1970) account—he also describes a resurgence of the phenomenon in the 1950s—makes it necessary to complicate Geschiere's (1999) claim that zombie witchcraft is a "new" phenomenon in Africa.

37. This phrase is also cited by Wade Davis (1988:75).

38. It was Monica Wilson (1951) who first spoke of witch beliefs as the standardized nightmares of a group.

CHAPTER 8

1. "US Military Gives 'Make Love, Not War' New Meaning," *Cape Times,* 17 January 2005, p.1. See also "Pentagon Reveals Rejected Chemical Weapons," *New*

*Scientist,* 15 January 2005; www.newscientist.com/article.ns?id=mg18524823.800, accessed 13 November 2005.

2. "'Brokeback' & Abu Ghraib: What's Our Problem With Gays," Jesse Kornbluth, *Huffington Post,* 20 February 2006; www.huffingtonpost.com/jesse-kornbluth/brokeback-abu-ghraib_b_16007.html; accessed 14 March 2006.

3. "Abu Ghraib Tactics Were First Used at Guantanamo," Josh White, *Washington Post,* 14 July 2005; www.washingtonpost.com/wp-dyn/content/article/2005/0713/AR2005071302380.html; accessed 14 November 2005.

4. "Comrade Clowns, My Inspiration," Pieter-Dirk Uys, *Cape Times,* 10 February 2005, p.9.

5. "Madiba Mourns: Obituary," Lloyd Gedye and Sapa, *Mail & Guardian,* 7–13 January 2005, p.3.

6. "Comrade Clowns, My Inspiration," Peter-Dirk Uys, *Cape Times,* 10 February 2005, p.9.

7. "HIV and AIDS in South Africa," *Avert.org,* March 2010; www.avert.org/aidssouthafrica.htm, accessed 16 March 2010.

8. "Hut by Hut, AIDS Steals a Middle Generation in a Southern Africa Town," *New York Times,* 28 November 2004, pp.1, 14, 15.

9. "Aids Takes a Grim Toll on African Families, Even After Death," *New York Times,* 16 December 1998, pp.1, 14.

10. Critics have accused TAC of downplaying the often severe side effects of ARV medication. Activists in the US, by contrast, have struggled to force pharmaceutical companies to acknowledge the complex consequences of treatment (Decoteau n.d.:14f). Optimistic claims for the "manageability" of AIDS drugs by activists in South Africa must be seen in relation to a history of assertions, made by so-called denialists, that ARVs are deadly poisons.

11. Also active on the national scene are the National Association of People With HIV/AIDS (NAPWA) which, while not as internationally visible as TAC, also organizes a network of support groups; the AIDS Law Project at the University of the Witwatersrand; and a string of local and translocal NGOs (Le Marcis 2004; Robins 2004).

12. Zackie Achmat, one of TAC's founders and its most charismatic embodiment, affirms that the movement strives to structure its activities according to the old anti-apartheid calendar of struggle. Thus, for example, it organizes a protest march in mid-February, from St. George's Cathedral to the Houses of Parliament in central Cape Town, to mark the opening session of the parliamentary year and the president's state of the nation address (personal communication).

13. In an interview on National Public Radio in Chicago in 2006, Achmat noted that TAC owed much to media techniques like those laid out by Act Up in its "AIDSdemographics"; *World View,* 12 April 2006.

14. "Turning Disease Into Political Cause: First AIDS, and Now Breast Cancer," Jane Gross, *New York Times,* 7 January 1991; http://query.nytimes.com/gst/fullpage.html?sec=health&res=9D0CE1DE1F38F934A35752C0A967958260, accessed 4 April 2006.

15. Directed by Darrell James Roodt, HBO, 2004; in isiZulu, with English subtitles.

16. This dis/location obtains even when exception becomes the rule and "emergency" arrangements become institutionalized (Agamben 2005:9).

17. "Drug Giants Made to Swallow Bitter Pill," Charlotte Denny and James Meek, *The Guardian,* 19 April 2001, p.12.

18. "Africa's Children Left Out of HIV Treatment Breakthrough," Stephen Lewis, *Sunday Independent,* 13 February 2005, p.9.

19. "Wave of Shame," John Pilger, *Mail & Guardian,* 7–13 January 2005, p.7.

# Bibliography

Ackermann, Lourens W.H.
  2004     The Legal Nature of the South African Constitutional Revolution."
           *New Zealand Law Review* 2004(4):633–79.
Acocks, John Phillip Harison
  1953     "Veld Types of South Africa." *Memoirs of the Botanical Survey of South
           Africa,* no.28. Pretoria: Division of Botany, Department of Agriculture.
Adam, Heribert, Frederik van Zyl Slabbert, and Kogila Moodley
  1998     *Comrades in Business: Post-Liberation Politics in South Africa.* Cape
           Town: Tafelberg.
Adorno, Theodor W.
  1981     *In Search of Wagner.* Translated by R. Livingstone. London: New Left
           Books.
Agamben, Giorgio
  1998     *Homo Sacer: Sovereign Power and Bare Life.* Translated by Daniel Heller
           Roazen. Stanford, CA: Stanford University Press.
  2005     *State of Exception.* Translated by K. Attell. Chicago: University of
           Chicago Press.
Agrama, Hussein Ali
  2005     "Law Courts and Fatwa Councils in Modern Egypt: An Ethnog-
           raphy of Islamic Legal Practice." PhD dissertation. Johns Hopkins
           University.
Alverson, Hoyt
  1978     *Mind in the Heart of Darkness: Value and Self-Identity Among the Tswana
           of Southern Africa.* New Haven, CT: Yale University Press.
Amin, Samir
  1989     *Eurocentrism.* Translated by Russell Moore. New York: Monthly Review
           Press.
  2010     "The Millennium Development Goals: A Critique from the South."
           *Monthly Review* 57(10):1–15.

Anderson, Benedict
   1991     *Imagined Communities: Reflections on the Origin and Spread of National-ism.* London: Verso.
Appadurai, Arjun
   1990     "Disjuncture and Difference in the Global Cultural Economy." *Public Culture* 2 (Spring):1–24.
   1996     *Modernity at Large: The Cultural Dimensions of Globalization.* Min-neapolis: University of Minnesota Press.
   2004     "The Capacity to Aspire in Cultural and Public Activism." In *Cultural and Public Activism,* (eds.) Vijayendra Rao and Michael Walton. Stan-ford, CA: Stanford University Press.
Ardener, Edwin W.
   1970     "Witchcraft, Economics, and the Continuity of Belief." In *Witchcraft Confessions and Accusations,* (ed.) Mary Douglas. London: Tavistock.
Arendt, Hannah
   1958     *The Human Condition.* Chicago: University of Chicago Press.
Ashforth, Adam
   2002     "An Epidemic of Witchcraft? The Implications of AIDS for the Post-Apartheid State." *African Studies* 61(1):121–42.
Balibar, Étienne
   2004     *We, the People of Europe? Reflections on Transnational Citizenship.* Translated by James Swenson. Princeton, NJ: Princeton University Press.
Barber, Benjamin R.
   1984     *Strong Democracy: Participatory Politics for a New Age.* Berkeley: Uni-versity of California Press.
Barkun, Michael
   1968     *Law Without Sanctions: Order in Primitive Societies and the World Community.* New Haven, CT: Yale University Press.
Barrow, John
   1806     *A Voyage to Cochinchina.* London: Cadell & Davies.
Barsh, Russel Lawrence
   1992     "Democratization and Development." *Human Rights Quarterly* 14(1):120–34.
Barth, Frederik
   1973     "Descent and Marriage Reconsidered." In *The Character of Kinship,* (ed.) Jack Goody. Cambridge: Cambridge University Press.
Bauman, Zygmunt
   2005     *Work, Consumerism and the New Poor.* Second edition. Maidenhead: Open University Press.
Bayart, Jean-François
   1993     *The State in Africa: Politics of the Belly.* New York: Longman.
Bell, Daniel
   1960     *The End of Ideology: On the Exhaustion of Political Ideas in the Fifties.* Glencoe, IL: Free Press.

Benjamin, Walter
  1968    *Illuminations.* Edited by Hannah Arendt, translated by Harry Zohn. New York: Harcourt, Brace & World.
  1978    "Critique of Violence." In *Reflections: Essays, Aphorisms, Autobiographical Writings.* Edited by Peter Demetz, translated by Edmund Jephcott. New York: Schocken Books.
  2005    *On the Concept of History.* Translated by Dennis Redmond; www.efn.org/~dredmond/Theses_on_History.html.

Berlant, Lauren
  1997    *The Queen of America Goes to Washington City: Essays on Sex and Citizenship.* Durham, NC: Duke University Press.

Bernal, Martin
  1987–    *Black Athena: The Afroasiatic Roots of Classical Civilization,* 3 volumes.
  2006    New Brunswick, NJ: Rutgers University Press.

Bhabha, Homi K.
  1994a    *The Location of Culture.* New York: Routledge.
  1994b    "Remembering Fanon: Self, Psyche and the Colonial Condition." In *Colonial Discourse and Post-Colonial Theory: A Reader,* (eds.) Patrick Williams and Laura Chrisman. New York: Columbia University Press.

Biehl, Joao
  2001    "Vita: Life in a Zone of Social Abandonment." *Social Text* 68, 19(3): 131–49.
  2004    "The Activist State: Global Pharmaceuticals, AIDS, and Citizenship in Brazil." *Social Text* 80, 22(3):105–32.
  2007    *Will to Live: AIDS Therapies and the Politics of Survival.* Princeton, NJ: Princeton University Press.

Bond, Patrick
  1997    "Fighting Neo-Liberalism: The South African Front." *Southern Africa Report Archive* 12(2); www.africafiles.org/article.asp?ID=3851.

Booth, Wayne C.
  1961    *The Rhetoric of Fiction.* Chicago: University of Chicago Press.
  1974    *The Rhetoric of Irony.* Chicago: University of Chicago Press.

Botswana, Republic of
  1970    *Report on the General Elections 1969.* Gaborone: Government Printer.
  1974    *Report to the Minister of State on the General Elections 1974.* Gaborone: Government Printer.

Bradbury, Malcolm
  1992    *Doctor Criminale.* New York: Penguin Books.

Braque, Georges
  1971    *Illustrated Notebooks, 1917–1955.* Translated by Stanley Appelbaum. New York: Dover.

Bratton, Michael
  2002    "Wide but Shallow: Popular Support for Democracy in Africa." *Afrobarometer.* Afrobarometer Working Paper no.19. Cape Town: Institute for Democracy in South Africa.

Bratton, Michael, and Robert Mattes
    2001    "Support for Democracy in Africa: Intrinsic or Instrumental?" *British Journal of Political Science* 31(3):447–74.

Bratton, Michael, Robert Mattes, and Emmanuel Gyimah-Boadi
    2005    *Public Opinion, Democracy, and Market Reform in Africa.* Cambridge: Cambridge University Press.

Brazier, Alex
    1989    *A Double Deficiency? A Report on the Social Security Act 1986 and People with Acquired Immune Deficiency Syndrome (AIDS), AIDS Related Complex (ARC), and HIV Infection.* London: Terrence Higgins Trust.

Brown, J. Tom
    1895    *Secwana Dictionary: Secwana–English and English–Secwana.* Frome, UK: Butler & Tanner for the London Missionary Society.

    1926    *Among the Bantu Nomads: A Record of Forty Years Spent Among the Bechuana.* London: Seeley Service.

Bull, Malcolm
    2004    "States Don't Really Mind Their Citizens Dying (Provided They Don't All Do It At Once): They Just Don't Like Anyone Else to Kill Them." *London Review of Books* 26(24):3–6.

Bundy, Colin
    1999    "Truth ... Or Reconciliation." *South Africa Report* 14(4); www.africafiles.org/article.asp?ID=3731.

Burchell, William J.
    1824    *Travels in the Interior of Southern Africa,* Volume 2. London: Longman, Hurst, Rees, Orme, Brown & Green.

Burridge, Kenelm O.L.
    1979    *Someone, No One: An Essay on Individuality.* Princeton, NJ: Princeton University Press.

Busby, Cecilia
    1997    "Permeable and Partible Persons: A Comparative Analysis of Gender and Body in South India and Melanesia." *Journal of the Royal Anthropological Institute* 3(2):261–78.

Butler, Judith P.
    1990    *Gender Trouble: Feminism and the Subversion of Identity.* New York: Routledge.

    1993    *Bodies That Matter: On the Discursive Limits of Sex.* New York: Routledge.

    1997    *The Psychic Life of Power: Theories in Subjection.* Stanford, CA: Stanford University Press.

    2004    *Precarious Life: The Power of Mourning and Violence.* New York: Verso.

Buur, Lars
    2001    "The South African Truth and Reconciliation Commission: A Technique of Nation-State Formation." In *States of Imagination: Ethnographic Explorations of the Postcolonial State,* (eds.) Thomas Blom Hansen and Finn Stepputat. Durham, NC: Duke University Press.

Campbell, John
    1822    *Travels in South Africa: Being a Narrative of a Second Journey,* 2 volumes. London: Westley.

Carlyle, Thomas
    1842    *On Heroes, Hero-Worship, and the Heroic in History.* New York: D. Appleton.

Carr, G.W., J.M. Robin, and R.W. Robinson
    1986    "Environmental Weed Invasion of Natural Ecosystems: Australia's Greatest Conservation Problem." In *Ecology of Biological Invasions: An Australian Perspective,* (eds.) R.H. Groves and J.J. Burdon. Canberra: Australian Academy of Science.

Carrithers, Michael, Steven Collins, and Steven Lukes
    1985    Preface. In *The Category of the Person: Anthropology, Philosophy, History,* (eds.) Michael Carrithers, Steven Collins, and Steven Lukes. Cambridge: Cambridge University Press.

Cassidy, John
    2010    "The Volcker Rule: Obama's Economic Adviser and His Battles over the Financial-Reform Bill." *New Yorker,* July 26, pp.25–30.

Castaño, Paula
    n.d.    "The Time of the Victims: Understandings of Violence and Institutional Practices in the National Commission of Reparation and Reconciliation in Colombia." PhD dissertation proposal. Department of Sociology, University of Chicago, 2009.

Cattelino, Jessica R.
    2008    *High Stakes: Florida Seminole Gaming and Sovereignty.* Durham, NC: Duke University Press.

Chabal, Patrick, ed.
    1986    *Political Domination in Africa.* Cambridge: Cambridge University Press.

Chakrabarty, Dipesh
    2000    *Provincializing Europe: Postcolonial Thought and Historical Difference.* Princeton, NJ: Princeton University Press.

Chalfin, Brenda
    2010    *Neoliberal Frontiers: An Ethnography of Sovereignty in West Africa.* Chicago: University of Chicago Press.

Chance, Kerry
    n.d.    "Living Politics." PhD dissertation proposal. Department of Anthropology, University of Chicago, 2007.

Chang, Ha-Joon
    2008    *Bad Samaritans: The Myth of Free Trade and the Secret History of Capitalism.* New York: Bloomsbury Press.
    2011    *23 Things They Don't Tell You About Capitalism.* New York: Bloomsbury Press.

Chari, Sharad
    2006    "Post-Apartheid Livelihood Struggles in Wentworth, South Durban." In *The Development Decade? Economic and Social Change in South*

*Africa, 1994–2004,* (ed.) Vishnu Padayachee. Cape Town: HSRC Press.

n.d.    "Apartheid Remains: Political Environs and the Biopolitics of Refusal." In *Imperial Debris: On Ruins and Ruination,* (ed.) Ann L. Stoler. Durham, NC: Duke University Press. [Forthcoming.]

Charlton, Roger

1993    "The Politics of Elections in Botswana." *Africa* 63(1):330–70.

Chatterjee, Partha

1997    *Our Modernity.* Rotterdam and Dakar: The South-South Exchange Programme for Research on the History of Development (SEPHIS) and the Council for the Development of Social Science Research in Africa (CODESRIA).

Clery, E.J.

1995    *The Rise of Supernatural Fiction, 1762–1800.* Cambridge: Cambridge University Press.

Cobley, Alan

2001    "Does Social History Have a Future? The Ending of Apartheid and Recent Trends in South African Historiography." Special issue for Shula Marks, (eds.) William Beinart, Saul Dubow, Deborah Gaitskell, and Isabel Hofmeyr. *Journal of Southern African Studies* 27(3):613–25.

Coetzee, John M.

2003    *Elizabeth Costello.* London: Secker & Warburg.

2008    *Diary of a Bad Year.* London: Vintage Books.

Coffee, John C. Jr.

1992    "Paradigms Lost: The Blurring of the Criminal and Civil Law Models— and What Can Be Done About It." *Yale Law Journal* 101(8):1875–93.

Cohen, David William

1994    *The Combing of History.* Chicago: University of Chicago Press.

Colclough, Christopher, and Stephen McCarthy

1980    *The Political Economy of Botswana.* Oxford: Oxford University Press.

Collins, Steven

1985    "Categories, Concepts or Predicaments? Remarks on Mauss's Use of Philosophical Terminology." In *The Category of the Person: Anthropology, Philosophy, History,* (eds.) Michael Carrithers, Steven Collins, and Steven Lukes. Cambridge: Cambridge University Press.

Comaroff, Jean

1974    "Barolong Cosmology: A Study of Religious Pluralism in a Tswana Town." PhD dissertation. University of London.

1980    "Healing and the Cultural Order." *American Ethnologist* 7(4):637–57.

1985    *Body of Power, Spirit of Resistance: The Culture and History of a South African People.* Chicago: University of Chicago Press.

1997    "Consuming Passions: Nightmares of the Global Village." In *Body and Self in a Post-Colonial World,* (ed.) Ellen Badone. Special issue of *Culture* 17(1–2):7–19.

2005    "The End of History, Again: Pursuing the Past in the Postcolony."

In *Postcolonial Studies and Beyond,* (eds.) Suvir Kaul, Ania Loomba, Matti Bunzl, Antoinette Burton, and Jed Esty. Durham, NC: Duke University Press.

n.d.       "Populism and Late Liberalism: A Special Affinity." In *Race, Religion, and Late Democracy,* (eds.) John Jackson and David Kyuman Kim. *The Annals of the American Academy of Political and Social Sciences.* [Forthcoming.]

Comaroff, Jean, and John L. Comaroff

1990       "Goodly Beasts and Beastly Goods: Cattle and Commodities in a South African Context." *American Ethnologist* 17(2):195–216.

1991       *Of Revelation and Revolution,* Volume 1: *Christianity, Colonialism, and Consciousness in South Africa.* Chicago: University of Chicago Press.

1993       Introduction. In *Modernity and Its Malcontents: Ritual and Power in Postcolonial Africa,* (eds.) Jean Comaroff and John L. Comaroff. Chicago: University of Chicago Press.

1999a      "Occult Economies and the Violence of Abstraction: Notes from the South African Postcolony." *American Ethnologist* 26(2):279–303.

2000a      "Millennial Capitalism: First Thoughts on a Second Coming." In *Millennial Capitalism and the Culture of Neoliberalism,* (eds.) Jean Comaroff and John L. Comaroff. Special edition of *Public Culture* 12(2):291–343.

2000b      "Naturing the Nation: Aliens, Apocalypse and the Postcolonial State." *Social Identities* 7(2):233–65; also *Journal of Southern African Studies* 27(3):627–51.

2003       "Second Comings: Neoprotestant Ethics and Millennial Capitalism in South Africa, and Elsewhere." In *2000 Years and Beyond: Faith, Identity and the Common Era,* (ed.) Paul Gifford with David Archard, Trevor A. Hart, and Nigel Rapport. London: Routledge.

2006a      "Figuring Crime: Quantifacts and the Production of the Unreal." *Public Culture* 18(1):209–46.

Comaroff, John L.

1974       "Chiefship in a South African 'Homeland.'" *Journal of Southern African Studies* 1:36–51.

1975       "Talking Politics: Oratory and Authority in a Tswana Chiefdom." In *Political Language and Oratory in Traditional Societies,* (ed.) Maurice Bloch. London: Academic Press.

1978       "Rules and Rulers: Political Processes in a Tswana Chiefdom." *Man* (NS) 13:1–20.

1987       "*Sui Genderis:* Feminism, Kinship Theory, and Structural Domains." In *Gender and Kinship: Essays Toward a Unified Theory,* (eds.) Jane F. Collier and Sylvia Yanagisako. Stanford, CA: Stanford University Press.

1990       "Bourgeois Biography and Colonial Historiography." *Journal of Southern African Studies* 16:550–62.

1994       "Democracy, Fried Chicken and the Anomic Bomb." *Cultural Survival* 18(2/3):34–39.

1995       "Ethnicity, Nationalism, and the Politics of Difference in an Age of

Revolution." In *Perspectives on Nationalism and War,* (eds.) John L. Comaroff and Paul C. Stern. Luxembourg: Gordon and Breach.

1998    "Reflections on the Colonial State, in South Africa and Elsewhere: Fragments, Factions, Facts and Fictions." *Social Identities* 4(3): 321–61.

2009    "Reflections on the Rise of Legal Theology: Law and Religion in the 21st Century." *Social Analysis* 53(1):193–216.

Comaroff, John L., and Jean Comaroff

1981    "The Management of Marriage in a Tswana Chiefdom." In *Essays on African Marriage in Southern Africa,* (eds.) Eileen Jensen Krige and John L. Comaroff. Cape Town: Juta.

1987    "The Madman and the Migrant: Work and Labor in the Historical Consciousness of a South African People." *American Ethnologist* 14(2):191–209.

1992    *Ethnography and the Historical Imagination.* Boulder, CO: Westview Press.

1997    *Of Revelation and Revolution,* Volume 2: *The Dialectics of Modernity on a South African Frontier.* Chicago: University of Chicago Press.

1999b   Introduction. In *Civil Society and the Political Imagination in Africa,* (eds.) John L. Comaroff and Jean Comaroff. Chicago: University of Chicago Press.

2006b   Introduction. In *Law and Disorder in the Postcolony,* (eds.) Jean Comaroff and John L. Comaroff. Chicago: University of Chicago Press.

2007    "Popular Justice in the New South Africa: Policing the Boundaries of Freedom." In *Legitimacy and Criminal Justice: International Perspectives,* (ed.) Tom R. Tyler. New York: Russell Sage Foundation.

2009    *Ethnicity, Inc.* Chicago: University of Chicago Press.

Comaroff, John L., and Simon A. Roberts

1981    *Rules and Processes: The Cultural Logic of Dispute in an African Context.* Chicago: University of Chicago Press.

Comaroff, Joshua A., and Gullivar Shepard

1999    "Lagos Charter: Case Studies in the African Informal. Harvard Project on the City: West Africa." MA thesis. Graduate School of Design, Harvard University.

Connell, Raewyn

2007    *Southern Theory: The Global Dynamics of Knowledge in Social Science.* Malden, MA: Polity.

Coombe, Rosemary J.

1998    *The Cultural Life of Intellectual Properties: Authorship, Appropriation, and the Law.* Durham, NC: Duke University Press.

Cooper, Frederick

2005    *Colonialism in Question: Theory, Knowledge, History.* Berkeley: University of California Press.

Coronil, Fernando

2004    "Latin American Postcolonial Studies and Global Decolonization." In

*The Cambridge Companion to Postcolonial Literary Studies,* (ed.) Neil
Lazarus. Cambridge: Cambridge University Press.

Corrigan, Philip, and Derek Sayer
1985    *The Great Arch: English State Formation as Cultural Revolution.* Oxford:
Basil Blackwell.

Crush, Jonathan
1999    "Fortress South Africa and the Deconstruction of Apartheid's Migration Regime." *Geoforum* 30(1):1–11.

Crowder, Michael
1988a   "Botswana and the Survival of Liberal Democracy in Africa." In
*Decolonization and African Independence,* (eds.) Prosser Gifford and
William R. Louis. New Haven, CT: Yale University Press.

1988b   *The Flogging of Phinehas McIntosh: A Tale of Colonial Folly and Injustice:
Bechuanaland 1933.* New Haven, CT: Yale University Press.

Crowder, Michael, Jack Parson, and Neil Q. Parsons
1990    "Legitimacy and Faction: Tswana Constitutionalism and Political
Change." In *Succession to High Office in Botswana,* (ed.) Jack Parson.
Athens: Ohio University Center for International Studies.

Dachs, Anthony J.
1972    "Missionary Imperialism: The Case of Bechuanaland." *Journal of
African History* 13(4):647–58.

Darian-Smith, Eve
1996    "Postcolonialism: A Brief Introduction." *Social and Legal Studies*
5(3):291–99.

2010    *Religion, Race, Rights: Landmarks in the History of Modern Anglo-
American Law.* Oxford: Hart Publishing.

Das, Veena, and Arthur Kleinman
2001    Introduction. In *Remaking a World: Violence, Social Suffering and Recovery,* (eds.) Veena Das, Arthur Kleinman, Margaret Lock, Mamphela
Ramphele, and Pamela Reynolds. Berkeley: University of California
Press.

Davidson, Basil
1992    *The Black Man's Burden: Africa and the Curse of the Nation-State.* New
York: Times Books.

Davis, Mike
1995    "Los Angeles After the Storm: The Dialectic of Ordinary Disaster."
*Antipode* 27(3):221–41.

2005    *The Monster at Our Door: The Global Threat of Avian Flu.* New York:
New Press.

Davis, Wade
1988    *Passage of Darkness: The Ethnobiology of the Haitian Zombie.* Chapel
Hill, NC: University of North Carolina Press.

Day, Jennifer A., W. Roy Siegfried, Gideon N. Louw, and Margaret L. Jarman, eds.
1979    *Fynbos Ecology: A Preliminary Synthesis.* South African National Scientific Programmes, Report no.40. Pretoria: Cooperative Scientific
Programme, Council for Scientific and Industrial Research.

Decoteau, Claire
    n.d.     "The Diseased Body Politic: The Bio-Politics of HIV/AIDS in South Africa." Paper presented at an international symposium on AIDS and the Moral Order. Institute for Social Anthropology, Free University of Berlin, March 3–6, 2005. Ms.

de Kock, Ingrid
    2004–5   "Body Maps." *New Contrast* 128(32):58–60.

Deleuze, Gilles
    1986     *Foucault.* Paris: Editions de Minuit.

Depestre, René
    1971     *Change.* Paris: Editions du Seuil.

Derrida, Jacques
    1974     *Of Grammatology.* Translated by Gayatri Spivak. Baltimore: Johns Hopkins University Press.
    1994     *Specters of Marx: The State of Debt, the Work of Mourning, and the New International.* Translated by Peggy Kamuf. New York: Routledge.

Desai, Ashwin
    2002     *We Are the Poors: Community Struggles in Post-Apartheid South Africa.* New York: Monthly Review Press.

Deutsch, Jan-George, Peter Probst, and Heike I. Schmidt, eds.
    2002     *African Modernities: Entangled Meanings in Current Debates.* Portsmouth, NH: Heinemann.

Diop, Cheikh Anta
    1955     *Nations nègres et culture: De l'antiquité nègre égyptienne aux problèmes culturels de l'Afrique noire d'aujourd'hui.* Paris: Présence Africaine.

Dirks, Nicholas B., ed.
    1992     *Colonialism and Culture.* Ann Arbor: University of Michigan Press.

Dirlik, Arif
    1990     "Culturalism as Hegemonic Ideology and Liberating Practice." In *The Nature and Context of Minority Discourse,* (eds.) Abdul R. JanMohamed and David Lloyd. New York: Oxford University Press.
    1996     "Looking Backwards in an Age of Global Capital: Thoughts on History in Third World Cultural Criticism." In *Pursuit of Contemporary East Asian Culture,* (eds.) X. Tang and S. Snyder. Boulder, CO: Westview Press.

Dlamini, Jacob
    2009     *Native Nostalgia.* Auckland Park: Jacana Media.

Dlhomo, Herbert Isaac Ernest
    1977     "Why Study Tribal Dramatic Forms?" In *Literary Theory of H.I.E. Dlhomo,* (eds.) Nick Visser and Tim Couzens. Special issue of *English in Africa* 4(2). [1939]

Duara, Prasenjit
    2007     "To Think Like an Empire." Review of *Colonialism in Question: Theory, Knowledge, History,* Frederick Cooper (Berkeley: University of California Press, 2005). *History and Theory* 46(2):292–98.

2009 Featured Review of *The Theft of History,* Jack Goody (New York: Cambridge University Press, 2006). *American Historical Review* 114: 405–07.

Dube, Pamela Sethunya

2002 "The Story of Thandi Shezi." In *Commissioning the Past: Understanding South Africa's Truth and Reconciliation Commission,* (eds.) Deborah Posel and Graeme Simpson. Johannesburg: Witwatersrand University Press.

Du Bois, William Edward Burghardt

1933 *The Souls of Black Folk: Essays and Sketches.* Chicago: A.C. McClurg.

Dumont, Louis

1970 *Homo Hierarchicus: An Essay on the Caste System.* Translated by M. Sainsbury. Chicago: University of Chicago Press.

Duncan, Ian

1992 *Modern Romance and Transformations of the Novel: The Gothic, Scott, Dickens.* Cambridge: Cambridge University Press.

Durham, Deborah, and Fred Klaits

2000 "Funerals and the Public Space of Mutuality in Botswana." *Journal of Southern African Studies* 28(4):777–95.

Durkheim, Emile

1938 *The Rules of Sociological Method.* Eighth edition. Edited by Sarah A. Solovay and John H. Mueller, translated by George E.G. Catlin. New York: Free Press.

2001 *The Elementary Forms of Religious Life.* Translated by Carol Cosman. New York: Oxford University Press. [1912]

du Toit, Fanie

1999 "Public Discourse, Theology and the TRC: A Theological Appreciation of the South African Truth and Reconciliation Commission." *Literature & Theology* 13(4):340–57.

Dyson, James

2010 *Ingenious Britain: Making the UK the Leading High Tech Exporter in Europe;* http://media.dyson.com/images_resize_sites/inside_dyson/assets/UK/downloads/IngeniousBritain.PDF.

Eisenstadt, Shmuel N., ed.

2002 *Multiple Modernities.* New Brunswick, NJ: Transaction Publishers.

Evans-Pritchard, Edward E.

1937 *Witchcraft, Oracles and Magic Among the Azande.* Oxford: Clarendon Press.

1940a "The Nuer of the Southern Sudan." In *African Political Systems,* (eds.) Meyer Fortes and Edward E. Evans-Pritchard. London: Oxford University Press for the International Institute of African Languages and Cultures.

1940b *The Nuer.* Oxford: Clarendon Press.

1956 *Nuer Religion.* Oxford: Clarendon Press.

Fabian, Johannes

1983 *Time and the Other: How Anthropology Makes Its Object.* New York: Columbia University Press.

Fanon, Frantz
  1967    *Black Skin, White Masks.* Translated by Charles Lam Markmann. New York: Grove Press.
Farer, Tom J.
  1989    "Democracy and Human Rights: Toward Union." *Human Rights Quarterly* 11(4):504–21.
Farmer, Paul
  2003    *Pathologies of Power: Health, Human Rights, and the New War on the Poor.* Berkeley: University of California Press.
Ferguson, James
  1993    "De-Moralizing Economies: African Socialism, Scientific Capitalism, and the Moral Politics of 'Structural Adjustment.'" In *Moralizing States and the Ethnography of the Present,* (ed.) Sally Falk Moore. American Ethnological Society Monograph Series, no.5. Arlington, VA: American Anthropological Society.
  1999    *Expectations of Modernity: Myths and Meanings of Urban Life on the Zambian Copperbelt.* Berkeley: University of California Press.
  2006    *Global Shadows: Africa in the Neoliberal World Order.* Durham, NC: Duke University Press.
Fields, Karen E.
  1985    *Revival and Rebellion in Colonial Central Africa.* Princeton, NJ: Princeton University Press.
Finnegan, William
  2010    "Comment: Borderlines." *New Yorker,* July 26, pp.19–20.
Fordred, Lesley
  1998    "Narrative, Conflict and Change: Journalism in the New South Africa." PhD dissertation. University of Cape Town.
Fortes, Meyer
  1953    "The Structure of Unilineal Descent Groups." *American Anthropologist* 55(1):17–41.
  1969    *Kinship and the Social Order: The Legacy of Lewis Henry Morgan.* London: Routledge & Kegan Paul.
  1973    "On the Concept of the Person Among the Tallensi." In *La Notion de Personne en Afrique Noire,* (ed.) Germaine Dieterlen. Paris: Éditions du Centre National de la Recherche Scientifique.
Fortes, Meyer, and Edward E. Evans-Pritchard
  1940    Introduction. In *African Political Systems,* (eds.) Meyer Fortes and Edward E. Evans-Pritchard. London: Oxford University Press for the International Institute of African Languages and Cultures.
Foucault, Michel
  1978    *History of Sexuality,* Volume 1: *An Introduction.* Translated by Robert Hurley. New York: Random House.
  1997    *The Politics of Truth.* Edited by Sylvère Lotringer, translated by Lysa Hochroth and Catherine Porter. New York: Semiotext(e).
  2008    *The Birth of Biopolitics: Lectures at the Collège de France, 1978–1979.* Edited by Michel Senellart, translated by Graham Burchell. New York: Palgrave.

Frank, Andre Gunder
  1971    *Capitalism and Underdevelopment in Latin America: Historical Studies of Chile and Brazil.* Harmondsworth: Penguin Books.
Friedman, Steven
  2007    *Power in Action: Democracy, Collective Action and Social Justice.* Research Report submitted to the Institute for Democracy in South Africa and the Ford Foundation. Pretoria: IDASA.
Fukuyama, Francis
  1992    *The End of History and the Last Man.* New York: Free Press.
Fullard, Madeleine, and Nicky Rousseau
  2008    "Uncertain Borders: The TRC and the (Un)Making of Public Myths." *Kronos* 34(1):215–39.
Gaskell, Elizabeth Cleghorn
  1855    *North and South.* London: Chapman & Hall.
Geschiere, Peter
  1997    *The Modernity of Witchcraft: Politics and the Occult in Postcolonial Africa.* Charlottesville: University of Virginia Press.
  1999    "Globalization and the Power of Indeterminate Meaning: Witchcraft and Spirit Cults in Africa and East Asia." In *Globalization and Identity: Dialectics of Flow and Closure,* (eds.) Birgit Meyer and Peter Geschiere. Oxford: Blackwell.
  2006    "Witchcraft and the Limits of the Law: Cameroon and South Africa." In *Law and Disorder in the Postcolony,* (eds.) Jean Comaroff and John L. Comaroff. Chicago: University of Chicago Press.
Geschiere, Peter, and Francis Nyamnjoh
  2000    "Capitalism and Autochthony: The Seesaw of Mobility and Belonging." In *Millennial Capitalism and the Culture of Neoliberalism,* (eds.) Jean Comaroff and John L. Comaroff. Special edition of *Public Culture* 12(2):423–52.
Gillett, Simon
  1973    "The Survival of Chieftaincy in Botswana." *African Affairs* 72(287):179–85.
Glaser, Barney G., and Anselm L. Strauss
  1967    *The Discovery of Grounded Theory: Strategies for Qualitative Research.* Chicago: Aldine.
Gluckman, Max
  1963    *Order and Rebellion in Tribal Africa.* London: Cohen & West.
Goffman, Erving
  1959    *The Presentation of Self in Everyday Life.* Garden City, NY: Doubleday.
Good, Kenneth
  1992    "Interpreting the Exceptionality of Botswana." *Journal of Modern African Studies* 30(1):69–95.
Goody, Jack
  2006    *The Theft of History.* New York: Cambridge University Press.
Gopnik, Adam
  2008    "The Back of the World: The Troubling Genius of G. K. Chesterton." *New Yorker,* July 7–14, pp.52–59.

Gordon, Jane Anna, and Neil Roberts
2009     "Introduction: The Project of Creolizing Rousseau." In *Creolizing Rousseau,* (eds.) Jane Anna Gordon and Neil Roberts. Special edition of *The CLR James Journal* 15(1):3–16.

Gramsci, Antonio
1988     *An Antonio Gramsci Reader: Selected Writings, 1916–1935.* Edited by David Forgacs. New York: Schocken Books.

Grandin, Greg, and Thomas Miller Klubock
2007     Introduction. In *Truth Commissions: State Terror, History, and Memory.* Special edition of the *Radical History Review* 97(Winter):1–10.

Guo, Jerry
2010     "How Africa Is Becoming the New Asia." *Newsweek,* March 1, pp.42–44.

Guyer, Jane I.
2004     *Marginal Gains: Monetary Transactions in Atlantic Africa.* Chicago: University of Chicago Press.

Hacking, Ian
1991     "Two Souls in One Body." *Critical Inquiry* 17(4):838–67.

Hall, Anthony Vincent
1979     "Invasive Weeds." In *Fynbos Ecology: A Preliminary Synthesis,* (eds.) Jennifer A. Day *et al.* South African National Scientific Programmes, Report no.40. Pretoria: Cooperative Scientific Programme, Council for Scientific and Industrial Research.

Halliwell, Stephen
2002     *The Aesthetics of Mimesis: Ancient Texts and Modern Problems.* Princeton, NJ: Princeton University Press.

Hannerz, Ulf
1989     "Notes on the Global Ecumene." *Public Culture* 1(2):66–75.

Hansen, Thomas Blom, and Finn Stepputat
2005     Introduction. In *Sovereign Bodies: Citizens, Migrants, and States in the Postcolonial World,* (eds.) Thomas Blom Hansen and Finn Stepputat. Princeton, NJ: Princeton University Press.

Hardt, Michael
1995     "The Withering of Civil Society." *Social Text* 45, 14(4):27–44.

Hardt, Michael, and Antonio Negri
2000     *Empire.* Cambridge, MA: Harvard University Press.

Harries, Patrick
1994     *Work, Culture, and Identity: Migrant Laborers in Mozambique and South Africa, c.1860–1910.* Portsmouth, NH: Heinemann.
2010     "From Public History to Private Enterprise: The Politics of Memory in the New South Africa." In *Historical Memory in Africa: Dealing with the Past, Reaching for the Future in an Intercultural Context,* (eds.) Mamadou Diawara, Bernard Lategan, and Jörn Rüsen. New York: Berghahn Books.

Hartog, François
2003     *Régimes d'historicité, Présentisme et expériences du temps.* Paris: Seuil.

Harvey, David
    1982    *The Limits to Capital.* Chicago: University of Chicago Press.
    1989    *The Condition of Postmodernity: An Enquiry into the Origins of Cultural Change.* Oxford: Blackwell.

Hegeman, Susan
    1991    "Shopping for Identities: 'A Nation of Nations' and the Weak Ethnicity of Objects." *Public Culture* 3(2):71–92.

Henner, Paul
    2009    *Human Rights and the Alien Tort Statute: Law, History and Analysis.* Chicago: ABA Publishing.

Hoad, Neville
    2005    "Thabo Mbeki's AIDS Blues: The Intellectual, the Archive, and the Pandemic." *Public Culture* 17(1):101–27.
    2007    *African Intimacies: Race, Homosexuality, and Globalization.* Minneapolis: University of Minnesota Press.

Hobsbawm, Eric J.
    1992    "Ethnicity and Nationalism in Europe Today." *Anthropology Today* 8(1):3–8.

Holm, John D.
    1987    "Elections in Botswana." In *Elections in Independent Africa,* (ed.) F.M. Hayward. Boulder, CO: Westview Press.

Holm, John D., and Patrick P. Molutsi, eds.
    1989    *Democracy in Botswana.* Athens: Ohio University Press/The Botswana Society.

Hourani, Albert
    1983    *Arabic Thought in the Liberal Age, 1799–1939.* Cambridge: Cambridge University Press.

Huffington, Arianna
    2010    *Third World America: How Our Politicians Are Abandoning the Middle Class and Betraying the American Dream.* New York: Crown.

Irvine, Judith T., and Susan Gal
    2000    "Language Ideology and Linguistic Differentiation." In *Regimes of Language: Ideologies, Polities, and Identities,* (ed.) Paul V. Kroskrity. Santa Fe, NM: School for American Research Press.

Jackson, Tim
    2009    *Prosperity Without Growth: Economics for a Finite Planet.* London: Earthscan.

Jacobson, David
    1996    *Rights Across Borders.* Baltimore: Johns Hopkins University Press.

Jeffery, Patricia, Roger Jeffery, and Andrew Lyon
    1989    *Labour Pains and Labour Power: Women and Childbirth in India.* London: Zed Books.

Jensen, Steffen
    2005    "Above the Law: Practices of Sovereignty in Surrey Estate, Cape Town." In *Sovereign Bodies: Citizens, Migrants, and States in the Postcolonial World,* (eds.) Thomas Blom Hansen and Finn Stepputat. Princeton, NJ: Princeton University Press.

Jones, Gareth Stedman
   1971   *Outcast London: A Study in the Relationship Between Classes in Victorian Society.* Oxford: Clarendon Press.
Joyce, Patrick
   1995   "The End of Social History?" *Social History* 20(1):73–91.
Junod, Henri A.
   1927   *Life of a South African Tribe,* Volume 2. Second edition. London: Macmillan.
Kahn, Jeffrey
   n.d.   "Quarantine and the Camp: HIV-Positive Haitians at Guantanamo Bay, Cuba." Paper written for the 21st Century Seminar, University of Chicago, Fall 2004. Ms.
Kapferer, Bruce, ed.
   2005   *The Retreat of the Social: The Rise and Rise of Reductionism.* Oxford: Berghahn Books.
Karlstrom, Mikael
   1996   "Imagining Democracy: Political Culture and Democratization in Buganda." *Africa* 66(4):485–505.
Kirtzman, Andrew
   2009   *Betrayal: The Life and Lies of Bernie Madoff.* New York: HarperCollins.
Kistner, Ulrike
   2003   *Commissioning and Contesting Post-Apartheid's Human Rights: AIDS, Racism, Truth and Reconciliation.* Münster: Lit Verlag.
   n.d.   "Adversities in Adherence: Paralogisms of 'Biological Citizenship' in South Africa." Paper presented at the 3rd European Conference on African Studies, Leipzig, 2009. Ms.
Klor De Alva, J. Jorge
   1995   "The Postcolonization of the (Latin) American Experience: A Reconsideration of 'Colonialism,' 'Postcolonialism,' and 'Mestizaje.'" In *After Colonialism: Imperial Histories and Postcolonial Displacements,* (ed.) Gyan Prakash. Princeton, NJ: Princeton University Press.
Konrad, Monica
   1998   "Ova Donation and Symbols of Substance: Some Variations on the Theme of Sex, Gender and the Partible Body." *Journal of the Royal Anthropological Institute* 4(4):643–67.
Koolhaas, Rem, and Edgar Cleijne
   2001   *Lagos: How It Works.* With Harvard Project on the City and 2X4, (ed.) Ademide Adelusi-Adeluyi. Baden: Lars Müller Publishers.
Kopytoff, Igor
   1987   "The Internal African Frontier: The Making of African Culture." In *The African Frontier,* (ed.) Igor Kopytoff. Bloomington: Indiana University Press.
Koselleck, Reinhart
   2002   *The Practice of Conceptual History: Timing History, Spacing Concepts.* Translated by Todd Samuel Presner. Stanford, CA: Stanford University Press.

Krotz, Esteban
  2005    "Anthropologies of the South: Their Rise, Their Silencing, Their Characteristics." *Journal of the World Anthropology Network* 1(1): 147–59.
Kruger, Frederick John
  1977    "Ecology and Management of Cape Fynbos: Towards Conservation of a Unique Biome Type." Paper presented to the South African Wild Life Management Association's Second International Symposium, Pretoria. Ms.
  1979    "Fire." In *Fynbos Ecology: A Preliminary Synthesis,* (eds.) Jennifer A. Day *et al.* South African National Scientific Programmes, Report no.40. Pretoria: Cooperative Scientific Programme, Council for Scientific and Industrial Research.
Kruger, Frederick John, ed.
  1978    *A Description of the Fynbos Biome Project.* A Report of the Committee for Terrestrial Ecosystems, National Programme for Environmental Sciences. Pretoria: Cooperative Scientific Programmes, Council for Scientific and Industrial Research.
Kymlicka, Will, and Wayne Norman
  2000    Introduction. In *Citizenship in Diverse Societies,* (eds.) Will Kymlicka and Wayne Norman. Oxford: Oxford University Press.
Laclau, Ernesto
  1990    *New Reflections on the Revolution of Our Time.* New York: Verso.
La Fontaine, Jean S.
  1985    "Person and Individual: Some Anthropological Reflections." In *The Category of the Person: Anthropology, Philosophy, History,* (eds.) Michael Carrithers, Steven Collins, and Steven Lukes. Cambridge: Cambridge University Press.
Lalu, Premesh
  2009    *The Deaths of Hintsa: Postapartheid South Africa and the Shape of Recurring Pasts.* Cape Town: HSRC Press.
Lambek, Michael
  1996    "The Past Imperfect: Remembering as a Moral Practice." In *Tense Past: Cultural Essays in Trauma and Memory,* (eds.) Paul Antze and Michael Lambek. London: Routledge.
Langer, Susanne K.
  1942    *Philosophy in a New Key: A Study in the Symbolism of Reason, Rite, and Art.* Cambridge, MA: Harvard University Press.
Lash, Scott
  1999    *Another Modernity: A Different Authenticity.* Oxford: Blackwell.
Lash, Scott, and John Urry
  1987    *The End of Organized Capitalism.* Madison: University of Wisconsin Press.
Latour, Bruno
  1993    *We Have Never Been Modern.* Translated by Catherine Porter. Cambridge, MA: Harvard University Press.

Lefkowitz, Mary R., and Guy Maclean Rogers, eds.
  1996    *Black Athena Revisited.* Chapel Hill: University of North Carolina
          Press.
Legassick, Martin C.
  1969    "The Sotho-Tswana Peoples Before 1800." In *African Societies in
          Southern Africa,* (ed.) Leonard M. Thompson. London: Heinemann
          Educational Books.
Le Marcis, Frédéric
  2004    "The Suffering Body of the City." *Public Culture* 16(3):453–77.
Lévi-Strauss, Claude
  1963    *Structural Anthropology,* Volume 1. Translated by Claire Jacobson and
          Brooke Grundfest-Schoepf. New York: Basic Books.
  1969    *The Elementary Structures of Kinship.* Translated by James Harle Bell,
          John Richard von Sturmer, and Rodney Needham. Boston: Beacon
          Press. [1949]
Levin, Adam
  2005    "Aidsafari: A Memoir of My Journey with AIDS." Cape Town: Zebra
          Press.
Levy, Jacob T.
  2000    *The Multiculturalism of Fear.* Oxford: Oxford University Press.
Lichtenstein, Henry (M.H.C.)
  1930    *Travels in Southern Africa,* Volume 2. Translated by A. Plumptre. Cape
          Town: Van Riebeeck Society.
Lienhardt, Godfrey
  1985    "Self: Public, Private. Some African Representations." In *The Category
          of the Person: Anthropology, Philosophy, History,* (eds.) Michael Car-
          rithers, Steven Collins, and Steven Lukes. Cambridge: Cambridge
          University Press.
Lijphart, Arend
  1995    "Self-Determination Versus Pre-Determination of Ethnic Minorities
          in Power-Sharing Systems." In *The Rights of Minority Cultures,* (ed.)
          Will Kymlicka. Oxford: Oxford University Press.
Lodge, David
  1988    *Nice Work.* London: Secker & Warburg.
Lodge, Tom
  1983    *Black Politics in South Africa Since 1945.* London: Longman.
Lomnitz, Claudio
  2006    "Latin America's Rebellion: Will the New Left Set a New Agenda?"
          *Boston Review,* September/October; http://bostonreview.net/BR31/
          lomnitz.php.
MacFarlane, Alan
  1978    *The Origins of English Individualism.* Oxford: Basil Blackwell.
Mackenzie, John
  1871    *Ten Years North of the Orange River.* Edinburgh: Edmonston & Douglas.
  1887    *Austral Africa: Losing It or Ruling It,* 2 volumes. London: Sampson
          Low, Marston, Searle & Rivington.

Macpherson, Crawford Brough
  1962    *The Political Theory of Possessive Individualism: Hobbes to Locke.* Oxford:
          Oxford University Press.
Makdisi, Saree S.
  1992    "The Empire Renarrated: *Season of Migration to the North* and the
          Reinvention of the Present." *Critical Inquiry* 18(4):804–20.
Mamdani, Mahmood
  1986    "Peasants and Democracy in Africa." *New Left Review* 156
          (March–April):37–40.
  1990    "State and Civil Society in Contemporary Africa." *Africa Development*
          15(3–4):47–70.
  1992    "Africa: Democratic Theory and Democratic Struggles." *Dissent*
          (Summer):312–318.
  1996    *Citizen and Subject: Contemporary Africa and the Legacy of Late Colo-
          nialism.* Princeton, NJ: Princeton University Press.
  2000    "The Truth According to the TRC." In *The Politics of Memory: Truth,
          Healing and Social Justice,* (eds.) Ifi Amadiume and Abdullah Am-
          Na'im. London: Zed Books.
  2002    "Amnesty or Impunity? A Preliminary Critique of the Report of the
          Truth and Reconciliation Commission of South Africa (TRC)." *Dia-
          critics* 32(3–4):33–59.
Mandel, Ernst
  1978    *Late Capitalism.* Translated by Joris De Bres. New York: Verso.
Mandela, Nelson
  1994    *Long Walk to Freedom: The Autobiography of Nelson Mandela.* Boston:
          Little, Brown & Company.
Mann, Kenneth
  1992    "The Middleground Between Criminal and Civil Law." *Yale Law
          Journal* 101(8):1795–1873.
Marks, Shula
  1978    "Natal, the Zulu Royal Family and the Ideology of Segregation." *Journal
          of Southern African Studies* 4(2):172–94.
  1997    "Rewriting South African History or the Hunt for Hintsa's Head."
          Bindoff Memorial Lecture, Queen Mary College, 1996. In *Rethinking
          South African History,* (eds.) S.M. McGrath, K. King, *et al.* Edinburgh:
          Edinburgh University Press.
Marx, Karl
  1967    *Capital: A Critique of Political Economy,* Volume 1. New York: Inter-
          national Publishers.
Masilela, Ntongela
  2003    "South African Literature in African Languages." In *Encyclopedia of
          African Literature,* (ed.) Simon Gikandi. New York: Routledge.
  n.d.    "New Negro Modernity and New African Modernity"; http://pzacad
          .pitzer.edu/NAM/general/modernity.pdf, 2003. Ms.
Matshoba, Mtutuzeli
  2002    "Nothing But the Truth: The Ordeal of Duma Khumalo." In

*Commissioning the Past: Understanding South Africa's Truth and Rec-onciliation Commission,* (eds.) Deborah Posel and Graeme Simpson. Johannesburg: Witwatersrand University Press.

Mauss, Marcel
1985    "A Category of the Human Mind: The Notion of Person, the Notion of Self." Translated by W.D. Halls. In *The Category of the Person: Anthropology, Philosophy, History,* (eds.) Michael Carrithers, Steven Collins, and Steven Lukes. Cambridge: Cambridge University Press. [1938]
1990    *The Gift: The Form and Reason for Exchange in Archaic Societies.* Translated by W.D. Halls. New York: W.W. Norton. [1967]

Maylam, Paul R.
1980    *Rhodes, the Tswana, and the British.* Westport, CT: Greenwood Press.

Mazzarella, William
2003    *Shoveling Smoke: Advertising and Globalization in Contemporary India.* Durham, NC: Duke University Press.
2006    "Internet X-Ray: E-Governance, Transparency, and the Politics of Immediation in India." *Public Culture* 18(3):473–505.

Mbeki, Govan
1964    *South Africa: The Peasant's Revolt.* Harmondsworth: Penguin Books.

Mbembe, Achille
1992a    "Provisional Notes on the Postcolony." *Africa* 62(1):3–37.
1992b    "The Banality of Power and the Aesthetics of Vulgarity in the Post-colony." *Public Culture* 4(2):1–30.
2001    *On the Postcolony.* Berkeley: University of California Press.
2002    "African Modes of Self-Writing." Translated by Steven Rendall. *Public Culture* 14(1):239–73.
2003    "Necropolitics." *Public Culture* 15(1):11–40.
2006    "On Politics as a Form of Expenditure." In *Law and Disorder in the Postcolony,* (eds.) Jean Comaroff and John L. Comaroff. Chicago: University of Chicago Press.
2008    "Aesthetics of Superfluity." In *Johannesburg: The Elusive Metropolis,* (eds.) Sarah Nuttall and Achille Mbembe. Johannesburg: Witwa-tersrand University Press.

Mbembe, Achille, and Sarah Nuttall
2004    "Writing the World from an African Metropolis." *Public Culture* 16(3):347–72.

McCarthy, Cormac
1992    *Blood Meridian or the Evening Redness in the West.* New York: Vintage Books.

McClintock, Anne
1992    "The Angel of Progress: Pitfalls of the Term 'Post-Colonialism.'" *Social Text* 31/32:84–98.

McMichael, Philip
1998    "Development and Structural Adjustment." In *Virtualism: A New*

*Political Economy,* (eds.) James G. Carrier and Daniel Miller. Oxford: Berg.

Meillassoux, Claude

1972 "From Reproduction to Production." *Economy and Society* 1(1):93–105.

Merry, Sally Engel

1988 "Legal Pluralism." *Law and Society Review* 22(5):869–96.

Mishra, Vijay, and Bob Hodge

1991 "What is Post(-)Colonialism?" *Textual Practice* 5(3):399–414.

Mitchell, Timothy

1988 *Colonising Egypt.* Berkeley: University of California Press.

Mitchell, W.J. Thomas

2009 "The Unspeakable and the Unimaginable: Word and Image in a Time of Terror." In *Dynamics and Performativity of Imagination: The Image Between the Visible and the Invisible,* (eds.) Bernd Huppauf and Christoph Wulf. New York: Routledge.

Modood, Tariq

2000 "Anti-Essentialism, Multiculturalism, and the 'Recognition' of Religious Groups." In *Citizenship in Diverse Societies,* (eds.) Will Kymlicka and Wayne Norman. Oxford: Oxford University Press.

Moffat, Robert

1842 *Missionary Labours and Scenes in Southern Africa.* London: John Snow.

Mokgoro, Yvonne

1994 "The Role and Place of Lay Participation, Customary and Community Courts in a Restructured Future Judiciary." In *Reshaping the Structures of Justice for a Democratic South Africa.* Papers of a conference of the National Association of Democratic Lawyers, Pretoria, October 1993. Pretoria: National Association of Democratic Lawyers.

Molema, Silas Modiri

1920 *The Bantu, Past and Present.* Edinburgh: W. Green & Son.

1966 *Montshiwa: Barolong Chief and Patriot, 1815–96.* Cape Town: Struik.

Moll, Eugene, and Glen Moll

1994 *Common Trees of South Africa.* Cape Town: Struik.

Molutsi, Patrick P., and John D. Holm

1989 Introduction. In *Democracy in Botswana,* (eds.) John D. Holm and Patrick P. Molutsi. Athens: Ohio University Press/The Botswana Society.

Moore, Sally Falk

1978 *Law as Process.* London: Routledge & Kegan Paul.

Morton, Gregory Duff

n.d. "The Household and Its Money: Making Investments and Remaking Families with *Bolsa Família.*" PhD dissertation proposal. Department of Anthropology, University of Chicago, 2010.

Mudimbe, Valentin Yves

1988 *The Invention of Africa: Gnosis, Philosophy, and the Order of Knowledge.* Bloomington: Indiana University Press.

Mumford, Meg
  2009     *Bertolt Brecht.* Abingdon: Routledge.
Munn, Nancy D.
  1986     *The Fame of Gawa: A Symbolic Study of Value Transformation in a Massim (Papua New Guinea) Society.* Cambridge: Cambridge University Press.
Murphy, Robert F., and Lionel Kasdan
  1959     "The Structure of Parallel Cousin Marriage." *American Anthropologist* 61:17–29.
  1967     "Agnation and Endogamy: Some Further Considerations." *Southwestern Journal of Anthropology* 23:1–14.
Murray, Colin
  1976     "Marital Strategy in Lesotho: The Redistribution of Migrant Earnings." *African Studies* 35(2):99–121.
Nancy, Jean-Luc
  1997     *The Sense of the World.* Translated by Jeffrey S. Librett. Minneapolis: University of Minnesota Press.
National Botanical Gardens
  1959     *The Green Cancers in South Africa.* Kirstenbosch: Control of Alien Vegetation Committee.
Ndebele, Njabulo S.
  1991     *Rediscovery of the Ordinary: Essays on South African Literature and Culture.* Johannesburg: Congress of South African Writers.
Niehaus, Isak
  1993     "Witch-Hunting and Political Legitimacy: Continuity and Change in Green Valley, Lebowa, 1930–1991." *Africa* 63(4):498–530.
  1995     "Witches of the Transvaal Lowveld and Their Familiars: Conceptions of Duality, Power and Desire." *Cahiers d'études africaines* 138–139, 35(2–3):513–40.
  2001     "Witchcraft in the New South Africa: From Colonial Superstition to Postcolonial Reality?" In *Magical Interpretations, Material Realities: Modernity, Witchcraft and the Occult in Postcolonial Africa,* (eds.) Henrietta L. Moore and Todd Sanders. London: Routledge.
Nietzsche, Friedrich
  1910     *The Genealogy of Morals: A Polemic.* Translated by Horace B. Samuel. Edinburgh: T.N. Foulis.
  1957     *The Use and Abuse of History.* Translated by Adrian Collins. New York: Macmillan.
Norris, Pippa
  2004     "Electoral Engineering: Voting Rules and Political Behavior." Cambridge: Cambridge University Press.
Nuttall, Sarah
  2009     *Entanglement: Literary and Cultural Reflections on Post-Apartheid.* Johannesburg: Witwatersrand University Press.

Olivera, Oscar, in collaboration with Tom Lewis
  2004    *Cochabamba! Water War in Bolivia.* Cambridge, MA: South End Press.
Ong, Aiwa
  1999    *Citizenship: The Cultural Logics of Transnationality.* Durham, NC:
        Duke University Press.
Oomen, Barbara M.
  2002    "Chiefs! Law, Power and Culture in Contemporary South Africa." PhD
        dissertation. University of Leiden.
  2005    *Chiefs in South Africa: Law, Power and Culture in the Post-Apartheid*
        *Era.* New York: Palgrave.
Organization of American Historians
  2004    *History, Democracy, and Citizenship: The Debate over History's Role in*
        *Teaching Citizenship and Patriotism.* A report commissioned by the
        Executive Board of the Organization of American Historians. Bloom-
        ington, IN: Organization of American Historians.
Orwell, George
  1933    *Down and Out in Paris and London.* London: Harper & Bros.
Osborne, Ken
  2003    "Teaching History in Schools: A Canadian Debate." *Journal of Cur-*
        *riculum Studies* 35(5):585–626.
Packer, George
  2009    "The Ponzi State: Florida's Foreclosure Disaster." *New Yorker,* February
        9, pp.81–93.
Palmié, Stephan
  n.d.    "Slavery, Historicism, and the Poverty of Memorialization." Ms.
Parson, Jack
  1984    *Botswana: Liberal Democracy and the Labor Reserve in Southern Africa.*
        Boulder, CO: Westview Press.
Patton, Cindy
  1988    Inventing African AIDS. *City Limits* 363 (September):15–22.
Petryna, Adriana
  2002    *Life Exposed: Biological Citizenship After Chernobyl.* Princeton, NJ:
        Princeton University Press.
Philip, John
  1828    *Researches in South Africa; Illustrating the Civil, Moral, and Re-*
        *ligious Condition of the Native Tribes,* 2 volumes. London: James
        Duncan.
Picard, Louis A.
  1987    *The Politics of Development in Botswana: A Model for Success?* Boulder,
        CO: L. Rienner.
Picard, Louis A., ed.
  1985    *The Evolution of Modern Botswana.* London: Rex Collings.
Pietz, William
  1985    "The Problem of the Fetish, I." *Res* 9 (Spring):5–7.
  1987    "The Problem of the Fetish, II." *Res* 13 (Spring):23–45.

1988    "The Problem of the Fetish IIIa: Bosman's Guinea and the Enlighten-
        ment Theory of Fetishism." *Res* 16 (Autumn):105–23.

Piot, Charles
2010    *Nostalgia for the Future: West Africa After the Cold War.* Chicago:
        University of Chicago Press.

Plaatje, Solomon Tshekisho
1996    *Selected Writings.* Edited by Brian Willan. Johannesburg: Witwatersrand
        University Press.

Pooley, Simon
2010    "Pressed Flowers: Notions of Indigenous and Alien Vegetation in South
        Africa's Western Cape, c. 1902–1945." *Journal of Southern African
        Studies* 36(3):599–618.

Posel, Deborah, and Graeme Simpson, eds.
2002    *Commissioning the Past: Understanding South Africa's Truth and
        Reconciliation Commission.* Johannesburg: Witwatersrand University
        Press.

Prakash, Gyan
1995    "Introduction: After Colonialism." In *After Colonialism: Imperial His-
        tories and Postcolonial Displacements,* (ed.) Gyan Prakash. Princeton,
        NJ: Princeton University Press.

Przeworski, Adam
1991    *Democracy and the Market: Political and Economic Reforms in East-
        ern Europe and Latin America.* Cambridge: Cambridge University
        Press.

1999    "Minimalist Conception of Democracy: A Defense." In *Democracy's
        Value,* (eds.) Ian Shapiro and Casiano Hacker-Cordón. Cambridge:
        Cambridge University Press.

Radcliffe-Brown, Alfred Reginald
1951    Introduction. In *African Systems of Kinship and Marriage,* (eds.) Alfred
        Reginald Radcliffe-Brown and Daryl Forde. London: Oxford Univer-
        sity Press for the International African Institute.

Rajan, Kaushik Sunder
2005    "Subjects of Speculation: Emergent Life Sciences and Market Log-
        ics in the United States and India." *American Anthropologist* 107(1):
        19–30.

Ralushai, N.V., M.G. Masingi, D.M.M. Madiba, *et al.*
1996    *Report of the Commission of Inquiry into Witchcraft Violence and
        Ritual Murders in the Northern Province of the Republic of South Af-
        rica* (To: His Excellency The Honourable Member of the Executive
        Council for Safety and Security, Northern Province). No publisher
        given.

Rancière, Jacques
2003    *The Philosopher and His Poor.* Edited by Andrew Parker, translated by
        John Drury, Corinne Oster, and Andrew Parker. Durham, NC: Duke
        University Press.

Ranger, Terence O.
   n.d.      "History Matters." Valedictory Lecture, University of Zimbabwe, 31
            May 2001. Ms.

Rankin, Ian
   2009     *The Complaints.* London: Orion Books.

Rassool, Ciraj, and Sandra Prosalendis, eds.
   2001     *Recalling Community in Cape Town: Creating and Curating the District
            Six Museum.* Cape Town: District Six Museum.

Read, Kenneth
   1955     "Morality and the Concept of the Person Among the Gahuku-Gama."
            *Oceania* 25(4):233–82.

Reitzes, M.
   1994     "Alien Issues." *Indicator* (South Africa) 12(1):7.

Renan, Ernest
   1882     *Qu'est-ce qu'une nation? Conférence faite en Sorbonne, le 11 mars 1882.*
            Second edition. Paris: Calmann Lévy.

Robins, Steven
   1998     "The Truth Shall Make You Free? Reflections on the TRC." *Southern
            Africa Report* (August):9–13.
   2004     "'Long Live Zackie, Long Live': AIDS Activism, Science and Citi-
            zenship After Apartheid." *Journal of Southern African Studies* 30(3):
            651–72.
   2005     "ARVs and the Passage from 'Near Death' to 'New Life': AIDS Activism
            and 'Responsibilized' Citizens in South Africa." IDS Working Paper
            251. Brighton: Institute of Development Studies.
   2006     "From 'Rights' to 'Ritual': AIDS Activism in South Africa." *American
            Anthropologist* 108(2):312–23.
   2008     *From Revolution to Rights in South Africa: Social Movements, NGOs and
            Popular Politics After Apartheid.* Woodbridge: James Currey.

Ross, Fiona
   2003     *Bearing Witness: Women and the Truth and Reconciliation Commission
            in South Africa.* London: Pluto Press.

Roxburgh, Charles, *et al.*
   2010     *Lions on the Move: The Progress and Potential of African Economies.*
            McKinsey Global Institute Report; www.mckinsey.com/mgi/
            publications/progress_and_potential_of_african_economies/pdfs/MGI
            _african_economies_full_report.pdf.

Rubin, Jonah
   2008     "Adjudicating the Salvadoran Civil War: Expectations of the Law in
            Romagoza." *PoLAR* 31(2):264–85.
   n.d.      "Historical Memory and the Making of Liberal-Democratic Citizens
            in Spain." PhD dissertation proposal. Department of Anthropology,
            University of Chicago, 2010.

Rushdie, Salman
   1981     *Midnight's Children.* London: Penguin Books.

Sachs, Albie
  2009    *The Strange Alchemy of Life and Law.* Oxford: Oxford University Press.
  n.d.    "Towards the Liberation and Revitalization of Customary Law." In *Law in the uBuntu of South Africa,* (eds.) Drucilla Cornell and Nyoko Muvangua. New York: Fordham University Press. [Forthcoming.]
Said, Edward W.
  1983    *The World, the Text, and the Critic.* Cambridge, MA: Harvard University Press.
Schapera, Isaac
  1938    *A Handbook of Tswana Law and Custom.* London: Oxford University Press for the International Institute of African Languages and Cultures.
  1940    "The Political Organization of the Ngwato in Bechuanaland Protectorate." In *African Political Systems,* (eds). Meyer Fortes and Edward E. Evans-Pritchard. London: Oxford University for the International Institute of African Languages and Cultures.
  1943    *Tribal Legislation Among the Tswana of the Bechuanaland Protectorate.* London: London School of Economics.
  1953    *The Tswana.* London: International African Institute.
  1970    *Tribal Innovators: Tswana Chiefs and Social Change, 1795–1940.* London School of Economics Monographs, no.43. London: Athlone Press.
Schapera, Isaac, and John L. Comaroff
  1991    *The Tswana.* Revised edition. London: Kegan Paul International.
Schmitt, Carl
  1996    *The Concept of the Political.* Translated by George Schwab. Chicago: University of Chicago Press.
Seabrook, John
  2010    "How to Make It: James Dyson Built a Better Vacuum. Can He Pull Off a Second Industrial Revolution?" *New Yorker,* September 20, pp.66–73.
Seme, Pixley ka Isaka
  1905–6  "The Regeneration of Africa." *Royal African Society* 4:75–81.
Shamir, Ronen
  2004    "Between Self-Regulation and the Alien Tort Claims Act: On the Contested Concept of Corporate Social Responsibility." *Law and Society Review* 38(4):635–64.
Sharp, John S.
  1998    "'Non-Racialism' and Its Discontents: A Post-Apartheid Paradox." *International Social Science Journal* 156, 50(2):243–52.
  1998    "Who Speaks for Whom? A Response to Archie Mafeje's 'Anthropology and Independent Africans: Suicide or End of an Era.'" *African Sociological Review* 2(1):66–73.

Shechtel, Lexi
    2010    "Drivers of Satisfaction with Democracy in Africa." *Stanford Journal of International Relations* 11(2):48–57.

Shepherd, Peter M.
    1984    "Botswana: A Watershed Election." *Africa Now* 44 (December): 27–28.

Shillington, Kevin
    1985    *The Colonisation of the Southern Tswana, 1870–1900.* Johannesburg: Ravan Press.

Sillery, Anthony
    1952    *The Bechuanaland Protectorate.* London: Oxford University Press.

Silverstein, Michael
    1976    "Shifters, Linguistic Categories, and Cultural Description." In *Meaning in Anthropology,* (eds.) Keith H. Basso and Henry A. Selby. New York: Harper & Row.
    1998    "Contemporary Transformations of Local Linguistic Communities." *Annual Review of Anthropology* 27:401–26.

Simpson, Graeme
    2002    "'Tell No Lies, Claim No Easy Victories': A Brief Evaluation of South Africa's Truth and Reconciliation Commission." In *Commissioning the Past: Understanding South Africa's Truth and Reconciliation Commission,* (eds.) Deborah Posel and Graeme Simpson. Johannesburg: Witwatersrand University Press.

Sinclair, M.
    1996    "Unwilling Aliens: Migrants in the New South Africa." *Indicator* (South Africa) 13(3):14–18.

Sontag, Susan
    1989    *Illness as Metaphor and AIDS and Its Metaphors.* New York: Farrar, Straus & Giroux.

South African Human Rights Commission
    2000    *Lindela at the Crossroads for Detention and Repatriation: An Assessment of the Conditions of Detention.* Johannesburg: South African Human Rights Commission.

Spivak, Gayatri Chakravorty
    1988    "Can the Subaltern Speak?" In *Marxism and the Interpretation of Culture,* (eds.) Carey Nelson and Lawrence Grossberg. Urbana: University of Illinois Press.

Stiglitz, Joseph E.
    2002    *Globalization and Its Discontents.* New York: W.W. Norton.
    2008    "Realign the Interests of Wall Street." Forum on "How to Save Capitalism: Fundamental Fixes for a Collapsing System," *Harper's Magazine* 317, 1902 (November):36–37.

Stoler, Ann Laura
    2002    *Carnal Knowledge and Imperial Power: Race and the Intimate in Colonial Rule.* Berkeley: University of California Press.

2006    "Intimidations of Empire: Predicaments of the Tactile and the Unseen." In *Haunted by Empire: Geographies of Intimacy in North American History,* (ed.) Ann Laura Stoler. Durham, NC: Duke University Press.

Stoler, Ann Laura, and Frederick Cooper
1997    "Between Metropole and Colony: Rethinking a Research Agenda." In *Tensions of Empire: Colonial Cultures in a Bourgeois World,* (eds.) Frederick Cooper and Ann Laura Stoler. Berkeley: University of California Press.

Strange, Susan
1986    *Casino Capitalism.* Oxford: Blackwell.

Strathern, Marilyn
1988    *The Gender of the Gift: Problems with Women and Problems with Society in Melanesia.* Berkeley: University of California Press.

Sundkler, Bengt G.M.
1961    *Bantu Prophets in South Africa.* Second edition. London: Oxford University Press for the International African Institute.

Swatuk, Larry A.
1999    "Botswana: The Opposition Implodes." *Southern Africa Report* 14(3):27–30.

Tagart, Edward Samuel B.
1933    "Report on the Conditions Existing Among the Masarwa in the Bamangwato Reserve of the Bechuanaland Protectorate." *Official Gazette of the High Commissioner for South Africa* 122, 12 May 1933.

Táíwò, Olúfémi
2010    *How Colonialism Preempted Modernity in Africa.* Bloomington: Indiana University Press.

Taylor, Charles M.
1989    *Sources of the Self: The Making of Modern Identity.* Cambridge, MA: Harvard University Press.
1992    "The Politics of Recognition." In *Multiculturalism and "The Politics of Recognition": An Essay,* (ed.) Amy Gutmann. Princeton, NJ: Princeton University Press.

Taylor, John P.
2010    "Janus and the Siren's Call: Kava and the Articulation of Gender and Modernity in Vanuatu." *Journal of the Royal Anthropological Institute* (NS) 16(2):279–96.

Thelen, David
2002    "How the Truth and Reconciliation Commission Challenges the Ways We Use History." *South African Historical Journal* 47:162–90.

Therborn, Göran
1995    *European Modernity and Beyond: The Trajectory of European Societies 1945–2000.* London: Sage.

Tlou, Thomas
1974    "The Nature of Batswana States." *Botswana Notes and Records* 6: 57–75.

Tomasic, Roman
    1991    *Casino Capitalism? Insider Trading in Australia*. With Brendan Pentony. Canberra: Australian Institute of Criminology.

Toscana, Alberto
    2005    "Capture." In *The Deleuze Dictionary*, (ed.) Adrian Parr. Edinburgh: Edinburgh University Press.

Tostevin, Matthew
    2010    "World Cup Showcases Africa's Bigger Changes." *The Big Issue*, July 9–30, pp.14–18.

Treichler, Paula A.
    1988    "AIDS, Homophobia, and Biomedical Discourse: An Epidemic of Signification." In *AIDS: Cultural Analysis/Cultural Activism*, (ed.) Douglas Crimp. Cambridge, MA: MIT Press.
    1999    *How to Have Theory in an Epidemic: Cultural Chronicles of AIDS*. Durham, NC: Duke University Press.

Tronti, Mario
    1980    "The Strategy of Refusal." *Semiotext(e)* 3:28–36.

Trouillot, Michel-Rolph
    2000    "Abortive Rituals: Historical Apologies in the Global Era." *Interventions* 2(2):171–86.

Tsing, Anna Lowenhaupt
    1993    *In the Realm of the Diamond Queen: Marginality in an Out-of-the-Way Place*. Princeton, NJ: Princeton University Press.

Turner, Terence
    2003    "Class Projects, Social Consciousness, and the Contradictions of 'Globalization.'" In *Globalization, the State and Violence*, (ed.) Jonathan Friedman. Walnut Creek, CA: Altamira Press.

Turner, Victor
    1967    *The Forest of Symbols: Aspects of Ndembu Ritual*. Ithaca, NY: Cornell University Press.

Tutu, Desmond Mpilo
    1984    *Hope and Suffering: Sermons and Speeches*. Grand Rapids, MI: Eerdmans.

Van Binsbergen, Wim
    1995    Aspects of Democracy and Democratisation in Zambia and Botswana. *Journal of Contemporary African Studies* 13(1):3–33.

Van Binsbergen, Wim, and Peter Geschiere
    1999    "Commodification and Identities: *The Social Life of Things* Revisited." Call for papers for an international conference; www.shikanda.net/general/gen3/research_page/commodca.htm.

Vanderbilt, Tom
    1997    "The Advertised Life." In *Commodify Your Dissent: Salvos from The Baffler*, (eds.) Thomas Frank and Matt Weiland. New York: W.W. Norton.

Veblen, Thorstein
    1899    *The Theory of the Leisure Class: An Economic Study in the Evolution of Institutions*. New York: Macmillan.

Vengroff, Richard
   1975      Traditional Political Structures in the Contemporary Context. *African Studies* 34(1):39–56.

Verdery, Katherine
   1999      *The Political Life of Dead Bodies: Reburial and Postsocialist Change.* New York: Columbia University Press.

Wace, Nigel
   1988      "Naturalized Plants in the Australian Landscape." In *The Australian Experience,* (ed.) R.L. Heathcote for the International Geographical Congress. Melbourne: Longman Cheshire.

Wagner, Roy
   1991      "The Fractal Person." In *Big Men and Great Men: Personifications of Power in Melanesia,* (eds.) Maurice Godelier and Marilyn Strathern. Cambridge: Cambridge University Press.

Wallerstein, Immanuel
   2004      *Alternatives: The United States Confronts the World.* Boulder, CO: Paradigm Publishers.

Walshe, Peter
   1971      *The Rise of African Nationalism in South Africa: The African National Congress, 1912–1952.* Berkeley: University of California Press.

Wasser, Hartmut
   2001      "What's Troubling Democracies in Europe and the US?" *Veranstaltungsdokumentation,* October. Bonn: Bundeszentrale für politische Bildung; www.bpb.de/veranstaltungen/OZD4SK,0,What%92s_Troubling_Democracies_in_Europe_and_the_US.html.

Watkins, Susan
   2010      "Editorial: Blue Labor?" *New Left Review* (Second Series) 63 (May):5–15.

Watney, Simon
   1990      "Missionary Positions: AIDS, 'Africa,' and Race." In *Out There: Marginalization and Contemporary Cultures,* (eds.) Russell Ferguson, Martha Glover, Trinh T. Minh-ha, and Cornell West. Cambridge, MA: MIT Press/New Museum of Contemporary Art.

Wedeen, Lisa
   2008      *Peripheral Visions: Publics, Power, and Performance in Yemen.* Chicago: University of Chicago Press.

Wee, C.J. Wan-ling
   2003      *Culture, Empire, and the Question of Being Modern.* Oxford: Lexington Books.

Weiss, Joseph
   n.d.       "Challenging Reconciliation: Disagreement and Interdeterminacy in Canada's Indian Residential Schools Truth and Reconciliation Commission." MA thesis. Department of Anthropology, University of Chicago, 2009.

White, Hylton J.
   2001      "Value, Crisis, and Custom: The Politics of Sacrifice in a Post-Apartheid Countryside." PhD dissertation. University of Chicago.

2004    "Ritual Haunts: The Timing of Estrangement in a Post-Apartheid Countryside." In *Producing African Futures: Ritual and Reproduction in a Neoliberal Age,* (ed.) Brad Weiss. Leiden: Brill.

White, Luise
1990    *The Comforts of Home: Prostitution in Colonial Nairobi.* Chicago: University of Chicago Press.

Willoughby, William Charles
1932    *Nature-Worship and Taboo: Further Studies in "The Soul of the Bantu."* Hartford, CT: Hartford Seminary Press.

Wilkinson, Richard, and Kate Pickett
2010    *The Spirit Level: Why Equality Is Better for Everyone.* London: Penguin Books.

Wilson, Monica
1951    "Witch Beliefs and Social Structure." *American Journal of Sociology* 56(4):307–13.

Wilson, Richard A.
2001    *The Politics of Truth and Reconciliation in South Africa: Legitimizing the Post-Apartheid State.* Cambridge: Cambridge University Press.

Worby, Eric
1998    "Tyranny, Parody, and Ethnic Polarity: Ritual Engagements with the State in Northwestern Zambia." *Journal of Southern African Studies* 24(3):560–78.

Worger, William H.
1987    *South Africa's City of Diamonds: Mine Workers and Monopoly Capitalism in Kimberley, 1867–1895.* New Haven, CT: Yale University Press.

Wright, Gwendolyn
1991    *The Politics of Design in French Colonial Urbanism.* Chicago: University of Chicago Press.

Young, Tom
1993    "Elections and Electoral Politics in Africa." *Africa* 63(3):299–312.

Žižek, Slavoj
n.d.    "Appendix: Multiculturalism, the Reality of an Illusion"; www.lacan.com/essays/?page_id=454.

# Index

251

# About the Authors

Jean Comaroff is the Bernard E. and Ellen C. Sunny Distinguished Professor of Anthropology at the University of Chicago and was the founding director of the Chicago Center for Contemporary Theory (3CT). John L. Comaroff is the Harold H. Swift Distinguished Professor of Anthropology at the University of Chicago, a Founding Fellow of 3CT, and Research Professor at the American Bar Foundation. Both are Honorary Professors at the University of Cape Town. Their most recent books include *Ethnicity, Inc.* (2009), *Zombies et frontières à l'ère néolibérale. Le cas de l'Afrique du Sud postcoloniale* (2010), and the co-edited *Law and Disorder in the Postcolony* (2006).